THE HISTORIC
WOODSTOCK
ART COLONY

The Arthur A. Anderson Collection

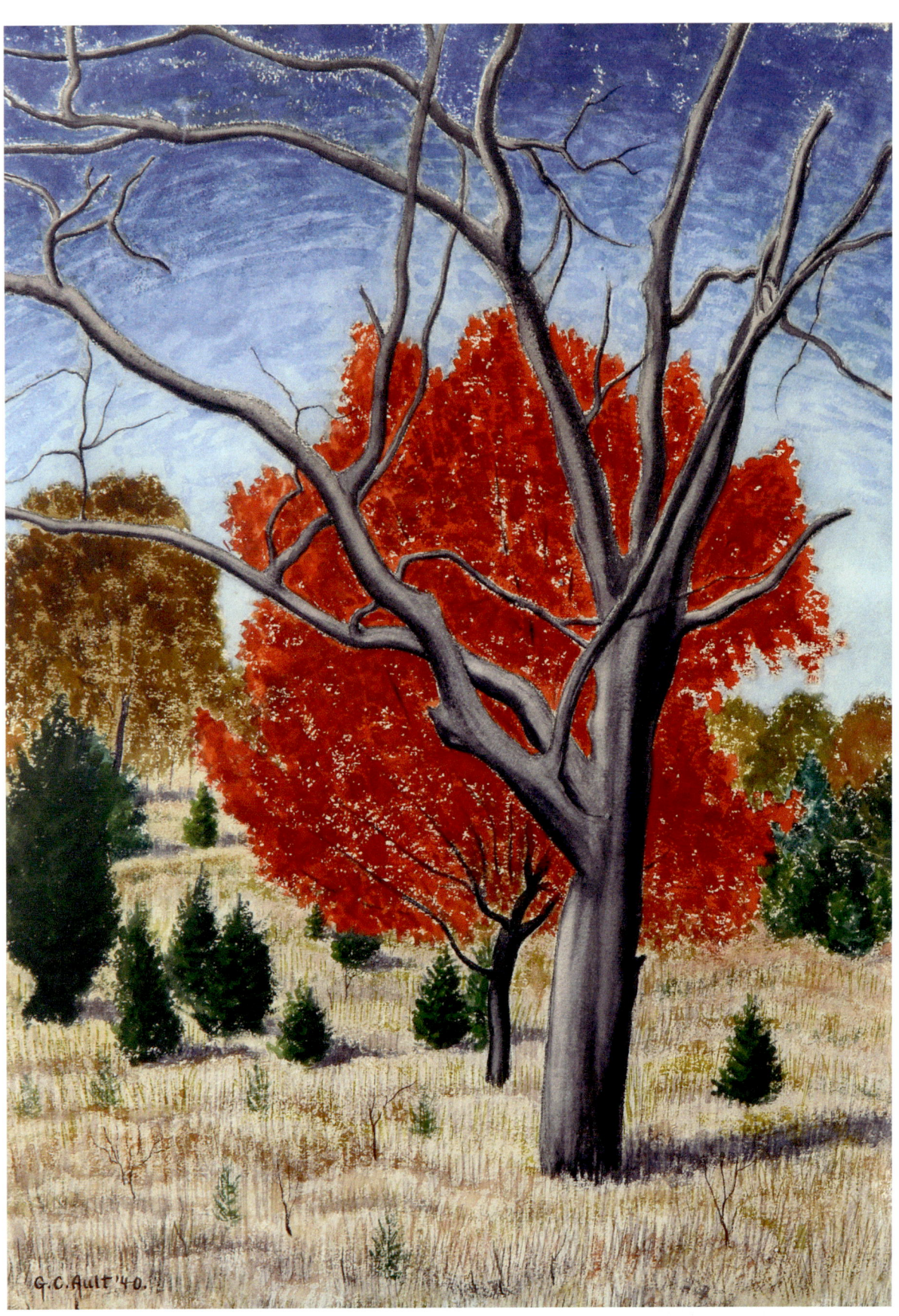

G.C.Ault '40.

THE HISTORIC
WOODSTOCK ART COLONY

The Arthur A. Anderson Collection

Karen E. Quinn

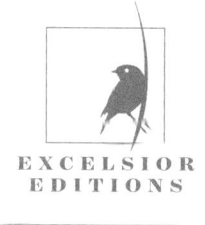

EXCELSIOR EDITIONS

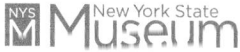

New York State Museum

Published by
STATE UNIVERSITY OF NEW YORK PRESS, ALBANY

© 2024 New York State Education Department

EXCELSIOR EDITIONS is an imprint of STATE UNIVERSITY OF NEW YORK PRESS
For information, contact State University of New York Press, Albany, NY
www.sunypress.edu

Library of Congress Cataloging-in-Publication Data

Names: New York State Museum, author, issuing body. | Quinn, Karen E., author.

Title: The historic Woodstock art colony : the Arthur A. Anderson
    collection / Karen E. Quinn.

Description: [Albany] : SUNY Press : New York State Museum, [2024] |
    Includes bibliographical references and index.

Identifiers: LCCN 2023045134 | ISBN 9781438497983 (paperback)

Subjects: LCSH: Art, American—New York (State)—Woodstock—20th
    century—Exhibitions. | Artist colonies—New York
    (State)—Woodstock—Exhibitions. | Anderson, Arthur A.—Art
    collections—Exhibitions. | Art—Private collections—New York
    (State)—Albany—Exhibitions. | New York State Museum—Art
    collections—Exhibitions.

Classification: LCC N6535.W66 N49 2024 | DDC
    709.73/07474734--dc23/eng/20240126

LC record available at https://lccn.loc.gov/2023045134

10   9   8   7   6   5   4   3   2   1

CONTENTS

The genesis of this publication is the magnificent gift from Arthur A. Anderson of his Historic Woodstock Art Colony Collection to the New York State Museum.

– Karen E. Quinn, Senior Historian/Curator, Art and Culture
New York State Museum

ACKNOWLEDGMENTS

The genesis of this publication is the magnificent gift from Arthur A. Anderson of his Historic Woodstock Art Colony Collection to the New York State Museum and the subsequent 2018–19 exhibition held at the museum. We are eternally grateful to Arthur for his generosity. Not only has he focused passionately on Woodstock and its artists, but he is also a curator's dream for the documentation and organization of his collection, expertly managed by Eric Lapp. Eric's devotion has been invaluable; he tirelessly answered questions, provided background information, and supported us as we worked on the exhibition and the book.

Mark Schaming, the Museum's director, wholeheartedly agreed with accepting the collection in its entirety—over fifteen hundred works. He understood its transformative nature and its educational potential in addition to its artistic importance.

Jennifer Lemak, chief curator of history, shepherded the acquisition of the collection and has overseen this project, making it seem effortless, in spite of its complexity. Also in the History Department, Bridget Enderle took on the organization of images for the book with her inimitable organizational skill. Emily Finelli and Mehna Reach worked with photographer Allison Munsell-Napierski to assure the high-quality production of all the illustrations.

The acquisition and processing of a collection of this scope required a museum-wide effort, from the initial transportation of the works, to exhibition, to publication. History staff supported all these endeavors— John Abeel, Kara Chambers, Robyn Gibson, Ashley Hopkins-Benton, Connie Frisbee Houde, Stephen Loughman, Aaron Noble, and Brad Utter. Throughout the Museum, other departments were also involved, including Exhibitions, Production, and Education and Visitor Services, among others. We are grateful to Ford Bailey, Kelley Feranec, Karen Glaz, Antonia Giuliano, Ethan Hacklin, Scott Heydrick, Chelsea Hildebrandt, Andrew Meier, Ben Karis, Nancy Kelley, Chris Kobuskie, Koren Lazarou, Kathleen Morehouse, Frank Moscowitz, Jessica Neidl, Alan Noble, Carrie Ross, Corianne Setzer, Daniel Stienstra, and Kathryn Weller for their contributions.

The beautiful design of this book was created by Christopher Havens. Donna Dixon edited, weaving the voices together, but keeping them distinct. Finally, the enthusiasm and support of the essay authors have made this project a pleasure: Jim Cox, Marianne S. Kearney, Susana Leval, John P. Murphy, Bruce Weber, Tom Wolf, and Arthur A. Anderson himself.

Karen E. Quinn
Senior Historian/Curator, Art and Culture
New York State Museum

Within the canon of American art, the Woodstock Art Colony is a far-reaching movement of national importance.

– Mark A. Schaming, Deputy Commissioner of Cultural Education
Director, New York State Museum

CONTRIBUTORS TO THE CATALOG

Arthur A. Anderson
Historic Woodstock Art Colony collector
Essay: Community and Congenial Spirits:
The Historic Woodstock Art Colony and Collection

James Cox
Director, James Cox Gallery at Woodstock
Essay: Woodstock and Kindred Spirits

Marianne S. Kearney
Granddaughter of George Bellows
Essay: A Rare Friendship

Susana Leval
Director Emerita of El Museo del Barrio
Essay: Julio De Diego: A Picaresque Journey in Art

John P. Murphy
The Philip and Lynn Straus Curator of Prints
and Drawings at The Frances Lehman Loeb Art
Center at Vassar
Essay: Arnold Wiltz: The Dreamlike Landscape

Karen E. Quinn
Senior Historian/Curator of Art and Culture
at the New York State Museum
Essay: Essay—"Rollicking humor and dry,
caustic comment": Caricatures by Peggy Bacon
in the Arthur A. Anderson Collection

Bruce Weber
Independent Scholar of American Art
Essay: Birge Harrison and the Woodstock School
of Landscape Painting

Tom Wolf
Professor of Art History and Visual Culture
at Bard College
Essay: Feminist Artists in the Early Woodstock
Art Colony

DIRECTOR'S FOREWORD

Since the inception of the New York State Museum in 1836, the institution has grown by the power of many visionaries and leaders in their fields. Botanist Amos Eaton, anthropologist Lewis Henry Morgan, engineer and Seneca tribal diplomat Ely Parker, and decorative arts collector Martin Wunsch are among those who built world-class private collections that trace New York State's cultural, human, and natural history, and then, with generosity and foresight, donated them to the State Museum. These critical artifacts, specimens, and works of art comprise the Museum's foundational collections.

In this tradition, the Historic Woodstock Art Colony: The Arthur A. Anderson Collection has become a State Museum foundational collection. In 2017 Arthur Anderson, an astute and deeply thoughtful collector, approached the Museum with the proposal to place his vast assemblage of artworks in our care. From the outset, Arthur's goal was about education—that his collection be used to inform not just scholars but learners at every level about the Woodstock Art Colony. State Museum curator Karen Quinn enthusiastically agreed to take in the collection, about fifteen hundred pieces, in its entirety.

The artworks in the Arthur A. Anderson collection were made over the course of about a hundred years, spanning the twentieth century, and all within the epicenter of Woodstock, New York, in the state's storied Hudson Valley. Without peer, this is the most comprehensive group of works of its kind, a singular collection. Within the canon of American art, the Woodstock Art Colony is a far-reaching movement of national importance. Of its many defining attributes are an unbridled freedom and variety of expression, encompassing both traditionalist and modernist approaches; a sense of place and of people; and evidence of a living community of eminently talented artists who came to live here from all over the country and the world. Taken together, the works epitomize Anderson's collecting vision. He is, in fact, more than just a collector of things. To be among these works with Arthur is a memorable experience. It's akin to watching someone revel in the presence of beloved old friends. His passion for and deep understanding of the works, the people, the place, and the backstories, is infectious. In coming to know Arthur and his collection, it became clear we needed to keep this family of works together for the purpose of study, exhibition, teaching, and to share with other museums and scholars.

Arthur has lived in the Woodstock area for many years and immersed himself in the place—the land, the houses, the studios, the words, the tales, and the atmosphere of a place that impacted art movements across New York and the nation. Along with amassing this collection, he is a ringmaster of scholars and others who have spent decades studying the artists of Woodstock. Through his generosity, Arthur has inspired other collectors to donate related important works to the Museum, building on the foundation of his gift to the state and enriching our educational reach.

In this volume, several experts have been drawn together by Arthur and Karen to speak to the importance of Woodstock in the history of American art. Together the contributors to this publication fuel our thinking; encourage us to take delight in viewing the works; and challenge, inspire, and compel us to learn more.

The State Museum is a better place for the thoughtful work of this grand partnership. We are especially grateful for Karen Quinn's dedication, endless curiosity, and insightful manner in which she shines a light on this foundational collection. We've all learned much as she's given voice to this distinctive choir of artists and the works she stewards. I am proud to be her colleague.

With this volume, we welcome you to learn about and enjoy the New York State Museum's Historic Woodstock Art Colony: The Arthur A. Anderson Collection.

Mark A. Schaming
Deputy Commissioner of Cultural Education
Director, New York State Museum

THE HISTORIC WOODSTOCK ART COLONY: THE ARTHUR A. ANDERSON COLLECTION

Introduction

Long before the famous music festival in 1969, Woodstock, New York, was home to what is considered America's first intentionally created year-round arts colony—founded in 1902 and still thriving over one hundred years later. Collecting the remarkable range of work produced there has been Arthur A. Anderson's focus for over three decades, resulting in the largest comprehensive assemblage of its type. The artists represented in it reflect the diversity of those who came to Woodstock, including Birge Harrison, Konrad Cramer, George Bellows, Julio de Diego, Peggy Bacon, Rolph Scarlett, and Yasuo Kuniyoshi, among many, many others. This variety is evident in the 1926 map of Woodstock artists' homes produced by Margaret and Rudolph Wetterau.

Arthur Anderson donated his entire collection—over fifteen hundred objects by almost two hundred artists—to the New York State Museum in 2017. This publication introduces to the public just a sample of the highlights of this extraordinary collection, which represents a body of work that together shaped art and culture in New York and forms a history of national and international significance. The works following each section were included in the New York State Museum's 2018–2019 exhibition *The Historic Woodstock Art Colony: The Arthur A. Anderson Collection.*

The Arthur A. Anderson Collection spans the twentieth century and includes works in all media: paintings, watercolors, pastels, drawings, prints, photographs, sculpture, ceramics, and even an easel and a hand-painted melodeon. It is augmented with archival material including letters, personal photographs, and manuscripts. With this breadth, Anderson has established a study collection, invaluable not only for the finished pieces, but for the insights related work such as sketches, studies, and primary source documents give into an artist's working process. This unique resource presents a fuller picture of, and gives greater context to, the artists who worked in Woodstock.

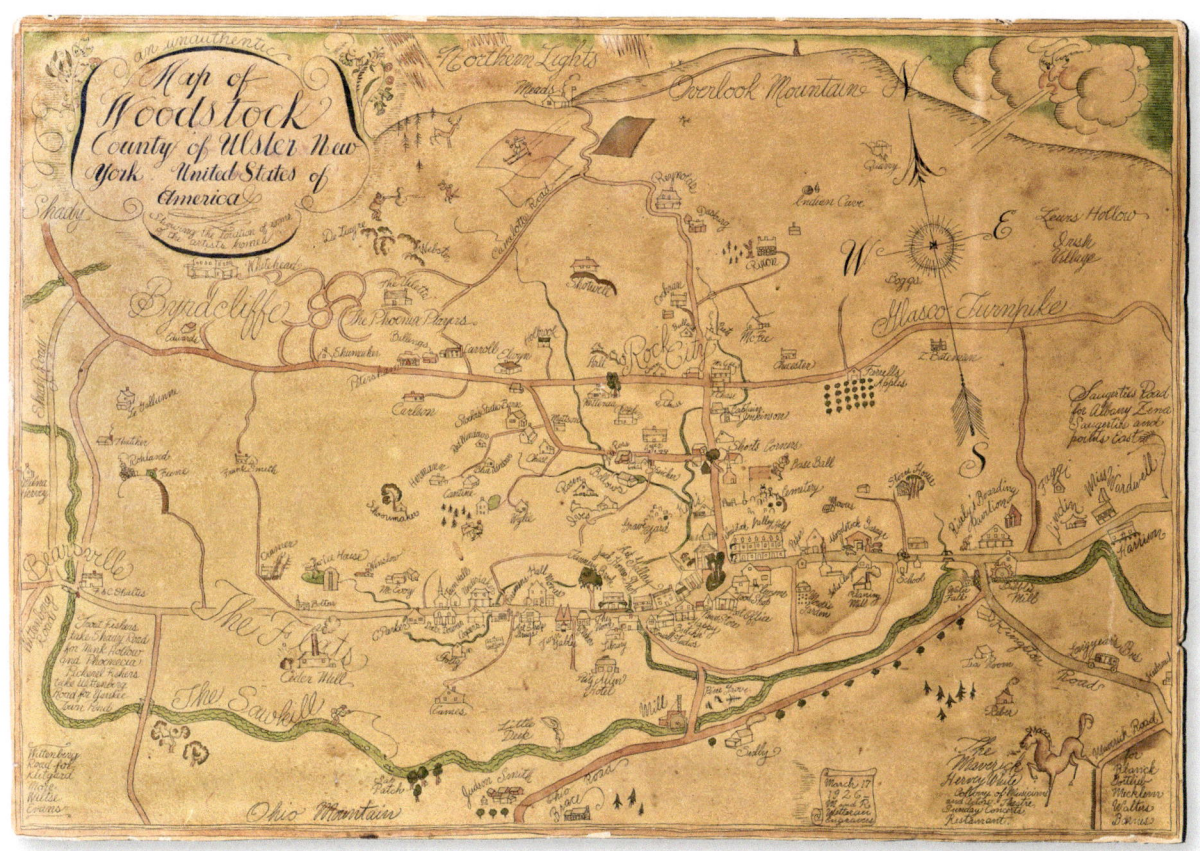

▲ Rudolph Wetterau (American, 1890–1953)
and Margaret Wetterau (American, 1894–1989)
*Map of Woodstock…Showing the location of
some of the artists' homes*, 1926
Ink on board

▶ Norbert Heermann (German, 1891–1966)
Lady With Red Lips, n.d.
Oil on canvas

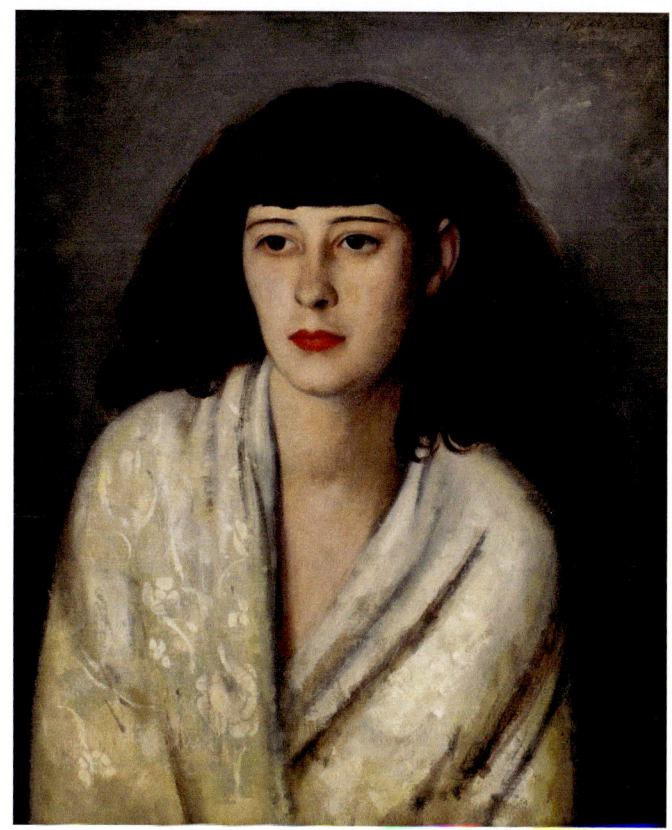

COMMUNITY AND CONGENIAL SPIRITS:
THE HISTORIC WOODSTOCK ART COLONY AND COLLECTION

—————— Arthur A. Anderson ——————

The door to this adventure opened when I fell in love with a lady with red lips in a Saugerties, New York, antique shop in 1990. Although it was financially imprudent for me to buy her, I did. This purchase led to a lifelong passion for creating a study collection of art and ephemera relating to the Historic Woodstock Art Colony.

I was told that *Lady with Red Lips* (p. 2) was painted by Norbert Heermann (1891–1966), a friend of the artist George Bellows, who also lived in Woodstock. The Woodstock connection between the two artists helped me to justify my purchase. However, afterward, I had buyer's remorse but was unable to return the painting, so I started to research and look for more art relating to George Bellows and his Woodstock circle. I was soon captivated by the fact that Bellows and others in Woodstock were especially creative, often drawing works on paper with a spontaneity that immediately demonstrated congeniality, wit, laughter, and fun. What I would soon come to learn and cherish were the connections among the Woodstock artists. These interpersonal and artistic connections fueled my curiosity and led me to meet and befriend my own circle of artists, scholars, curators, and gallerists with their own unique ties to Woodstock. For this, I am forever grateful. Shortly after my interest in George Bellows blossomed, I had the opportunity to meet and visit Jean Bellows Booth, his daughter, at her home in California. Booth educated me about her father and his circle of friends and graciously made the family archive accessible to me. Whenever I was in California, I always enjoyed visiting and spending time with Jean. One piece in my collection I am particularly fond of is a pencil drawing by George of Jean as a baby. In thinking about the connections, it always touched me that she was named after her father's best friend, Eugene Speicher, one of my favorite artists.

Jean Bellows Booth connected me to her longtime Woodstock friend, Aileen Cramer, in 2002. Aileen was the daughter of Woodstock artists Konrad Cramer and his wife, Florence Ballin Cramer. Aileen was a grande dame of Woodstock and a senior trustee and co-founder of the Woodstock Artists Association (WAA). As a newcomer to the Woodstock art collecting scene, I was invited to become a WAA trustee.

I was introduced to Aileen at a reception. She began our conversation by asking, "What on earth, Mr. Anderson, do you know about Woodstock Art?" I replied, "Very little, Miss Cramer, but I plan to learn from you and the WAA collection." After that, we got along famously, and she even offered to show me treasures from the Cramer family collection.

One piece that immediately struck me was her father's fifteenth anniversary wedding gift to her mother, a small handmade artist's book with intimate love poems and drawings. That book has pride of place in my collection. Another Woodstock grande dame and angel for building the collection was Kiriki de Diego Metzo, daughter of Woodstock artist Julio de Diego. Through her wisdom and foresight, we obtained his archive to build upon and celebrate Woodstock's artistic heritage.

Like the Woodstock artists, I had a circle of congenial spirits who shared my thirst for the art of Woodstock. Tom Fletcher opened an art gallery in Woodstock in 1992 and had a special gift for finding art in Woodstock artists' estates—and lots of it. Tom also had a wonderful talent for collecting fascinating stories about artists he represented, and he provided detailed provenance of the pieces he sold. I loved learning about the background stories and interconnections among the artists. Another like-minded individual was Jim Cox. Over the years his gallery and auctions were invaluable resources. Around 2004, halfway through my Woodstock collecting journey, Jim brought to my attention the availability of the original 1926 Wetterau map. This iconic map showed the location of many of the artists' homes in the Woodstock community and provided me with a list of more than one hundred artists living in the Woodstock art colony which motivated me to expand my collection.

For me, art collecting, as in business and adventure, is about people and extended family. So many friends and colleagues have contributed to the building of this collection. My business, Morgan Anderson Consulting, allowed me the financial freedom to acquire new artwork and build the collection and meet my circle of Woodstock kindred spirits along the way. While there are too many to name individually, a few stand out in my mind. Art "detective" and scholar Tram Combs, gallerist Tom French, conservators St. Julian Fishburne and Mike Densen, museum mentor Neil Trager, and valued colleague Eric Lapp. The list and my circle of congenial spirits go on and on.

The Historic Woodstock Art Colony Collection includes more than fifteen hundred works by 183 artists, with related archival materials and an art library that I collected over three decades. The Historic Woodstock Art Colony was never a singular style or school, which made it so interesting for me to collect. Its artists were diverse individuals who came from different cultural and geographic backgrounds. Their styles reflect a broad range: tonalist, realist, modernist, and even abstract. Notwithstanding its differences, the Woodstock Art Colony prospered with its distinct and fascinating community and continues today with an ever greater diversity of arts, crafts, music, dance, film, and other creative endeavors.

> *"After the end of the War, Woodstock was probably the best place for an artist to be…so many congenial spirits…a whole group… we all backed each other up…marvelous parties and balls… picnics and swimming…a great sense of fun and play."*
>
> – Denny Winters, Woodstock artist

After more than thirty years of building and living with this collection, my next challenge was figuring out what to do with it. I felt that it was a legacy collection, but it was also a study collection where the art could be used to educate the public and tell stories about the Woodstock Colony as a community and "congenial spirits."[1] Ideally, the collection would need to be kept together as a whole in perpetuity, in a safe and well-cared-for place, and most importantly, be used. My hope was that the collection would reintroduce the Historic Woodstock Art Colony to the American art canon. It would also inform art estates and collectors that an ideal place exists to place their Woodstock treasures; this is happening.

I had discussions with many East Coast museums, but the New York State Museum stood out as the right and best place. The oldest state museum in the United States, it has comprehensive collections relating to all aspects of New York's natural history, human history, culture, and art. Its mission is to inform and educate the general public, with a particular focus on K-12 students.

As a result of my donation, my circle of congenial spirits now includes senior historian and art curator Karen Quinn, chief curator of history Jennifer Lemak, museum director Mark Schaming, and their many contributing staff, to whom I express gratitude. In three short years, COVID notwithstanding, these folks accomplished a comprehensive exhibition (2019), and a conference with Woodstock scholars, created K-12 teacher lesson plans and podcasts, and facilitated unlimited lending of the collection to other museums including the Samuel A. Dorsky Museum in 2023. The pièce de résistance is this book on the collection.

I envision that the art in the Historic Woodstock Art Colony collection will be used to tell a cultural and social history of these artists as a group of "congenial spirits" and I look forward to future scholars and art lovers bringing forth more connections to these treasured works. My sincere appreciation and thanks to one and all. ■

Note

1. The phrase "congenial spirits" is borrowed from Woodstock artist Denny Winters. Born and raised in provincial Western Michigan, she went to "exciting" Chicago to study art, then as an artist to "boring" Los Angeles, and eventually to Woodstock after WW II. Winters observed: "After the end of the War, Woodstock was probably the best place for an artist to be...so many congenial spirits...a whole group...we all backed each other up...marvelous parties and balls... picnics and swimming... a great sense of fun and play." Her new friends in Woodstock included artists from around the world: Philip Guston, Fernand Léger, Yasao Kuniyoshi, Fletcher Martin, and Julio de Diego. From Bruce Weber, *Arriving at Byrdcliff*, November 5, 2022, blog, accessed at *learningwoodstockartcolony.com*.

THE HISTORIC WOODSTOCK ART COLONY: THE ARTHUR A. ANDERSON COLLECTION

Byrdcliffe Arts Colony

In 1902 the Byrdcliffe Arts Colony was established in Woodstock.[1] The year-round utopian community promoted the Arts and Crafts movement, which emphasized individual, hand-crafted work over mass production. Wealthy Englishman Ralph Radcliffe Whitehead and his wife, Jane Byrd McCall, along with writer Hervey White and artist Bolton Brown, founded the colony; its name was derived from the middle names of the Whiteheads, who financed the project.

Byrdcliffe drew artisans from across all media: furniture makers, painters, printmakers, photographers, metalworkers, weavers, ceramicists, and others, as well as writers and musicians. Classes were offered, and notable teachers included cofounder Bolton Brown, Hermann Dudley Murphy, Birge Harrison, and William Schumacher.

Brown, Harrison, and Murphy all worked in a soft-focus, Tonalist style often associated with painting at Byrdcliffe and seen here in their canvases *Valley and Sky (Tonalist Mountains)*, *St. Lawrence River Sunset*, and *The Shower of Sunset (Woodstock)* (p. 9), respectively. In works such as *The Woodchopper* (p. 8), Schumacher, however, favored a more modernist approach. Brown experimented with several media in addition to painting, including ceramics and lithography (pp. 51–56, "Bolton Brown and Lithography.") Other artists who worked in more than one medium included Eva Watson-Schütze, who painted *Yellow Callas* (p. 10), but also earned a reputation as a photographer, and Zulma Steele, who developed her own pottery she called "Zedware," designed and decorated furniture, made prints and paintings, and designed textiles.

Byrdcliffe continues to flourish today under the auspices of the Woodstock Byrdcliffe Guild.

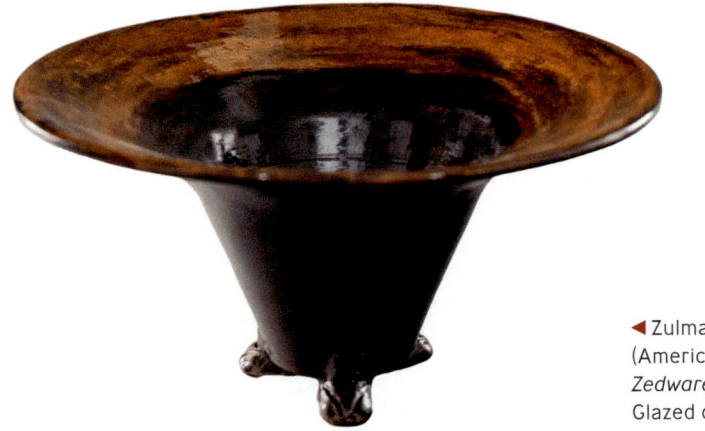

◀ Zulma Steele
(American, 1881–1979)
Zedware Bowl, c. 1935
Glazed ceramic

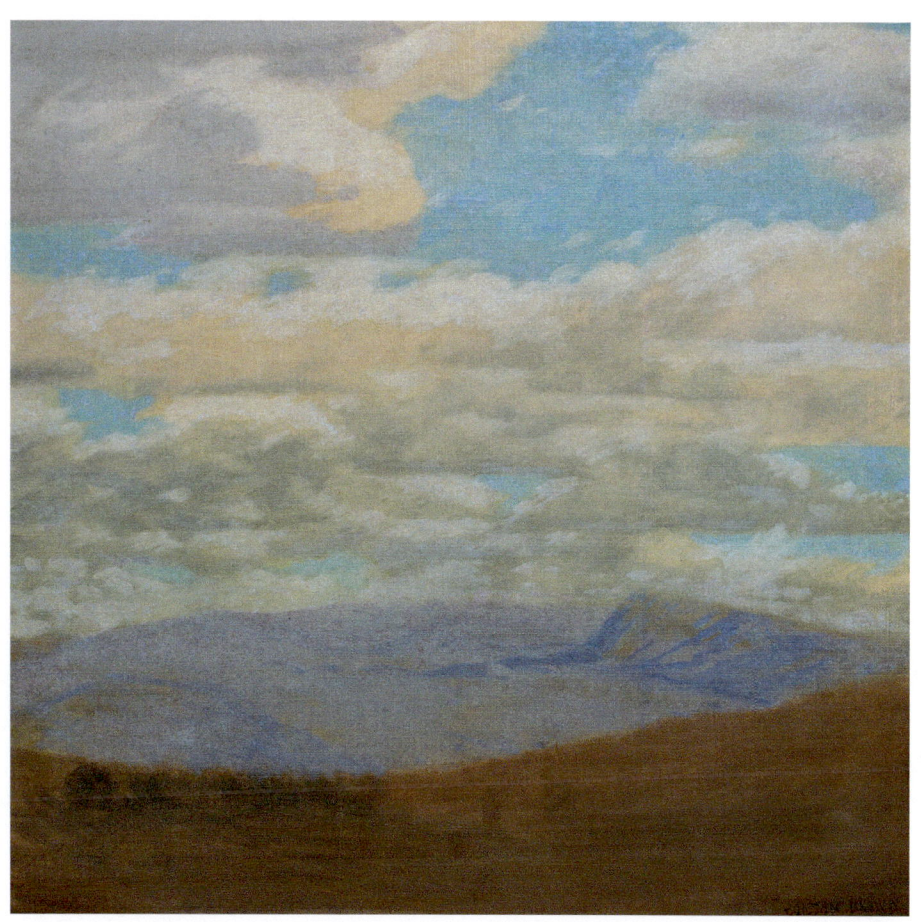

▶ Bolton Brown
(American, 1864–1936)
Valley and Sky (Tonalist Mountains), 1904
Oil on canvas

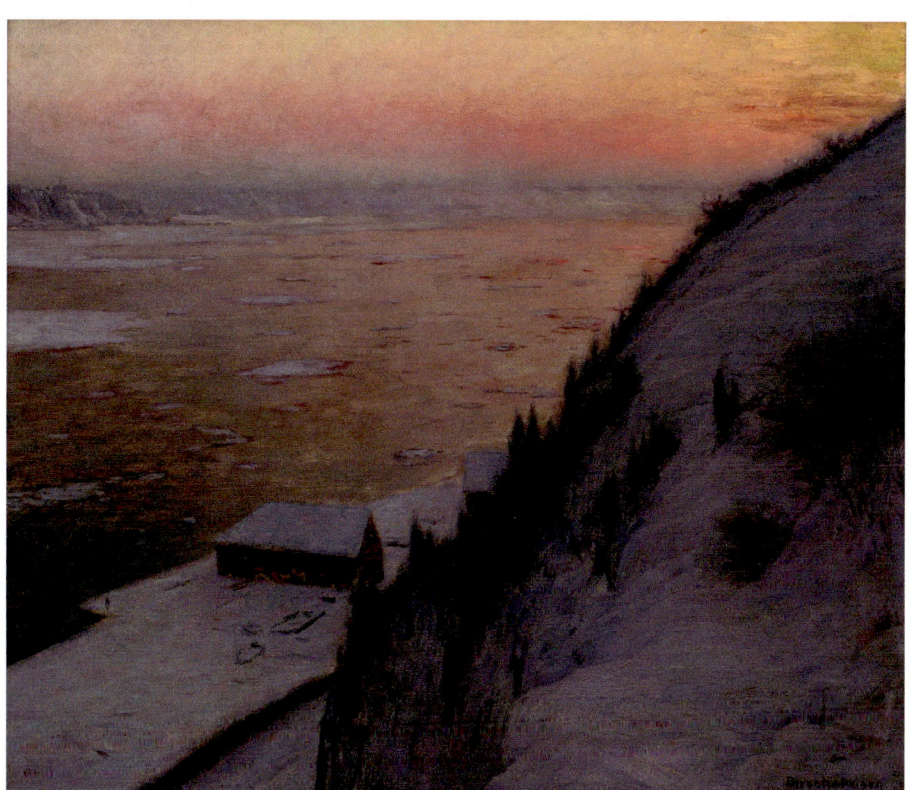

▶ Birge Harrison
(American, 1854–1929)
St. Lawrence River Sunset, n.d.
Oil on canvas

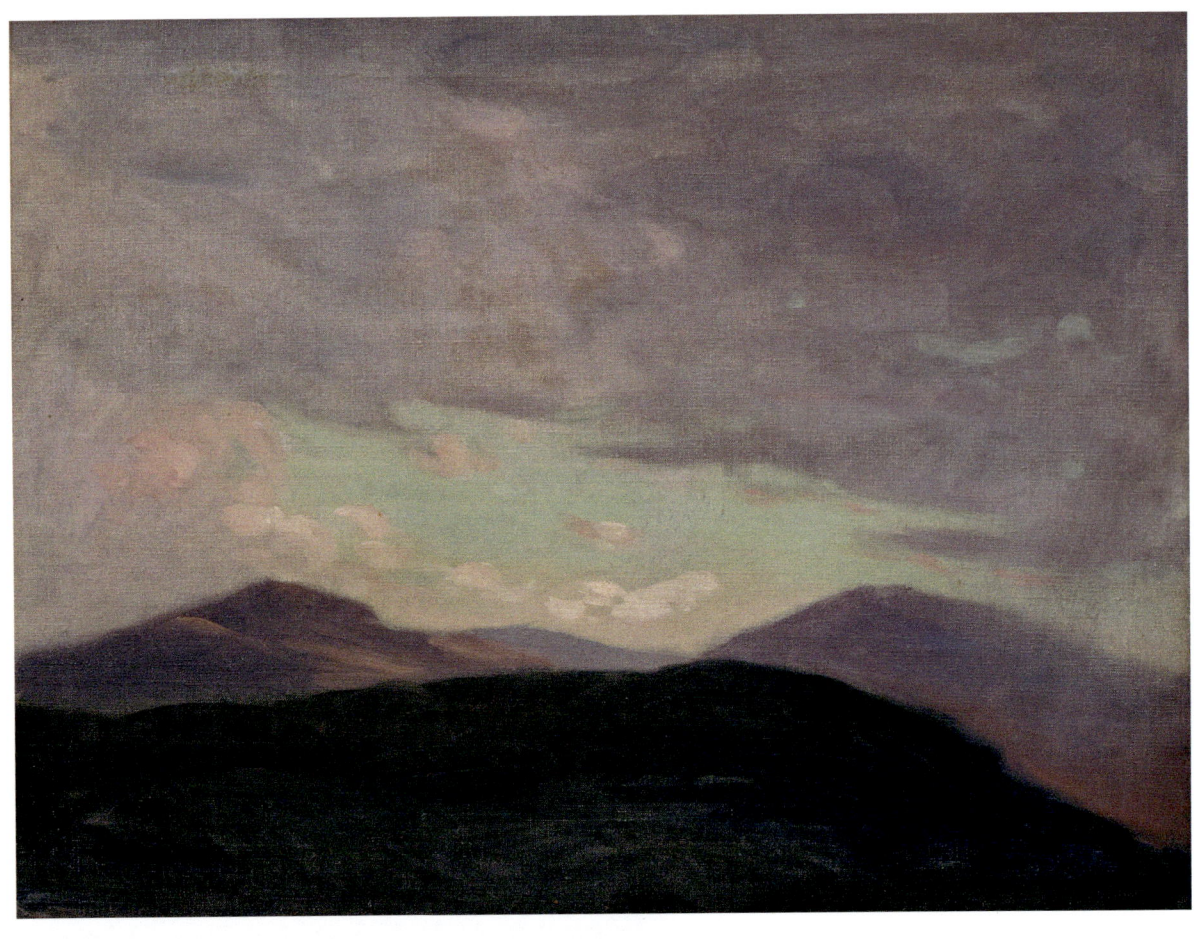

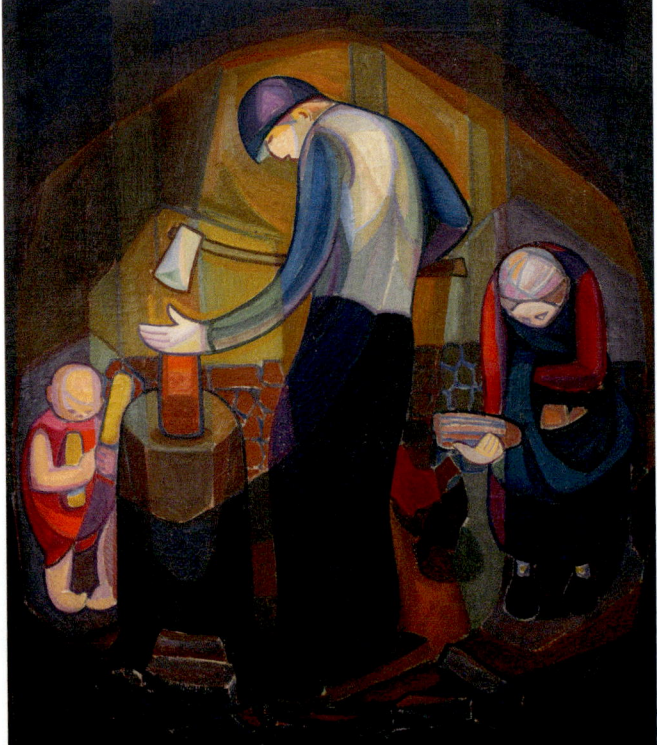

◀ William Schumacher
(American, born Belgium, 1870–1930)
The Woodchopper, 1920
Oil on canvas

▼ Bolton Brown
(American, 1864–1936)
Bowl, 1930
Polychrome glazed ceramic earthenware

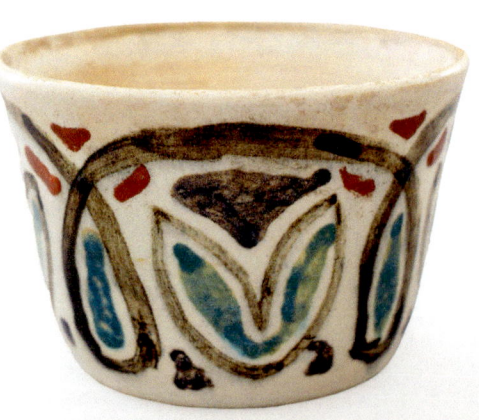

◄ Hermann Dudley Murphy
(American, 1867–1945)
*The Shower of Sunset
(Woodstock)*, 1904
Oil on canvas

► Bolton Brown
(American, 1864–1936)
Summer Shower, 1920
Lithograph on paper

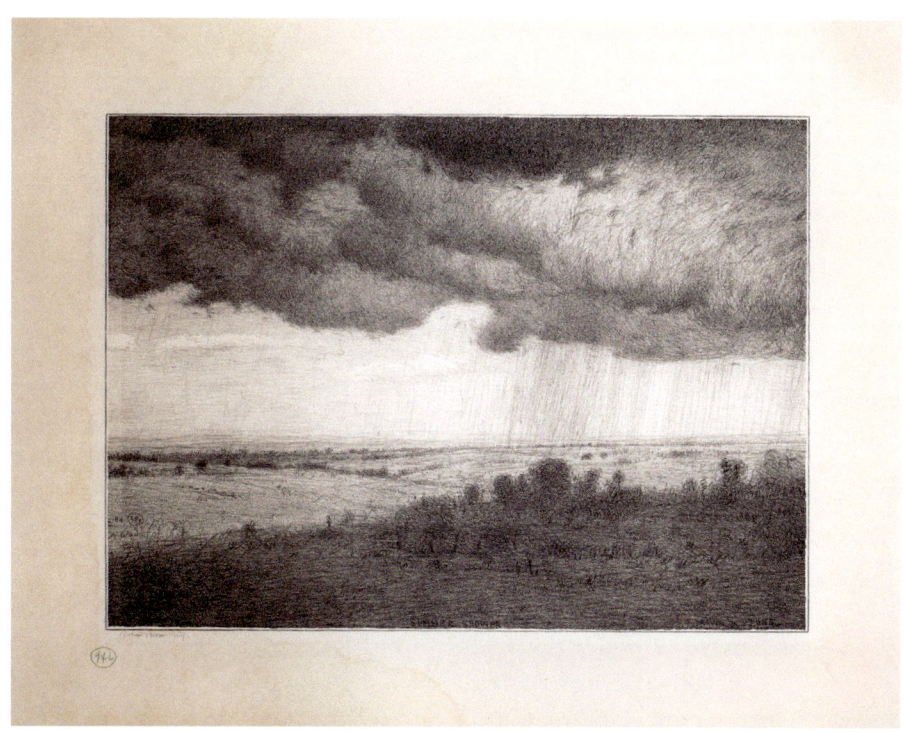

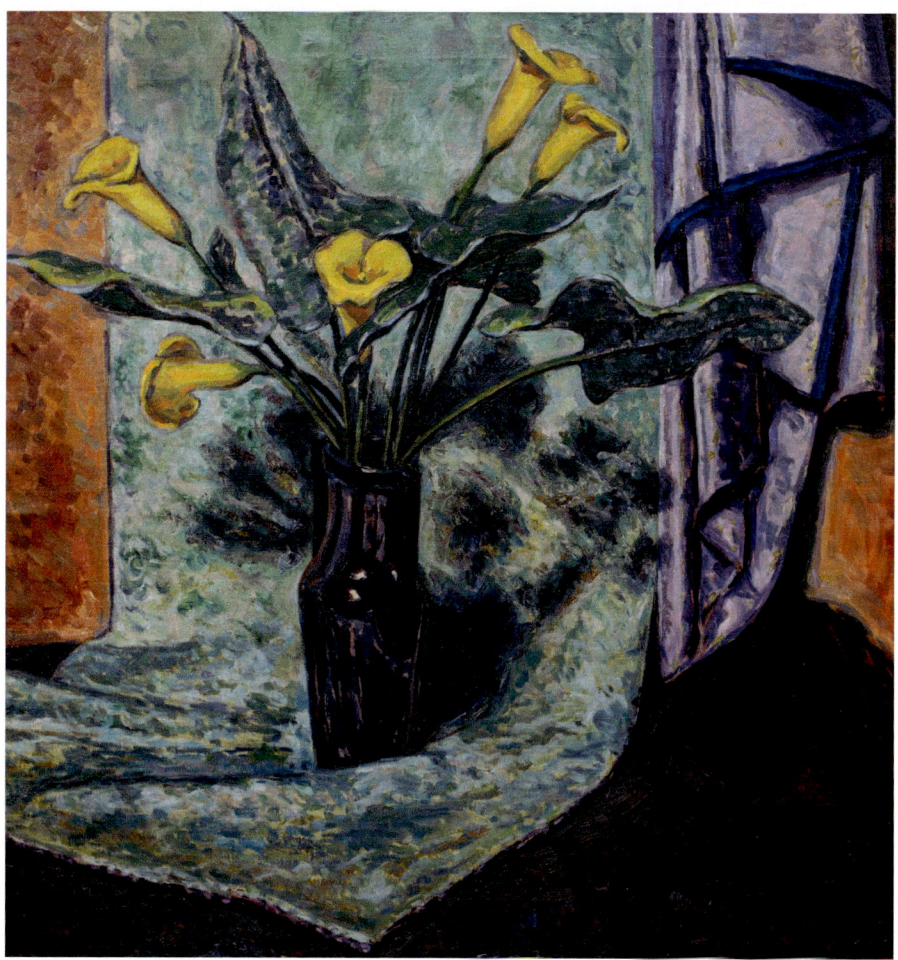

► Eva Watson-Schütze
(American, 1867–1935)
Yellow Callas, 1929
Oil on canvas

BIRGE HARRISON AND THE WOODSTOCK SCHOOL OF LANDSCAPE PAINTING

Bruce Weber

The Woodstock School of Landscape Painting was in operation from 1906–1922 under the auspices of the Art Students League of New York. The school's first teacher and director was Birge Harrison, who had a major impact on the art produced in the art colony's early years. Harrison originally came to Woodstock in 1904 when he accepted his friend Ralph Radcliffe Whitehead's offer to teach at Byrdcliffe and take over Hermann Dudley Murphy's position as the painting instructor and head of the school. After a summer of teaching at Byrdcliffe, Harrison took a year's sabbatical so that he could devote himself fully to painting. In 1905 the Art Students League in New York decided to move their summer school from Old Lyme, Connecticut, where it had been in operation for four years under the leadership of Frank Vincent DuMond. John F. Carlson, who studied with Harrison at Byrdcliffe, suggested moving the school to Woodstock and helped recruit Harrison for the job. He served as Harrison's assistant and followed him as the director of the school from 1911–1917. Harrison settled in Woodstock for the remainder of his life but spent extensive time away.

By the time of his arrival in Woodstock, Harrison was working in the soft, ethereal atmospheric Tonalist style for which he became well-known. In the 1890s, he had come under the stylistic sway of the landscape paintings of James Abbott McNeil Whistler. Whistler's landscapes inspired several American artists to adopt an interest in tonal painting, employ the use of a single, dominant color, and translate the spirit and mood of nature through the expressive simplification of color, line, and composition. His followers joined with other American landscape painters of the period, many of whom were inspired by the late works of George Inness and similarly come under the stylistic banner of Tonalism. The artists viewed nature as an agent for transporting the soul to a pure and ideal state—one where man contemplates the beauty and harmony of the natural world and the immaterial aspects of the universe. The Tonalists were drawn to the cultivated landscapes common to the French Barbizon School.

In Woodstock, Harrison favored painting snow-covered low-lying rural wintertime landscapes in the lowering light of day or featuring the rising moon. He typically liked to include a stream or waterway running back into the distance, where forms are vaguely defined. He utilized warm colors to enliven cooler hues and favored asymmetrical compositions—an outgrowth of his study and admiration of Japanese prints. Sometimes he chose to accentuate the emptiness of the setting and included a lone figure in the composition.

Under Harrison's influence, Woodstock's landscape painters favored picturing fragmentary or spare bits of nature (such as the corner of a field, a glimpse of a waterway or forest

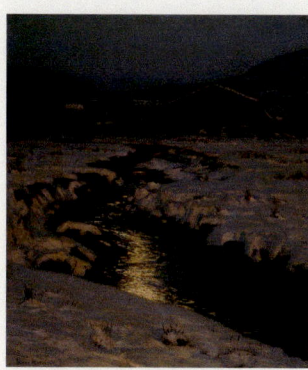

▲ Birge Harrison
(American, 1854–1929)
*Woodstock Meadows
in Winter,* 1909
Oil on canvas

interior, a simple line of trees, or an empty or near empty parcel of land). They were interested and sensitive to abstract design, and often indicated the presence of human life and settlement through the inclusion of a clearing, fence, path, vehicle, barn or house. Other concerns revolved around the evocation of mood, fluid brushwork, and a palette dominated by a single hue.

In 1912, a year after retiring from teaching at the League's school, Harrison authored the article "Painting at Woodstock: The Work of a Group of American Landscape Painters." He praised the ambitions and accomplishments of the school, which he believed had "become the most important and successful institution of its kind in the world," lauding the subjects within half a mile of the white steeple of the old Dutch Reformed Church, which marks the center of the village community. First, there is the winding Sawkill, with its mills, its falls and its long reaches of quiet water, overhung with branching trees; then the gleaming white houses of the little village itself, seen from the flat meadows, which are intersected everywhere with gently flowing streams and still pools; then the farms, the fields, the forest and the eternal soaring mountains. The picture material…is infinitely varied…This is partly due to the fact that Woodstock Valley is a valley only in name; for while to the west the view is hedged in by the twin peaks of Tonshe and Tiestoneck, and north and south rise the heights of Overlook and Ohayo mountains, to the east the horizon lies far an open as the plains of Holland, and the view stretches away across fifteen miles of wood and meadow to the valley of the Hudson River, whose vapors rise roseate in the early morning sunlight or shroud in pale mystery the rising moon.[1]

Harrison further related that the League inaugurated the school of landscape painting with a course extending over five months, from May to November, instead of the usual six weeks or two months which had been the rule in summer classes heretofore, that many of the more serious students found even this too short a limit, and that "Woodstock now has a considerable winter colony, consisting largely of graduates of the class who have become regular exhibitors in the great annual exhibitions of the country."[2] The group included Carlson, Alfred Hutty, Frank Swift Chase, John Folinsbee, Florence Ballin Cramer, Harry-Leith Ross, Marion Bullard, Cecil Chichester, Allen Dean Cochran, Walter Goltz, George Macrum, Anita M. Smith, Edna Thurber, John William Bentley, Neil Macdowell Ives and Jean Paul Slusser.

Harrison retired from teaching in 1911 but continued to maintain a connection with the Woodstock School of Landscape Painting and its students. His home remained a center of artistic activity. Harrison and his wife Jenny ran an open house every Sunday where Harrison was known to have an open ear to the voices of young artists. An art writer of the period remarked that "The establishment of [the] successful school [in Woodstock] was a [pursuit] that [Harrison] rode for a period of [six] years [including his time at Byrdcliffe]…He himself holds the successful building up of this little group of… students to a school of over 150 serious men and women to be the most important and valuable work of his life."[3] ■

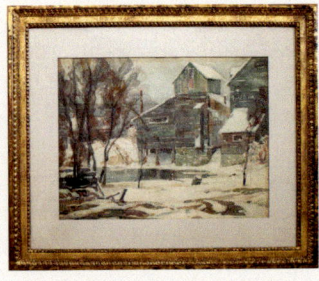

▲ John F. Carlson
Grey Mills, c. 1920
Watercolor on paper

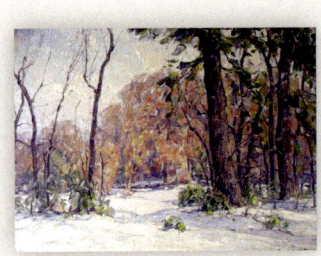

▲ Frank Swift Chase
Early Snow, n.d.
Oil on canvas

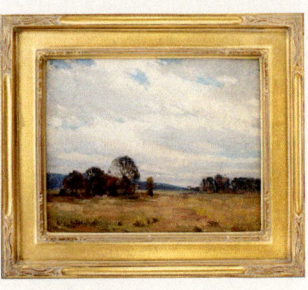

▲ Alfred Hutty
Summer Landscape, 1925
Oil on board

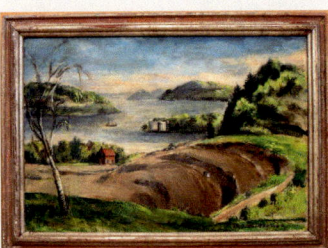

▲ Florence Ballin Cramer
Hudson River at Rondout, c. 1938
Oil on canvas

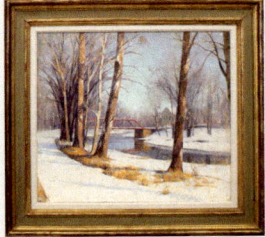

▲ Allen Cochran
Winter Stream, n.d.
Oil on canvas

Notes

1. Birge Harrison, "Painting at Woodstock," *Arts and Decoration* 2 (May 1912): 247–248.

2. Harrison, 248.

3. Charles Louis Borgmeyer, "Birge Harrison: Poet Painter," *The Fine Art Journal* 29 (October 1913): 605.

> The door to this adventure opened when I fell in love with a lady with red lips in a Saugerties, New York, antique shop in 1990.

> – Arthur A. Anderson, Historic Woodstock Art Colony collector

FEMINIST ARTISTS IN THE EARLY WOODSTOCK ART COLONY

Tom Wolf

From the time of the founding of Byrdcliffe, the original artists' colony in Woodstock, New York, in 1902, women artists have played a vital role in Woodstock's art scene. Byrdcliffe was intentionally created as a place to nurture artists by Ralph Radcliffe Whitehead, a wealthy Englishman who had absorbed the ideals of the Arts and Crafts movement while studying at Oxford with John Ruskin. Whitehead had several accomplices in his project of establishing a place for artists and craftspeople to pursue their work in a beautiful natural setting, remote from polluted cities. Primary among them was Hervey White, in many ways Whitehead's opposite: poor, but with charisma and generosity of spirit that made him a magnet for artists. The two first met at Hull House, the socially concerned settlement house founded by Jane Addams in Chicago. There they were introduced to each other by Charlotte Perkins Gilman, one of the primary voices of the first wave of feminism at the start of the twentieth century. Before turning to writing, Gilman aspired to be an artist and was married to an artist, Charles Walter Stetson. Their troubled marriage inspired her famous feminist short story, "The Yellow Wallpaper" (1892). She published her influential book, *Women and Economics*, in 1899 (and gave Whitehead a personal copy) and would become a frequent visitor to Byrdcliffe, where her presence helped set the tone of Woodstock as a place for independent women.

Whitehead and his team erected thirty buildings, most of which are still standing, in a lovely, forested setting. He invited artists and craftspeople to the colony and gave them financial support, and several women benefited from his generosity, including artists Zulma Steele and Edna Walker, weaver Marie Little, metal worker Bertha Thompson with her sister, Annie, and the team of ceramicists, Edith Penman and Elizabeth Hardenburgh. Steele and Walker lived together in the Byrdcliffe house named Angelus for close to twenty years and were essential members of the team that designed the Arts and Crafts style furniture that was manufactured in the early days of the colony. That production lasted only a short time, due to the expense of making such finely crafted furniture, and then Steele turned to painting luminous landscapes of her surroundings, such as *Mountain Landscape,* where the people pulling a cart are dwarfed by the extensive landscape that surrounds them. This traditional theme is rendered in a modern manner with an abruptly cropped composition energized by thick, spontaneous strokes of paint, while in the background one of the Catskill mountains glows with mingled

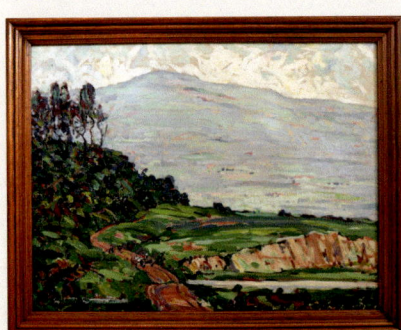

▲ Zulma Steele
Mountain Landscape, 1920
Oil on canvas

pastel hues. This is the sort of painting she exhibited in the 1915 exhibition for woman's suffrage discussed later in this essay.

Whitehead's wife, Jane, was an artist who also had known John Ruskin when she spent time in England, even painting watercolors side by side with him. In her opinion, by 1910 the number of women at Byrdcliffe had too much outnumbered the men: "This place has improved, but there is a lack of men, as usual. Stevens and the two engineers are good, but the thirty women want some more and some older men."[1] But women kept being drawn to the nurturing Woodstock culture: single women, married women, and members of same-sex couples. The sculptor Abastenia St. Leger Eberle spent several summers there in the 1910s after she had exhibited her radical feminist sculpture, *The Slave Trader*, of a brutal-looking man auctioning off a demure nude young woman, at the famous Armory Show in New York in 1913. One of her most esteemed tabletop sculptures was set in Woodstock: *Windy Doorstep*, with its hard-working woman sweeping a staircase as her clothes billow in the breeze. Eberle supported herself as a sculptor, no easy feat, making commercial works such as her *Mermaid* plaque, a small, decorative piece depicting a floating female figure rendered with the curving, contours and flowing hair of the Art Nouveau style.

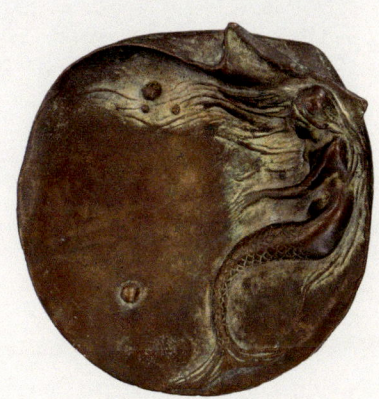

▲ Abastenia St. Leger Eberle
Mermaid, n.d.
Bronze

Mermaid presents an imaginary half-human woman, but there were more realistic nudes depicted by Woodstock's women artists. Eva Watson-Schütze had worked closely with Alfred Stieglitz, the influential advocate for photography as fine art, but after she married University of Chicago German professor Martin Schütze in 1901, the couple divided their lives between Chicago and Byrdcliffe. She became the most highly regarded photographer in the colony, working in a soft-focus, Pictorialist style. Her *Portrait of Two Children by Waterfall* is an Edenic image of purity and innocence, as the two nude kids stand upright, paralleling the vertical bands of falling water and looking frankly out at the viewer. Her photograph of her husband exercising in a Woodstock quarry is more extreme, a rare artistic image of a nude male made by a woman. Watson-Schütze had studied with the great Philadelphia artist Thomas Eakins, who was a pioneer of photographing unclothed models. Among the few precedents for her striking photograph of her husband nude are the photographs

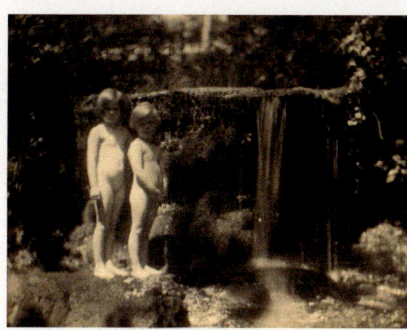

▲ Eva Watson-Schütze
Portrait of Two Children by Waterfall, 1902
Photograph

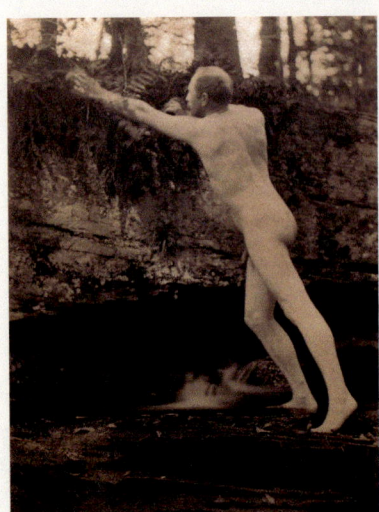

▲ Eva Watson-Schütze
Martin Schütze at a Quarry, 1902
Photograph

by Eakins's wife, Suzanne McDowell, of her artist husband; the intimacy of their relationships with their spouses emboldened both women to make images that were radical for their time. In Watson-Schütze's, Martin is exercising, engaging in the practice of physical fitness that was part of Byrdcliffe's ideology. His face is hardly visible, typical of the modesty surrounding images of the nude at the time. This was a period when female art students were not permitted to work from unclothed models, or at best were segregated into women-only classes for this training that was considered essential for artists.[2] So Dewing Woodward's Blue Dome Society in Woodstock, dedicated to painting and drawing nude models outdoors, by men and women artists, was quite daring.

Woodward settled in Woodstock around 1907 with her partner, Louise Johnson, and founded the Blue Dome Society, after spending years in the Paris art world and teaching art in various locations in the United States. Her paintings often featured lissome women in the forest, integrated with the foliage that surrounds them, as in *Woodland Nude* (p. 29) where the figure's face is hidden as she moves gracefully towards the light shining through the leaves. Alfred Hutty was one of the male artists who participated in the Blue Dome Fraternity, and his handsome drawing of a model raises the distinction between "naked" and "nude," as her hairband suggests that she is undressed, as opposed to Woodward's woman who is in a pure state of nudity, one with the nature that surrounds her.[3] Such an ideal vision is typical of Woodward's outdoor nudes, which despite their pleasant appearance were quite radical at the time. Her painting *Paper Dolls* offers a different type of innocence, that of a young girl seriously involved in her play. Images of children, and of peaceful maternity, were commonplace in works by women artists in the early twentieth century, who wanted to project an image of virtue and responsibility as they campaigned for the right to vote that was denied them until 1920.[4]

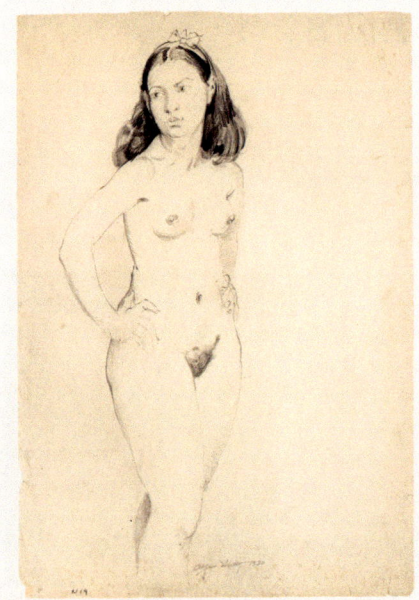

▲ Alfred Hutty
Nude Study, 1930
Graphite on paper

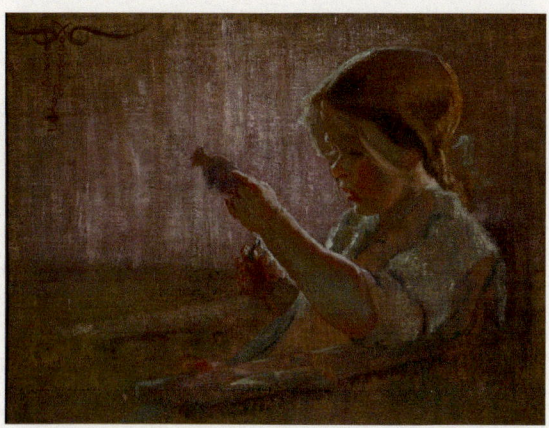

▲ Dewing Woodward (American, 1856–1950)
Paper Dolls, 1913
Oil on canvas

Scenes with children dominated the historic exhibition in support of women's suffrage held at the Macbeth Gallery in New York in 1915, with Woodstock women well represented among the exhibiting artists.[5] Eberle, the sculptor, was one of the organizers, as was Alice Morgan Wright, from nearby Albany. Woodstockers Grace Mott Johnson and Myra Musselman Carr were among the sculptors exhibiting, while Zulma Steele, Marion Bullard, and Ethel Canby donated paintings to the cause. From its origins as an artists' colony, Woodstock's artist population included many feminist women. The tradition of productive, aware women artists continued for well over a century, with artists like Peggy Bacon, Doris Lee and many others, a tradition that is still vital today and includes Mary Frank, Joan Snyder, Arlene Shechet, and more. ■

Notes

1. Jane Byrd McCall Whitehead to Ralph Radcliffe Whitehead, July 11, 1910, Downs Collection, Winterthur Museum. Quoted in Tom Wolf, "Byrdcliffe's History," *Byrdcliffe: An American Arts and Crafts Colony*, Nancy E. Green, ed. (Ithaca, NY: Herbert F. Johnson Museum of Art, Cornell University, 2004), 31.

2. This practice was discussed by Linda Nochlin in her pioneering feminist essay, "Why Have There Been No Great Women Artists," *ARTNews* (January 1971).

3. For the naked versus the nude see Kenneth Clark, *The Nude: A Study in Ideal Form*, (Princeton, NJ: Princeton University Press, 1972).

4. Paula Hayes Harper, "Votes for Women? A Graphic Episode in the Battle of the Sexes," *Art and Architecture in the Service of Politics*, Henry A. Millon and Linda Nochlin, eds. (Cambridge, MA: MIT Press, 1978), 8.

5. Mariea Caudill Dennison, "Babes for Suffrage: 'The Exhibition of Painting and Sculpture by Women Artists for the Benefit of the Woman Suffrage Campaign," *Woman's Art Journal* 24 No. 2 (Autumn 2003–Winter 2004): 24–30.

THE HISTORIC WOODSTOCK ART COLONY:
THE ARTHUR A. ANDERSON COLLECTION

Maverick Arts Colony

Hervey White left Byrdcliffe in 1904 and purchased a nearby farm to establish what would become the Maverick Arts Colony, a community more bohemian than Byrdcliffe. Early on, the colony attracted mostly writers and musicians, though by the 1920s visual artists of wide-ranging approaches and working in a plethora of media had a large presence, too. Some, like Harry Gottlieb, succumbed to the lure of the surrounding pastoral scenery and produced landscapes, even though he was better known as a social realist figurative artist. Robert Chanler decorated a melodeon with a lively suite of jesters and musicians, much in the spirit of the colony. Pioneering ceramicist Carl Walters created both functional and whimsical pieces including *Fan Dancer*. John Flannagan, one of the first American sculptors to practice direct carving, also worked in bronze, including the abstracted *Maternal Bird* (p. 21).

In 1910 White launched the Maverick Press, which published original literary and artistic material. A theater and concert hall was also built on the grounds. In 1915 White staged the first Maverick Festival, which would provide the main economic support for the colony. He laid out its genesis in a manuscript in the collection. Held annually on the night of the August full moon, the festival featured music, dancing, food and drink, and attendees dressed in creative costumes. *Lydia* (p. 22) is believed to depict the daughter of a musician in costume. The Festival is often seen as the forerunner to the famous Woodstock Music and Art Fair that was held in Bethel, New York, in 1969. Every summer Maverick Concerts still take place in the concert hall built by Hervey White in 1916 and graced by the monumental *Maverick Horse* carved by John Flannagan.

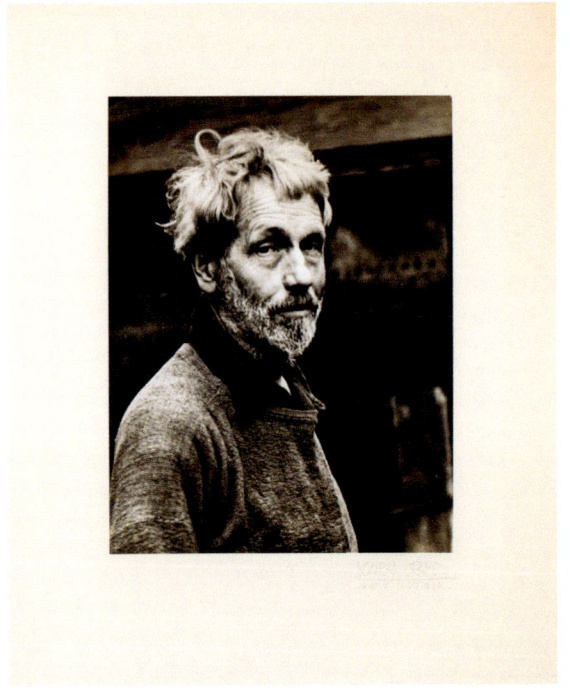

◄ Konrad Cramer (American, born Germany, 1888–1963)
Hervey White, c. 1920
Photograph

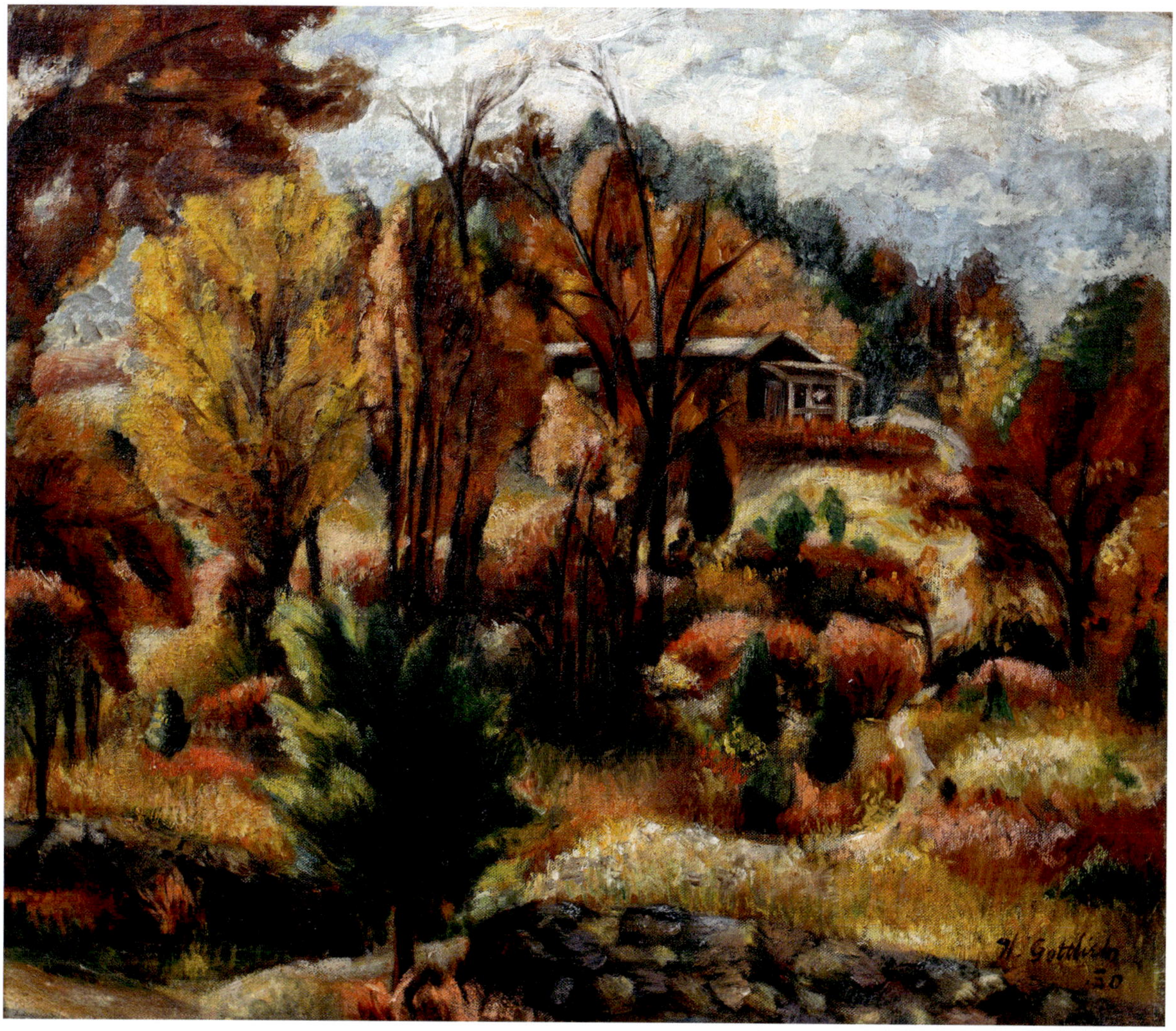

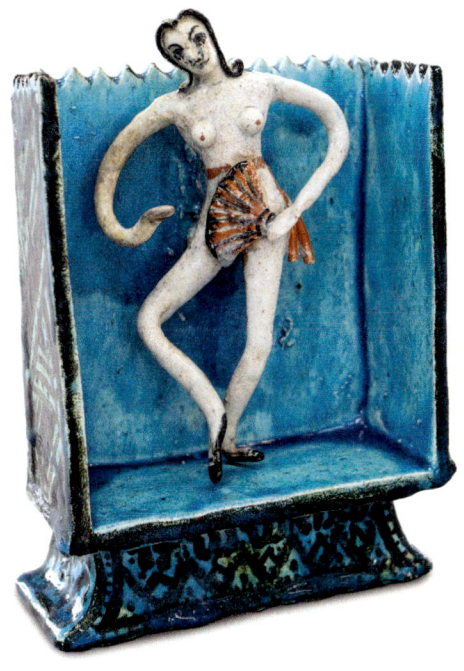

▲ Harry Gottlieb (American, born Romania, 1895–1992)
Autumn in Woodstock, 1930
Oil on canvas

▶ Carl Walters (American, 1883–1955)
Fan Dancer, 1923
Glazed terracotta

The First Maverick Festival.

by

Hervey White

It all began with a well that went down down into the bowels of the mountain and refused to produce any water. Fifteen hundred and sixty five dollars read the order which was signed for the final little trickle. Four cottages had been built for the well, another debt of another fat fifteen hundred. How would I ever raise the three thousand. Inspiration, or desperation? ... I'll give a show!

The cottages were rented to musicians. Leon Barzin was the most probable that season. "Could you get up an orchestra and give a concert?" I asked. He replied he could do it for three hundred dollars.

Ivan Narodny had one cottage, his wife was a singer. I broached the idea to them. They were all enthusiasm in a moment. Nothing like the Russian fire for talking. Away we blazed: we could get their friend "Lada" for a dancer. Pavlova would allow us to use her name. She might be present. The composer Gilbert would come We could use his name. A whole sheaf of names was unfolded. Also Narodny roamed the woods for a stadium, and decided

◀ Hervey White
(American, 1866–1944)
The First Maverick Festival,
1928 manuscript,
subsequently published in
The Saturday Morning,
Woodstock, New York,
August 31, 1928.

▼ Robert Winthrop Chanler
(American, 1872–1930)
Maverick Melodeon, n.d.
Hand-painted Mason &
Hamlin melodeon organ

▼ John Flannagan
(American, 1895–1942)
Maternal Bird, n.d.
Bronze

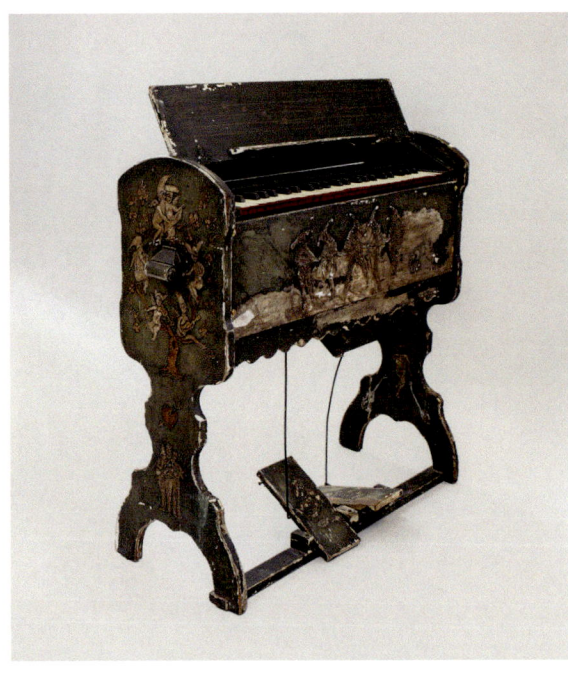

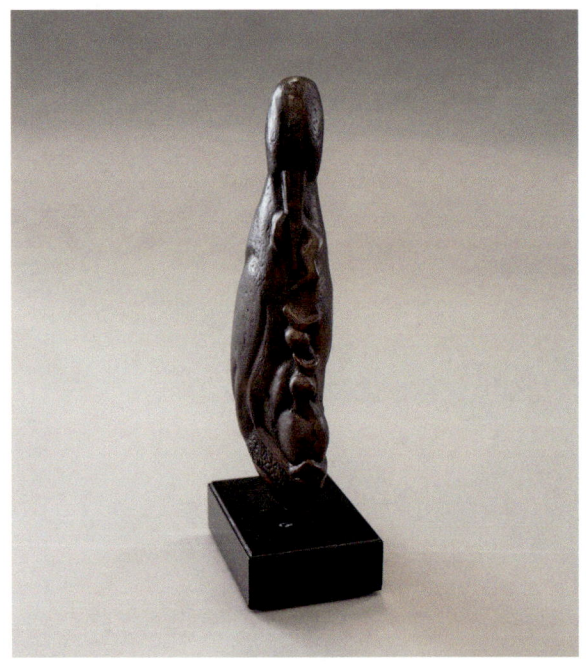

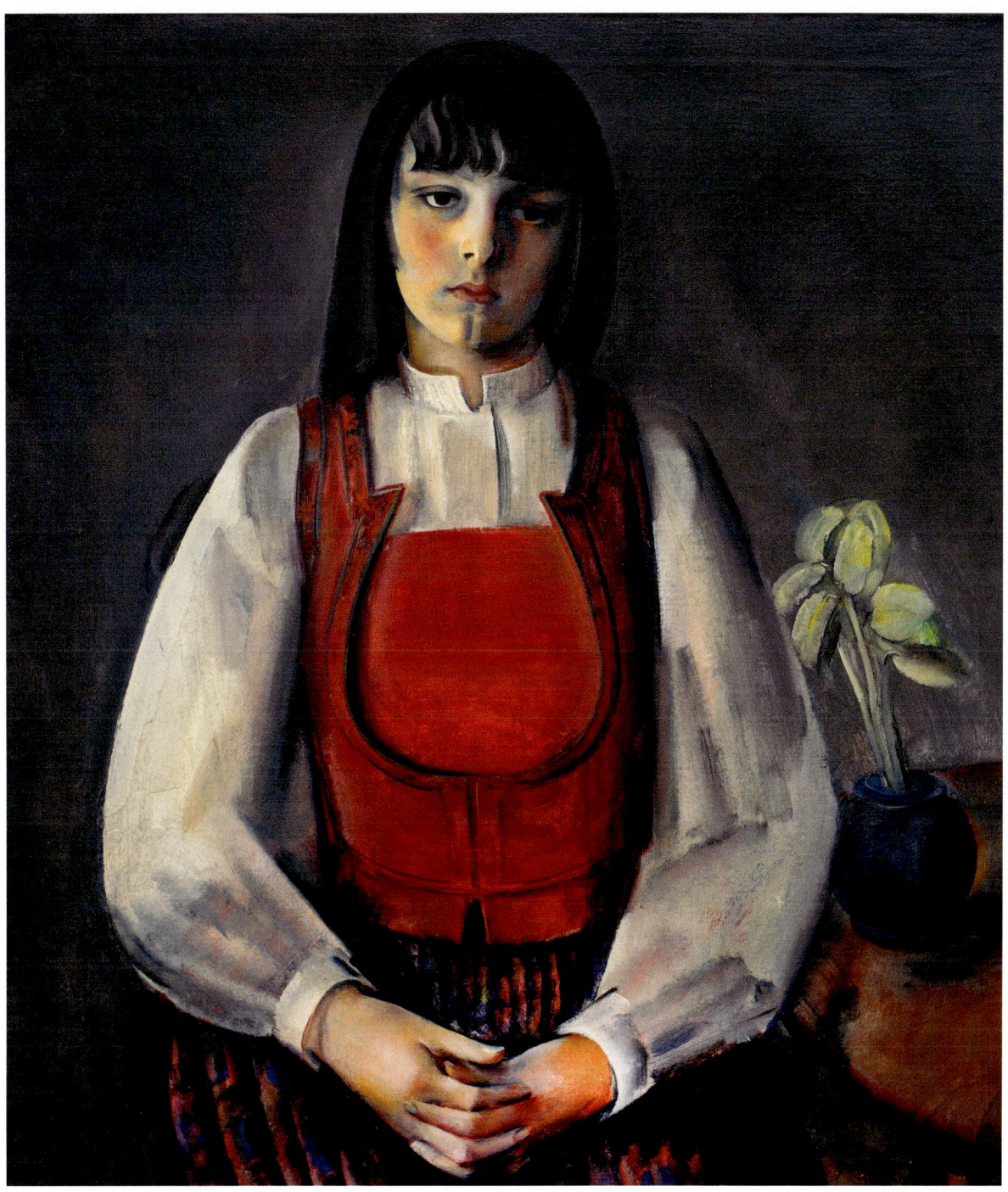

▲ John Carroll (American, 1892–1959)
Lydia, c. 1925
Oil on canvas

THE HISTORIC WOODSTOCK ART COLONY:
THE ARTHUR A. ANDERSON COLLECTION

Art Students League

In 1906 the Art Students League moved its summer school to Woodstock. The League had been founded in New York City in 1875 as an alternative to the mainstream National Academy of Design and had become one of the most important art schools in the country. From 1906 to 1922, and again from 1947 to 1979, the Art Students League brought as many as 200 students to the Woodstock area each year.

Birge Harrison taught at the summer school in Woodstock for the first five years. He had been the painting instructor at Byrdcliffe in 1904 (p. 7) and indeed there was much overlap of artists, both students, and teachers, among the various organizations in Woodstock. As Harrison noted, "The desire is to develop a number of individual painters and not to develop a 'school.'"[1] Landscape was emphasized as much as the figurative tradition, and naturally, given the beautiful, bucolic setting, it became the prevailing subject for many artists working in Woodstock.

Throughout the 1910s and 1920s, Woodstock artists associated with the Art Students League worked in a variety of styles, often combining inspiration from several sources. Some favored Birge Harrison's subtle Tonalist approach while others, including Cecil Chichester leaned towards the painterly brushstrokes and light of Impressionism. Frank Swift Chase and Henry Billings employed the jewel-like tones of the Post-Impressionist palette. In his landscapes, Arnold Blanch drew on the realism of his teachers at the Art Students League, including Robert Henri and John Sloan. Many defy categorization; George Ault's *Autumn Hillside* is unusual in an oeuvre known for its austerity and surreal qualities.

Although landscape may have come to dominate many artists' works, some eschewed the subject. Peggy Bacon, for example, focused on people she observed, often with great humor (see essay pp. 33–36). Likewise, Lucile Blanch, who treated a range of topics including Woodstock landscapes, could also turn to figures, notably in a series of circus performers. More traditional portraiture is represented by canvases such as *Two Sisters* (p. 28), Judson Smith's painting of his daughters. In sculpture, realist work was produced by Grace Mott Johnson, Paul Fiene, and Gertrude Vanderbilt Whitney. Finally, Dewing Woodward founded the Blue Dome Fraternity, combining the nude figure and landscape (something not promoted by the Art Students League) and seen in *Woodland Nude* (p. 29).

▶ George Ault (American, 1891–1948)
Autumn Hillside, 1940
Gouache on paper

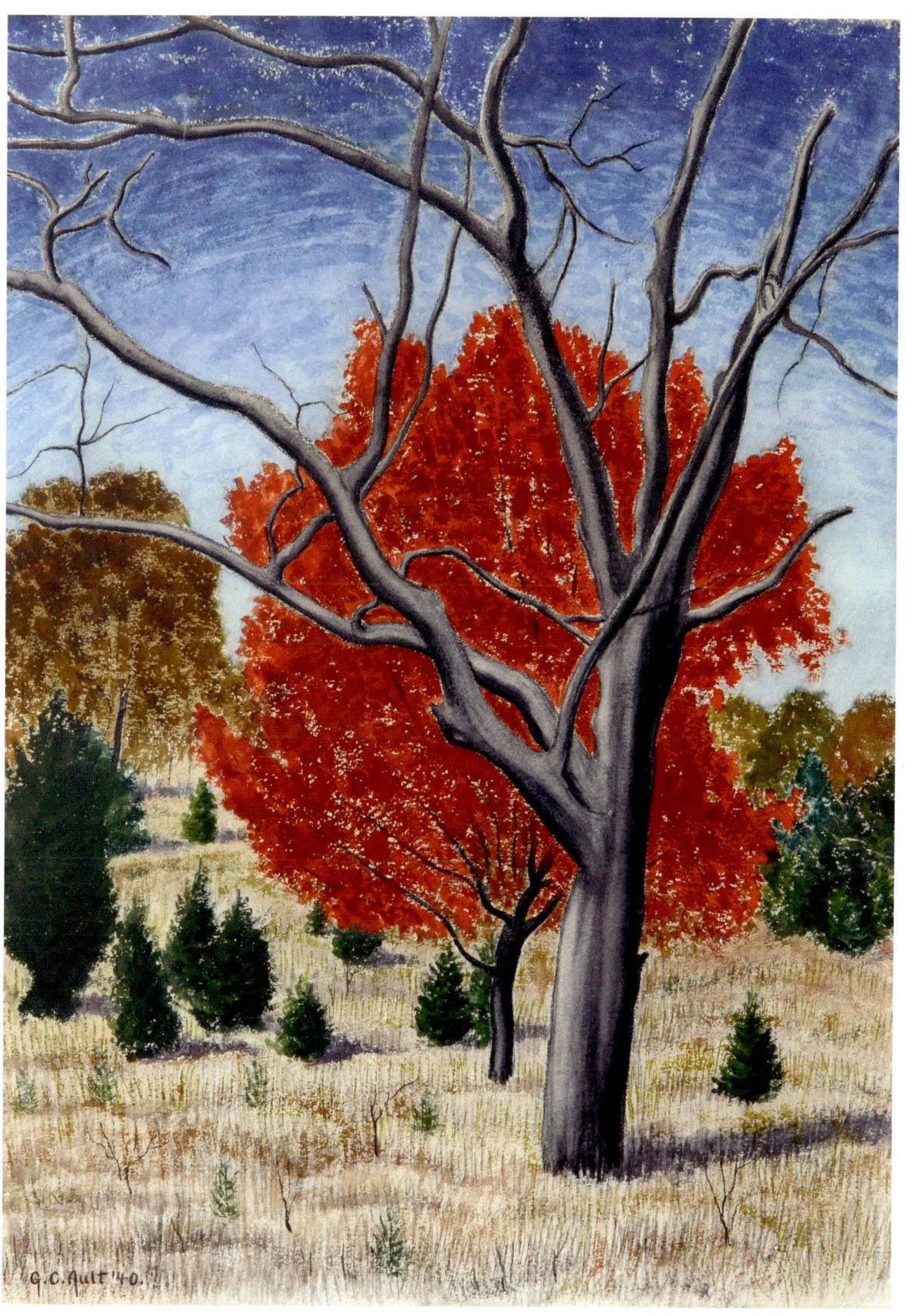

▼ Henry Billings (American, 1901–1985)
Backyard Garden Path, n.d.
Oil on canvas

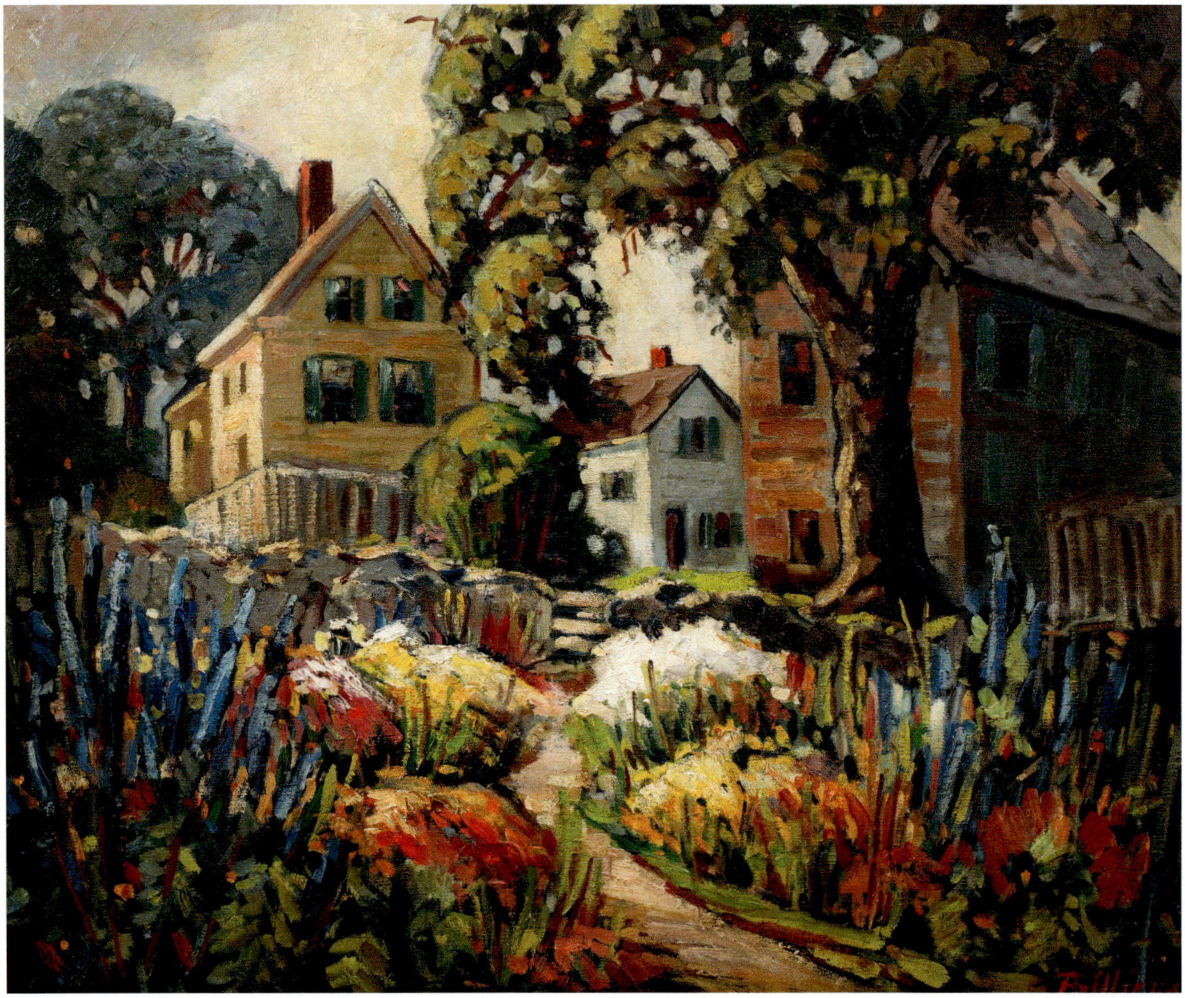

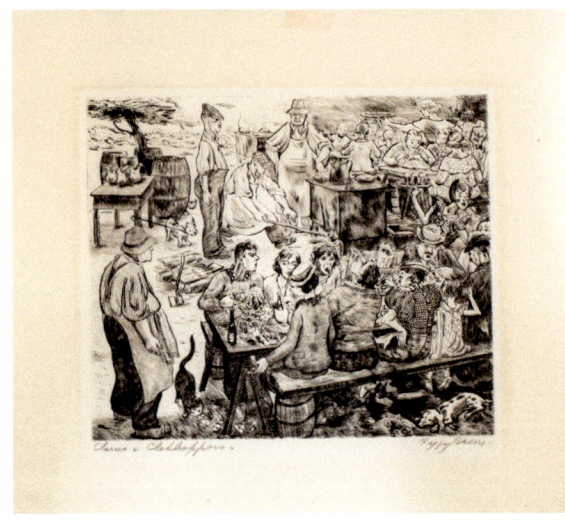

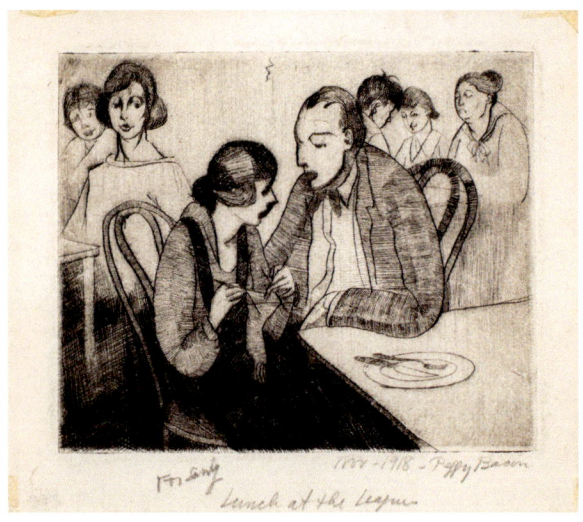

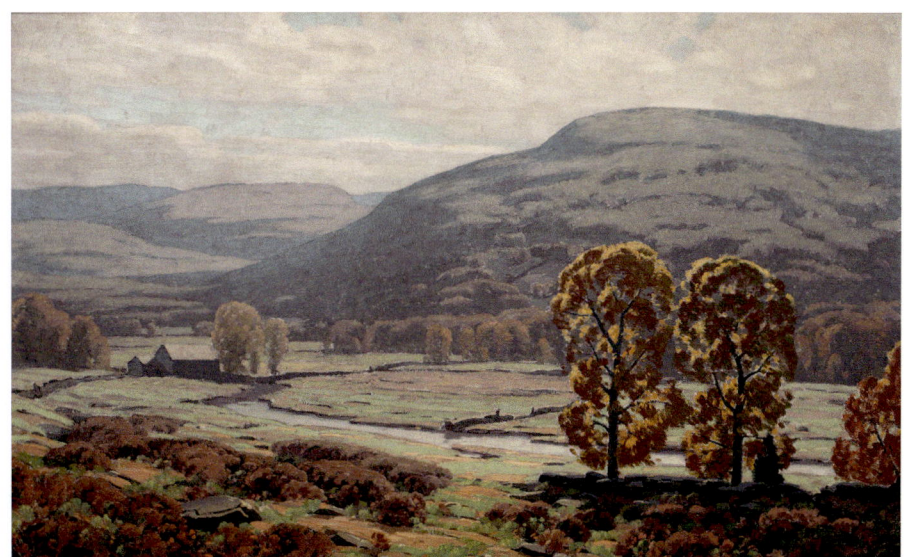

► Cecil Chichester
(American, 1891–1963)
*Willow Valley Near
Woodstock*, c. 1925
Oil on canvas

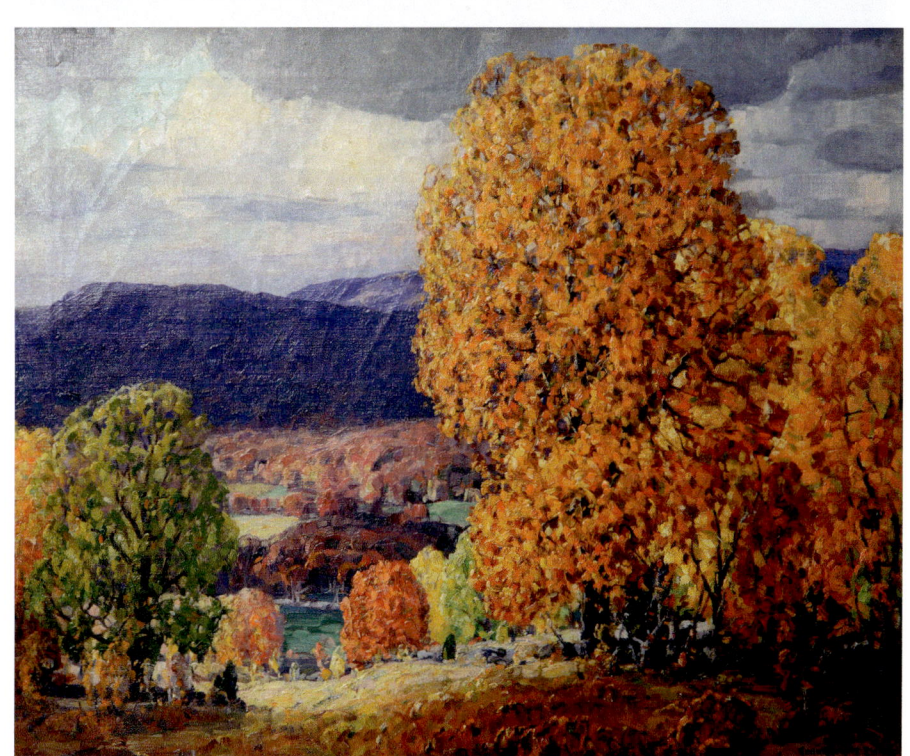

► Frank Swift Chase
(American, 1886–1958)
Catskills at Woodstock, 1927
Oil on canvas

◄ Peggy Bacon
(American, 1895–1987)
Clams and Clodhoppers, 1933
Dry point on paper

◄ Peggy Bacon
(American, 1895–1987)
Lunch at the League, c. 1918
Etching on paper

▼ Arnold Blanch (American, 1896–1968)
Woodstock Farm, 1926
Watercolor on board

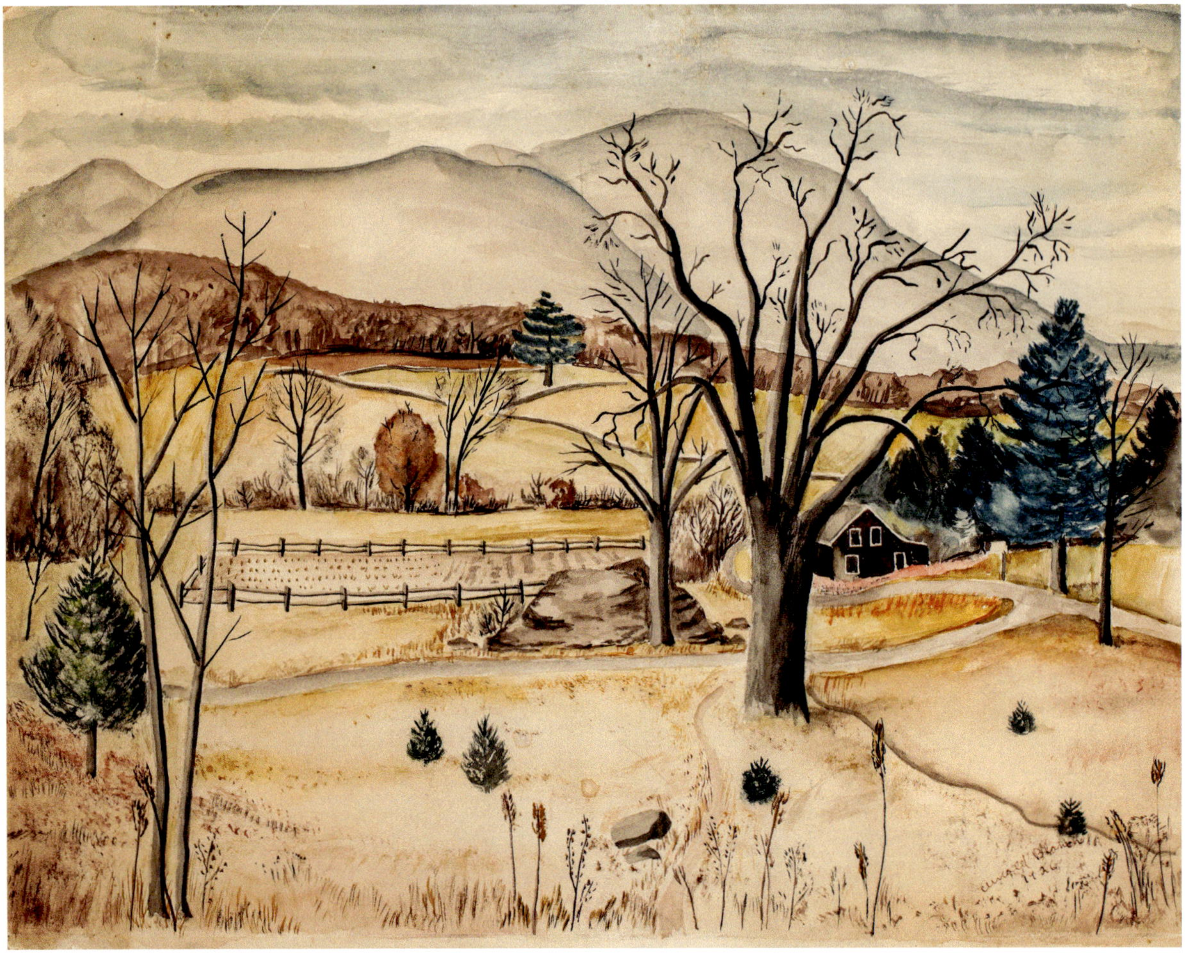

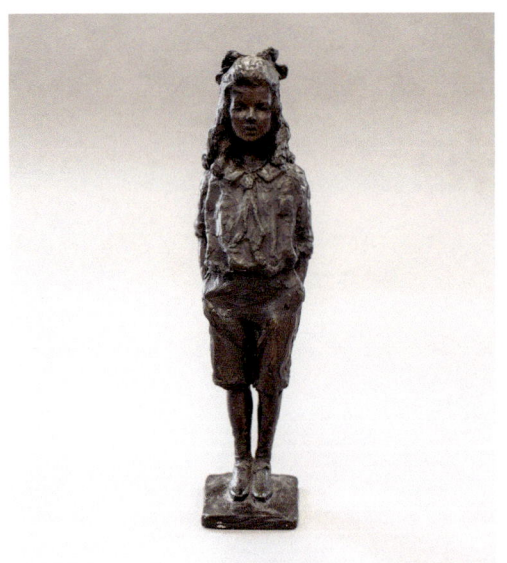

◄ Gertrude Vanderbilt Whitney (American, 1875–1942)
Young Girl, or Wallflower, 1913
Plaster with patina finish

Perhaps best known as an art patron and the founder of the museum that bears her name—the Whitney Museum of American Art—Gertrude Vanderbilt Whitney was also a sculptor who had studied at the Art Students League, garnered numerous public commissions, and whose strong ties to Woodstock and its artists began in the 1920s. This small-scale sculpture depicts her daughter Barbara at age ten.

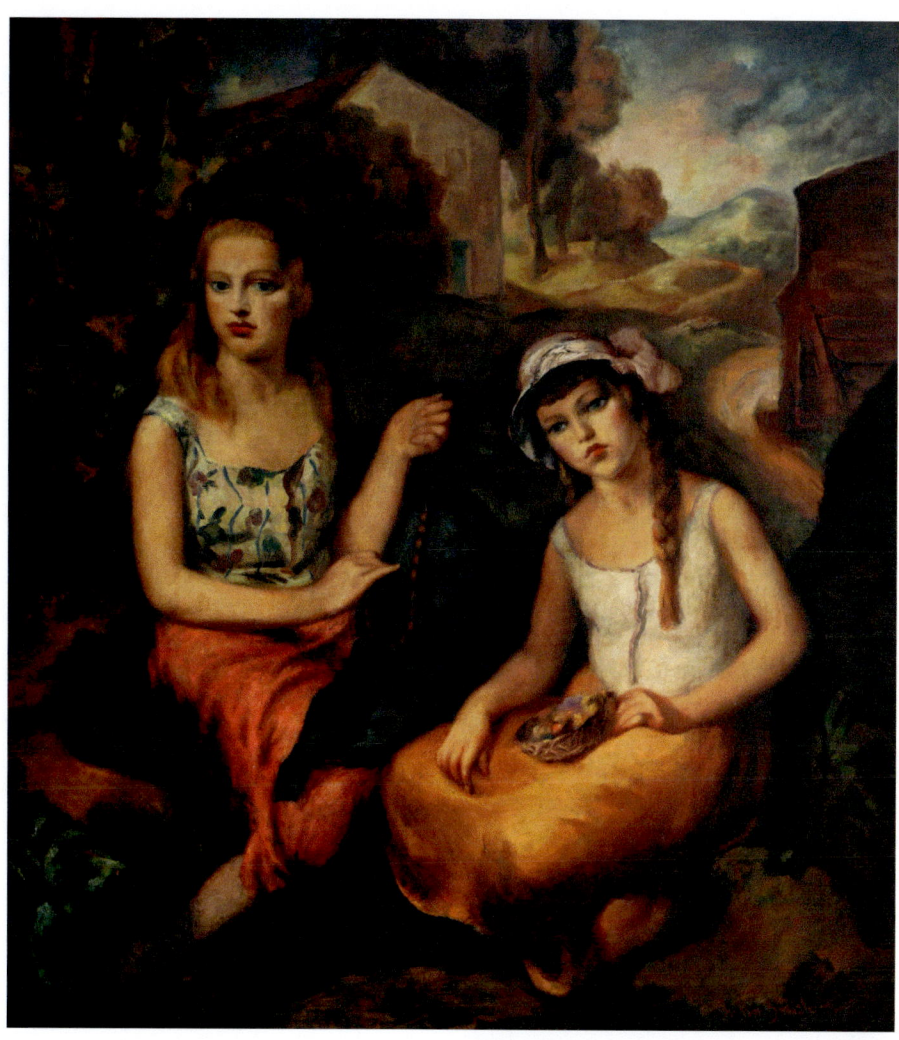

▶ Judson Smith
(American, 1880–1962)
Two Sisters, 1923
Oil on canvas

▶ Grace Mott Johnson
(American, 1882–1967)
*Young Greyhound
(Greyhound Pup)*, 1911
Bronze

▶ Paul Fiene (American,
born Germany, 1899–1949)
*Portrait Bust of the Artist
(Paul Fiene)*, 1932
Plaster

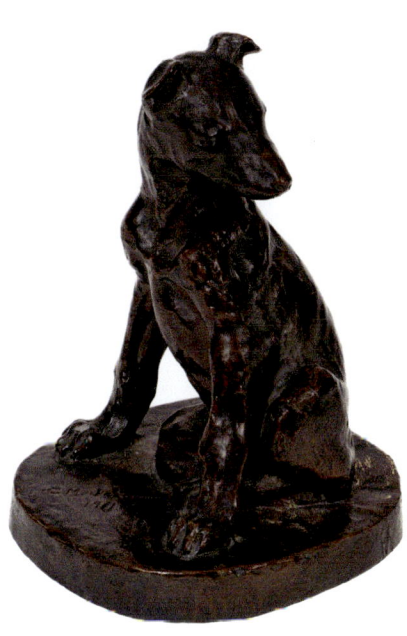

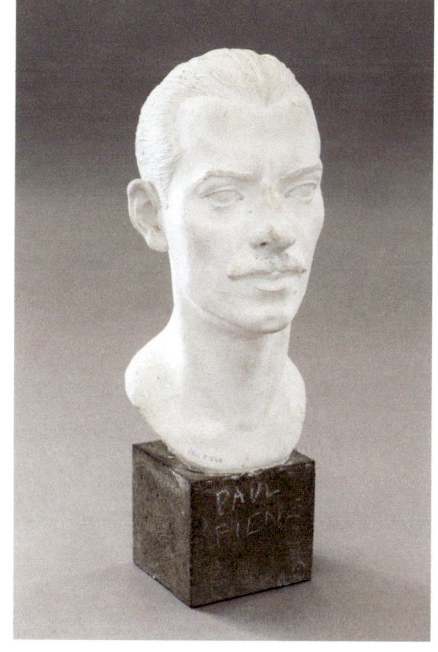

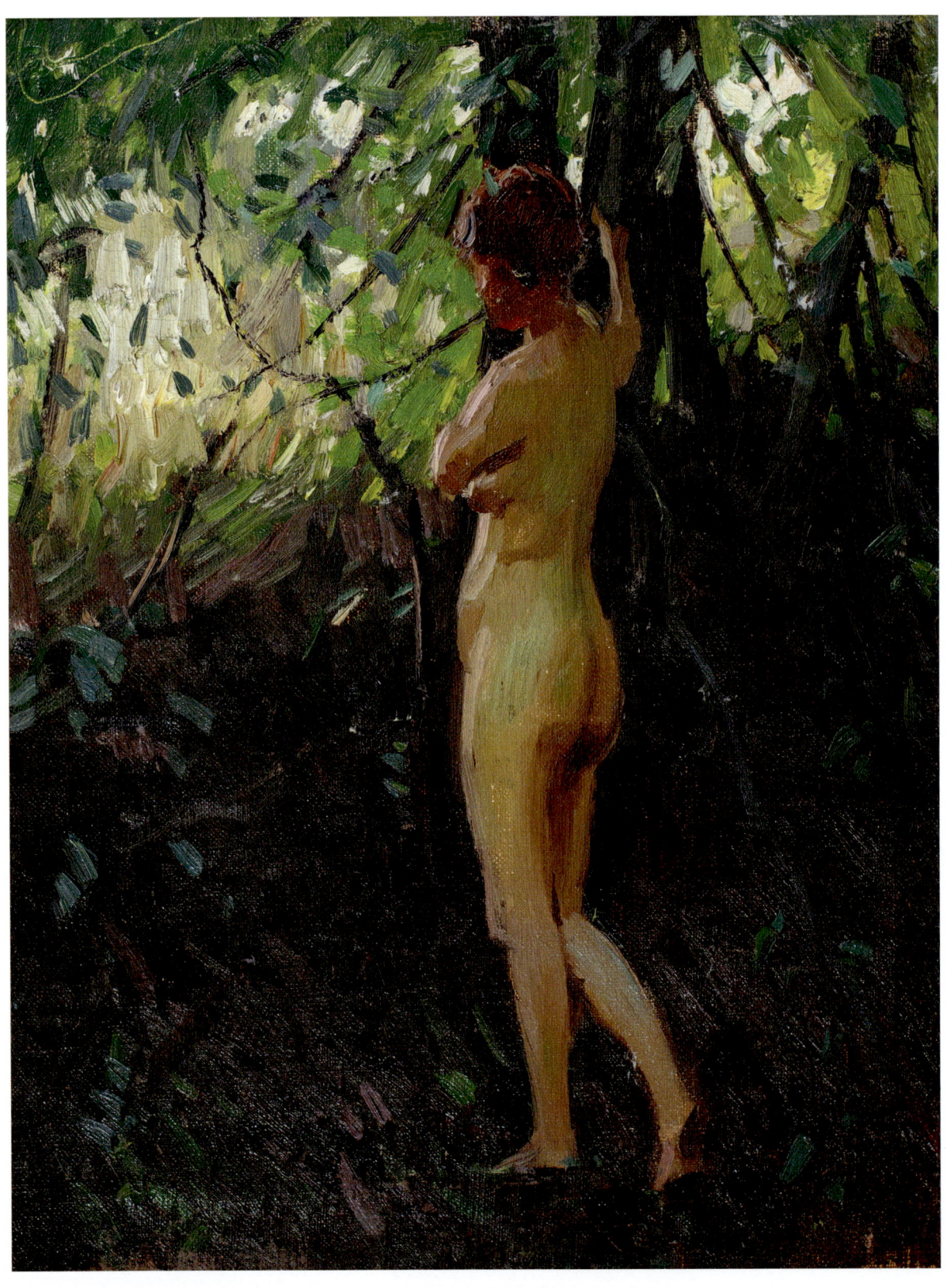

▲ Dewing Woodward (American, 1856–1950)
Woodland Nude, c. 1915
Oil on canvas

► Alexander Brook
(American, 1898–1980)
Cottage on a Hillside, 1935
Oil on canvas

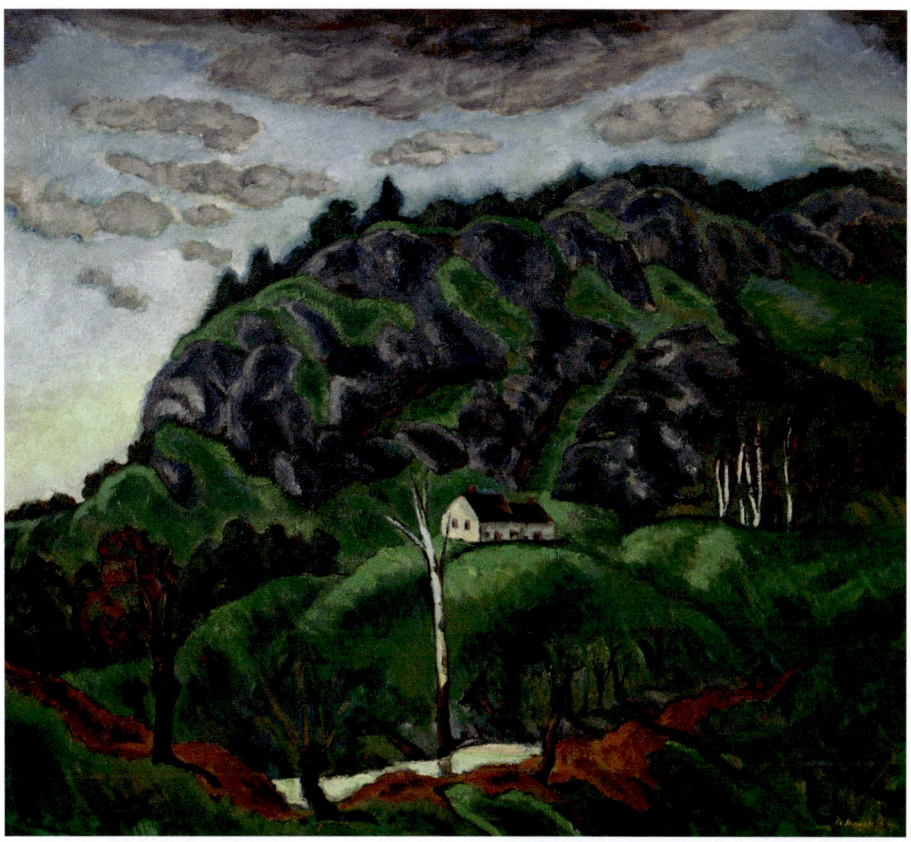

► Lucile Blanch
(American, 1895–1981)
Circus Acrobats, 1930
Watercolor on paper

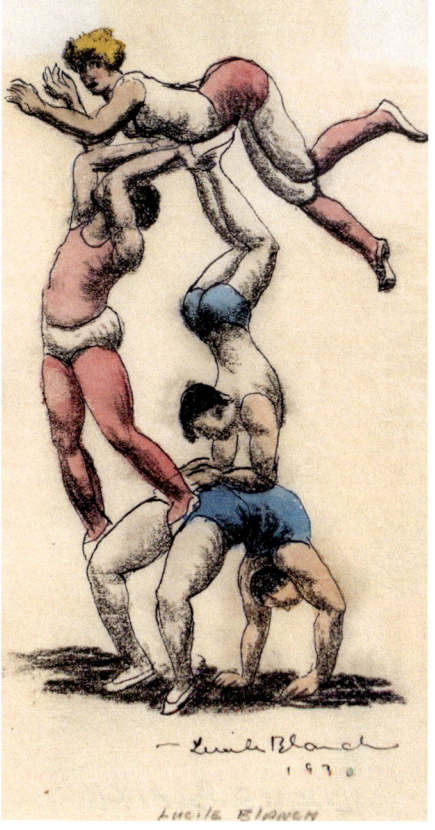

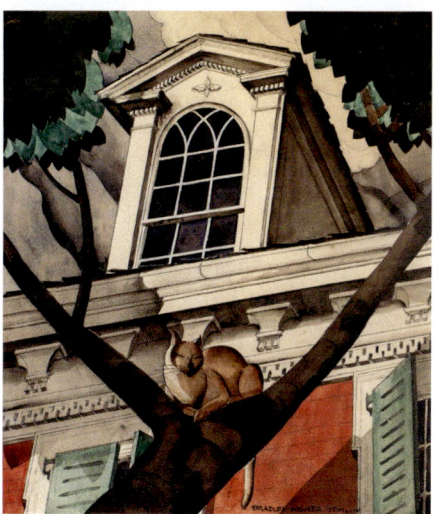

▲ Bradley Walker Tomlin
(American, 1899–1953)
*House with Dormer
and Cat*, 1926
Watercolor and pen
and ink on paper

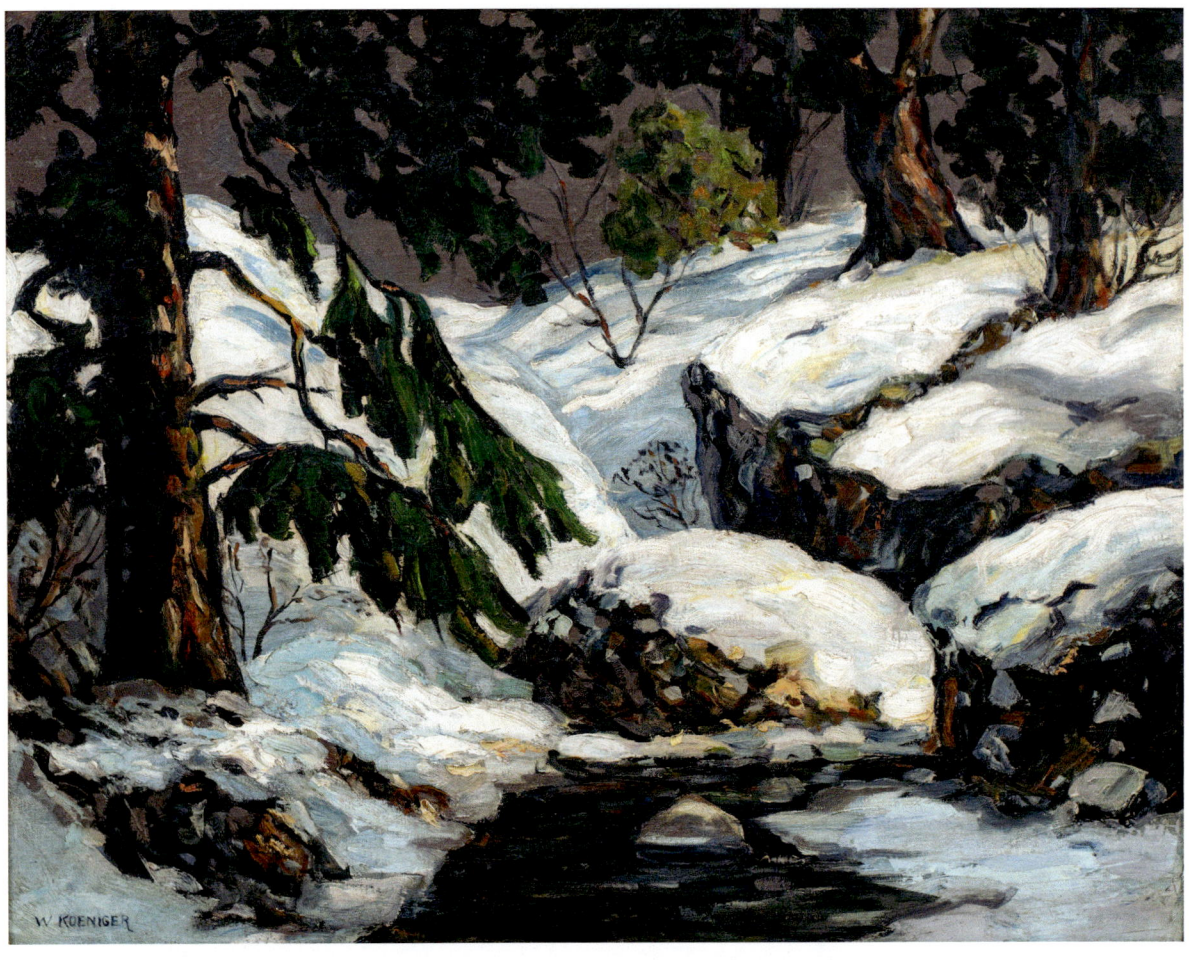

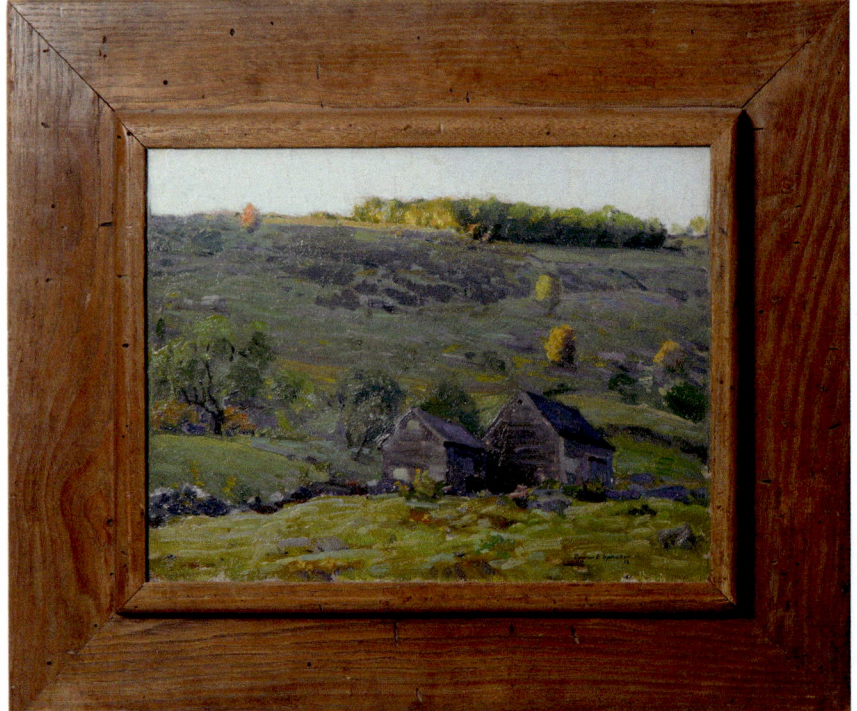

▲ Walter Koeniger (American, born Germany, 1881–1943)
Catskill Winter Stream, c. 1925
Oil on canvas

◄ Eugene Speicher (American, 1883–1962)
Last of the Sun, 1913
Oil on board

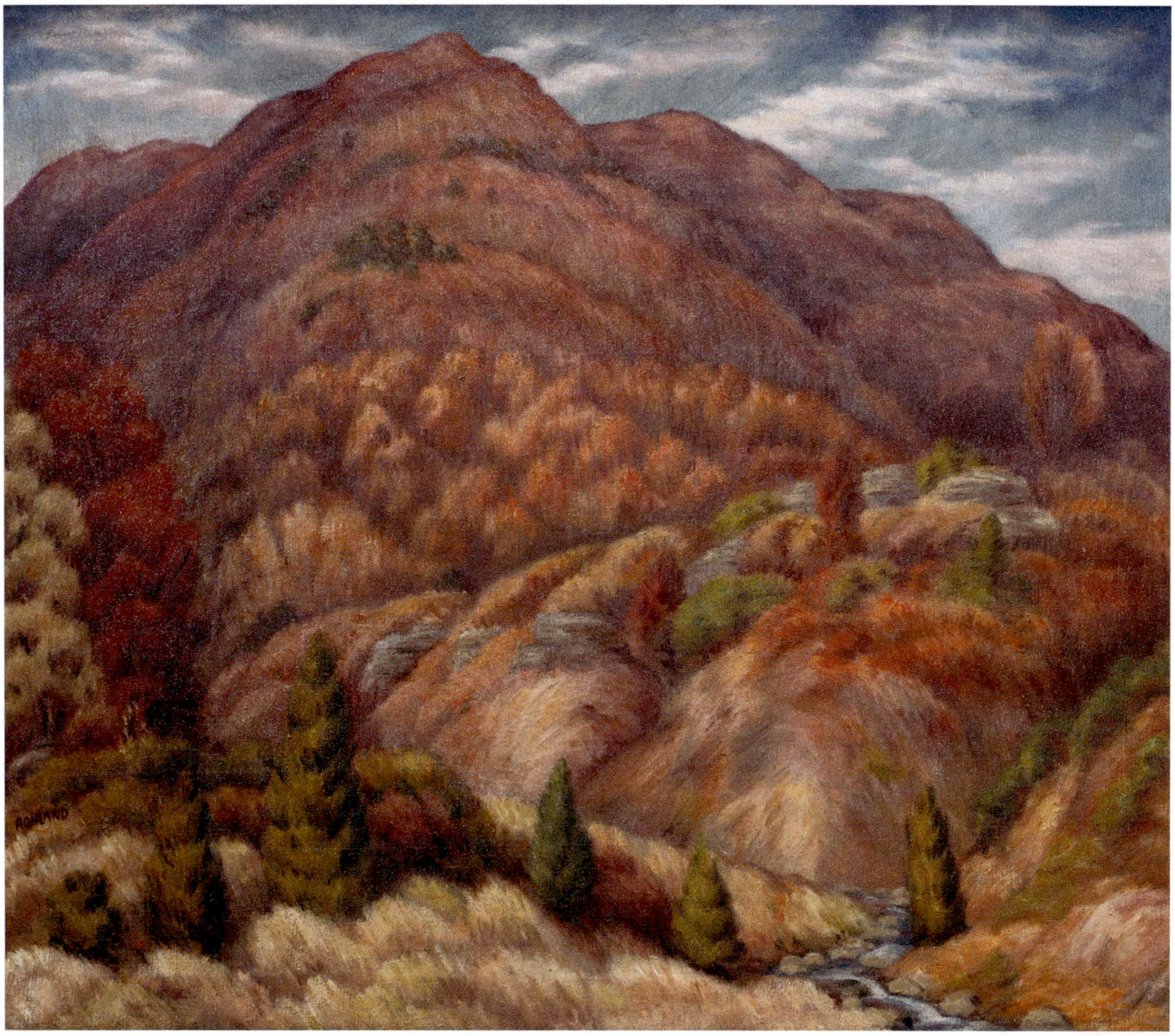

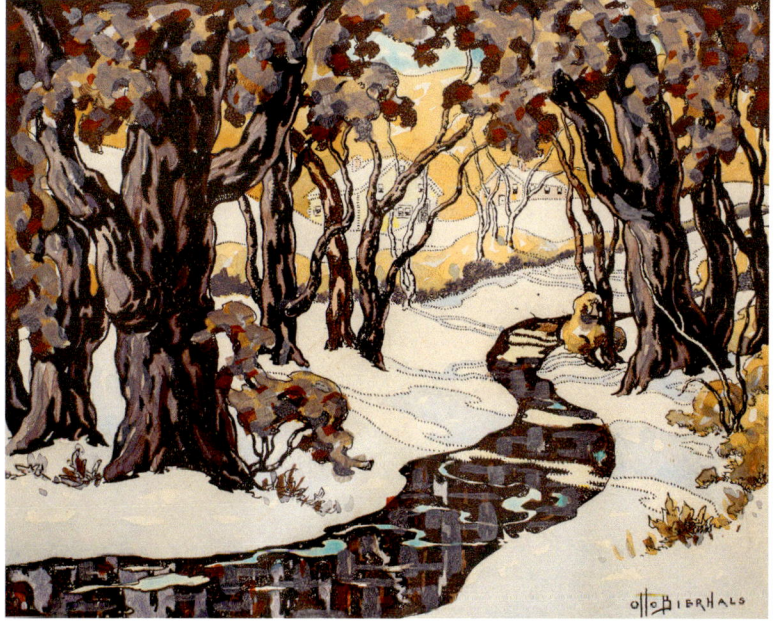

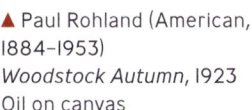
▲ Paul Rohland (American,
1884–1953)
Woodstock Autumn, 1923
Oil on canvas

▶ Otto Bierhals (American,
born Germany, 1879–1944)
Path in Woods, c. 1935
Hand-colored lithograph on paper

"ROLLICKING HUMOR AND DRY, CAUSTIC COMMENT": CARICATURES BY PEGGY BACON IN THE ARTHUR A. ANDERSON COLLECTION

Karen E. Quinn

Peggy Bacon (1895–1987) studied painting at the Art Students League from 1915 to 1920, but was self-taught at printmaking, the medium with which she is most closely associated.[1] During a prolific career, she produced drawings, poetry, and short stories for a variety of magazines, and illustrated some sixty books, fifteen of which she wrote.[2] She liked the immediacy first of the drypoint printmaking process, then lithography. "I love drypoint and I think that actually it gives you the same wonderful satisfaction that carving in stone must give to a person."[3] She began to experiment with the process around 1918 while at the Art Students League when she and a friend were shown an unused printing press. *Lunch at the League* (p. 25), an early effort, established her approach—a dense style of outlined figures filled in with different textures achieved by careful hatching and crosshatching to create a range of tones.

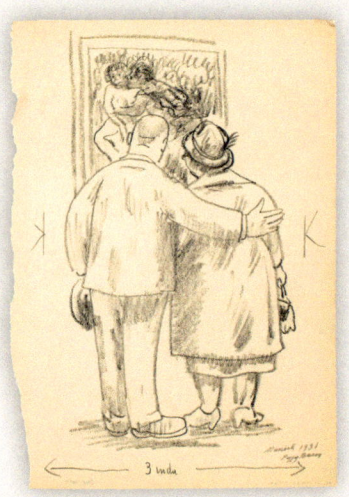

▲ Peggy Bacon
Art Gallery #2, 1931
Conte crayon on paper

At around the same time, Bacon first attempted caricatures of her peers at the Art Students League in a class taught by George Bellows. She went on to produce them as drawings, prints, and pastels for some two decades; of the more than thirty Bacon works in the Historic Woodstock Art Colony: Arthur A. Anderson Collection, almost all are caricature sketches and prints. Her subjects were people she saw regularly, including friends, but also complete strangers. Her perceptive observations led her to create images ranging from the warmly humorous to those that are savagely witty. *Art Gallery #2* depicts the former approach in which a portly couple—with heads together and the man's arm around the woman—views a painting of lusty lovers, perhaps imagining that it is, or once was, a reflection of themselves. On the other hand, in *Black Eye*, whose subject is identified as the Woodstock artist John Carroll, Bacon exaggerated Carroll's features, apparently injured in an altercation. The resulting comical image is even more

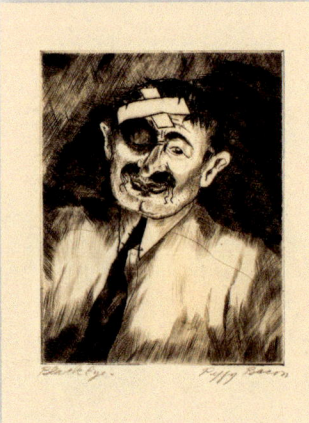

▲ Peggy Bacon
Black Eye "John Carroll", n.d.
Dry point on paper

amusing when compared to George Bellows's lithograph of a handsome Carroll, making it hard to believe it is the same sitter (p. 43). Even Bellows's own caricature of Carroll is more subdued in tone (p. 44).

In 1919 Bacon enrolled in the Art Students League summer school in Woodstock and lived there from 1921 to 1926 with her husband, Alexander Brook, whom she had met at the League in the city and married in 1920. Unlike many artists in Woodstock, including Brook (p. 30), Bacon did not feature landscape as her subject of choice but instead continued to focus on the people in her orbit. She studied with modernist Andrew Dasburg there (p. 58), but also associated with a wide variety of artists working in other styles, including her former teacher George Bellows and his circle: Eugene Speicher, Robert Henri, and Leon Kroll.[4] Bacon's drawing of Speicher captures a likeness of the artist with a few expressive strokes—in his characteristic bow tie and dark, round glasses. Sketched on notepad paper, the immediacy of this small treasure is one example of what makes the scope of the Arthur A. Anderson Collection and its role as a study collection so special.

Bacon's caricatures culminated in the publication of *Off With Their Heads* in 1934. The book featured thirty-nine images ranging from caricatures of Georgia O'Keeffe to Franklin Roosevelt, each accompanied by a brief, insightful physical description of the sitter, the verbal equivalent to the wittiness of her caricature. The artist, writer, and critic Guy Pène du Bois was one subject. The preliminary sketch is in the Anderson Collection; the resulting book illustration remained close to the original, though with a darker face and clothing.[5] Bacon's written assessment begins, "Rich pot-roast effect. Color warm, ruddy, winey. Goopy-fish eyes, skidding off at outer corners. Nose mashed crooked…Air of the keen, worldly bon-viveur with a lively lear [sic] and a

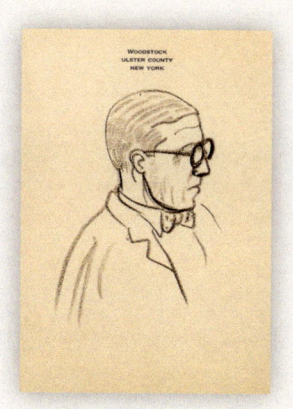

▲ Peggy Bacon
Portrait of Eugene Speicher, 1921
Conte crayon on paper

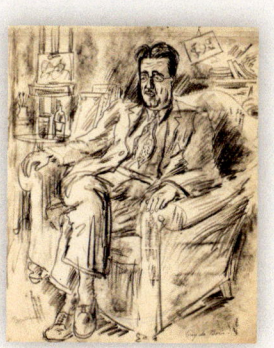

▲ Peggy Bacon
Guy Pène du Bois, 1935
Conte crayon on paper

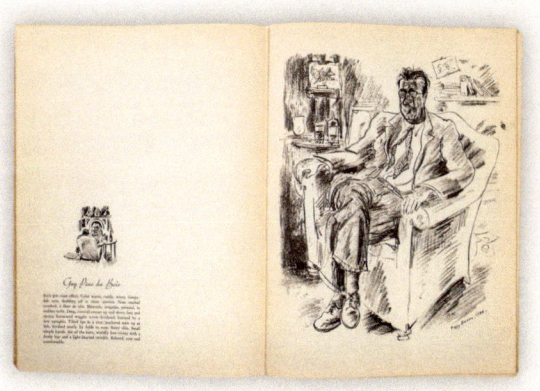

▲ Peggy Bacon,
Off With Their Heads, 1934, n.p.
New York, Robert M. McBride & Company

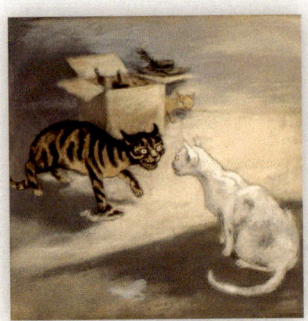

▲ Peggy Bacon,
Two Cats, n.d.
Pastel on paper

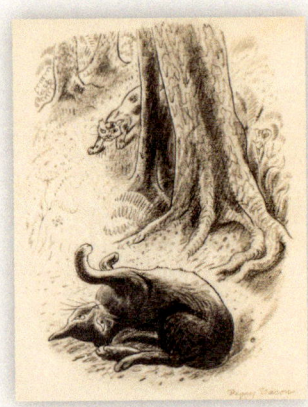

▲ Peggy Bacon,
Come Play With Me, n.d.
Lithograph on paper

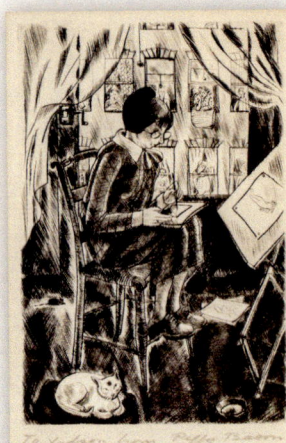

▲ Peggy Bacon,
Lady Artist, n.d.
Etching on Paper

light-hearted twinkle."[6] Words and sketch conjure the personality as well as the image of Pène du Bois, making the artist come alive for the reader.

Cats, for which Bacon had an affinity and depicted her entire career, were also frequently subjected to caricature. "We always had dynasties of cats around home when I was growing up…I loved them dearly and enjoyed them as personalities and as models," she noted.[7] They appeared as supporting characters in larger compositions such as *Clams and Clodhoppers*, along with their canine counterparts (p. 25). In the foreground, a well-fed feline enjoys the shellfish of the title offered by the woman in a hat, Bacon herself. Based on the number of empty shells on the ground, she has been very generous to the scavenger. The dog to the right and one in the background seem to have been less fortunate in their acquisition of treats.

Cats are featured more prominently in two other works on paper: *Two Cats* and *Come Play with Me*. In *Come Play with Me*, the animal in the foreground lies on its back in a seemingly impossible twist of its legs and torso. A second feline, crouched behind a tree, slinks towards the first, appearing to be readying to attack more than intending to play. In *Two Cats*, the felines of the title face off over the striped one's coveted catch; a third lurks behind a box. Their exaggerated, lumpy bodies, expressive ears, and wide, glowering eyes are the result of years of careful study by someone who has lived with cats and understands their physical quirks. With an economy of line, Bacon captures the traits of the felines with the same insightfulness as she did with her human subjects.

Bacon did not spare herself in her caricatures. As noted, she appeared in profile in *Clams and Clodhoppers* and she also included herself in *Off With Their Heads* (p. 34), scathingly describing herself as "Pin-head, parsimoniously covered with thin dark hair, on a short dumpy body…"[8] *Lady Artist* is a gentler self-portrait, where she depicted herself working on a drypoint in her studio with a serene feline at her side. A variety of figures in each window across the way fills the background with humorous details.

Her keen eye never rested—as she said, "The thing that keeps any artist's work alive and healthy is the constant observation and recording that should be part of his daily life like breathing."[9] ■

Notes

1. William Murrell, *Peggy Bacon* (Woodstock, New York: William M. Fisher, 1922), n.p. Art critic Murrell wrote a group of books called "Younger Artist Series" including this one on Bacon with an early assessment of her skills.

2. For general biographical information on Bacon see Roberta K. Tarbell, *Peggy Bacon: Personalities and Places* (Washington, DC.: National Collection of Fine Arts, 1975). For Bacon in Woodstock see Tom Wolf, *Peggy Bacon: Cats and Caricatures* (Woodstock, New York: Woodstock Artists Association and Museum, 2011) and Bruce Weber, "Peggy Bacon: Caricaturist, Observer, & Printmaker of the Woodstock Art Colony," April 2022: https://www.learningwoodstockartcolony.com/post/peggy-bacon-caricaturist-observer-printmaker-of-the-woodstock-art-colony. On Bacon's caricatures: Wendy Wick Reaves, *Celebrity Caricature in America*, (New Haven, Connecticut: Yale University Press, 1998), 247–253.

3. Oral history interview with Peggy Bacon, May 8, 1973. Archives of American Art, Smithsonian Institution (https://www.aaa.si.edu/collections/interviews/oral-history-interview-peggy-bacon-12376)

4. For images of Speicher, see also Bellows, *Eugene Speicher drawing on a Stone* (p. 43), and the middle figure in *Four Friends* (p. 37). For Speicher's work see Speicher, *Last of the Sun* (p. 31) and *Farmer in Overalls*, (p. 39); for Kroll, (p. 42); for Henri, (p. 41).

5. The image also appeared as an etching in 1933 called *The Hangover*.

6. Peggy Bacon, *Off With Their Heads* (New York, Robert M. McBride & Company, 1934), n.p.

7. Interview, Peggy Bacon.

8. Bacon, *Off With Their Heads*

9. Interview, Peggy Bacon.

THE HISTORIC WOODSTOCK ART COLONY: THE ARTHUR A. ANDERSON COLLECTION

George Bellows and His Circle

In 1920, at the invitation of Eugene Speicher, George Bellows spent his first summer in Woodstock. Bellows belonged to the Ashcan School, a loosely associated group of early twentieth-century artists working in New York City who favored urban subjects, often gritty in nature. They painted in a realist style that was in contrast to the prevailing and popular academic approaches. Both Speicher and Bellows had studied with leading Ashcan School artist, Robert Henri, in New York.

Bellows became, in many respects, the backbone of Arthur Anderson's collection and is richly represented by over 150 works, the most of any artist. The subjects cover the full range of Bellows's themes over the course of his career, from quick sketches to finished prints. The three versions of *Hungry Dogs*, his first attempt at lithography,

show him experimenting with the same literal "Ashcan" image. *Sniped* (p. 40), a World War I subject depicting a wounded or dead soldier surrounded by comrades in a trench was published in *Collier's* on July 13, 1918, with a story on combat titled "Something," by Donal Hamilton Haines. Bellows based his war works on published accounts and images. The largest group of works in the collection, however, centers on Bellows's family and friends. *Four Friends* depicts Leon Kroll, Bellows, Eugene Speicher, and Robert Henri. Work by each colleague is included as well. The wives of Speicher, Bellows, and Henri are featured in *Elsie, Emma, and Marjorie* (p. 40). More personal and humorous is the group of caricatures Bellows sketched, including Henri, John Carroll, Charles Rosen, and even a self-portrait.

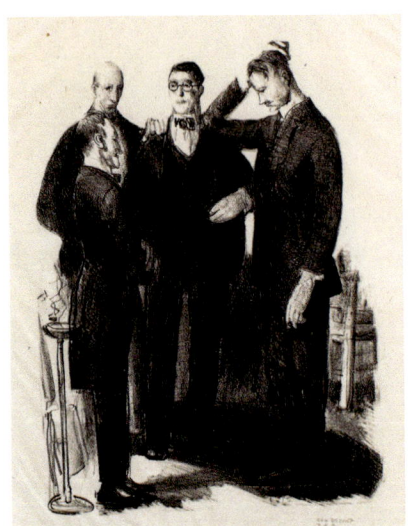

◀ George Bellows (American, 1882–1925)
Four Friends, 1921
Lithograph on paper

▶ George Bellows (American, 1882–1925)
Hungry Dogs, 1916
Lithograph on paper

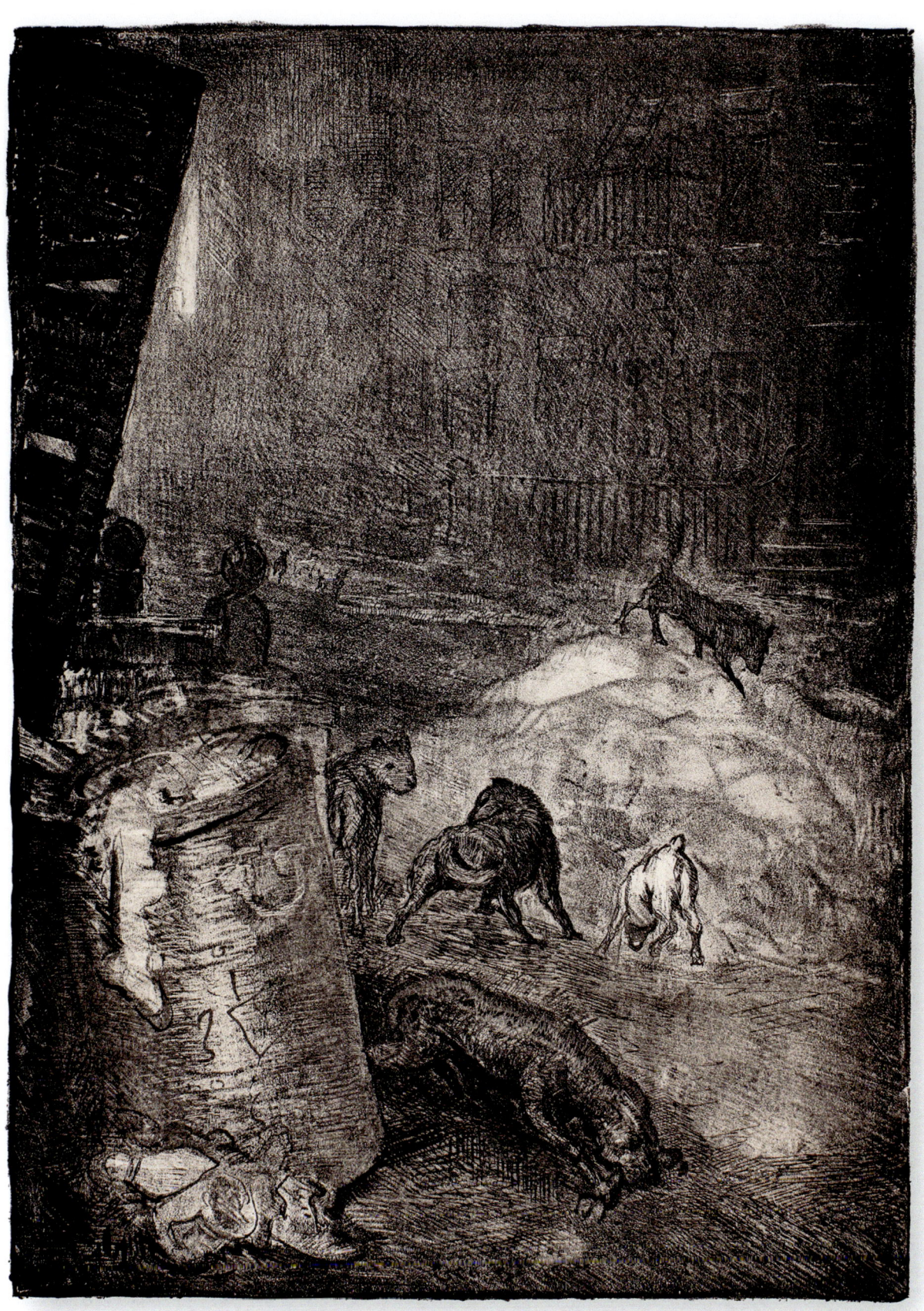

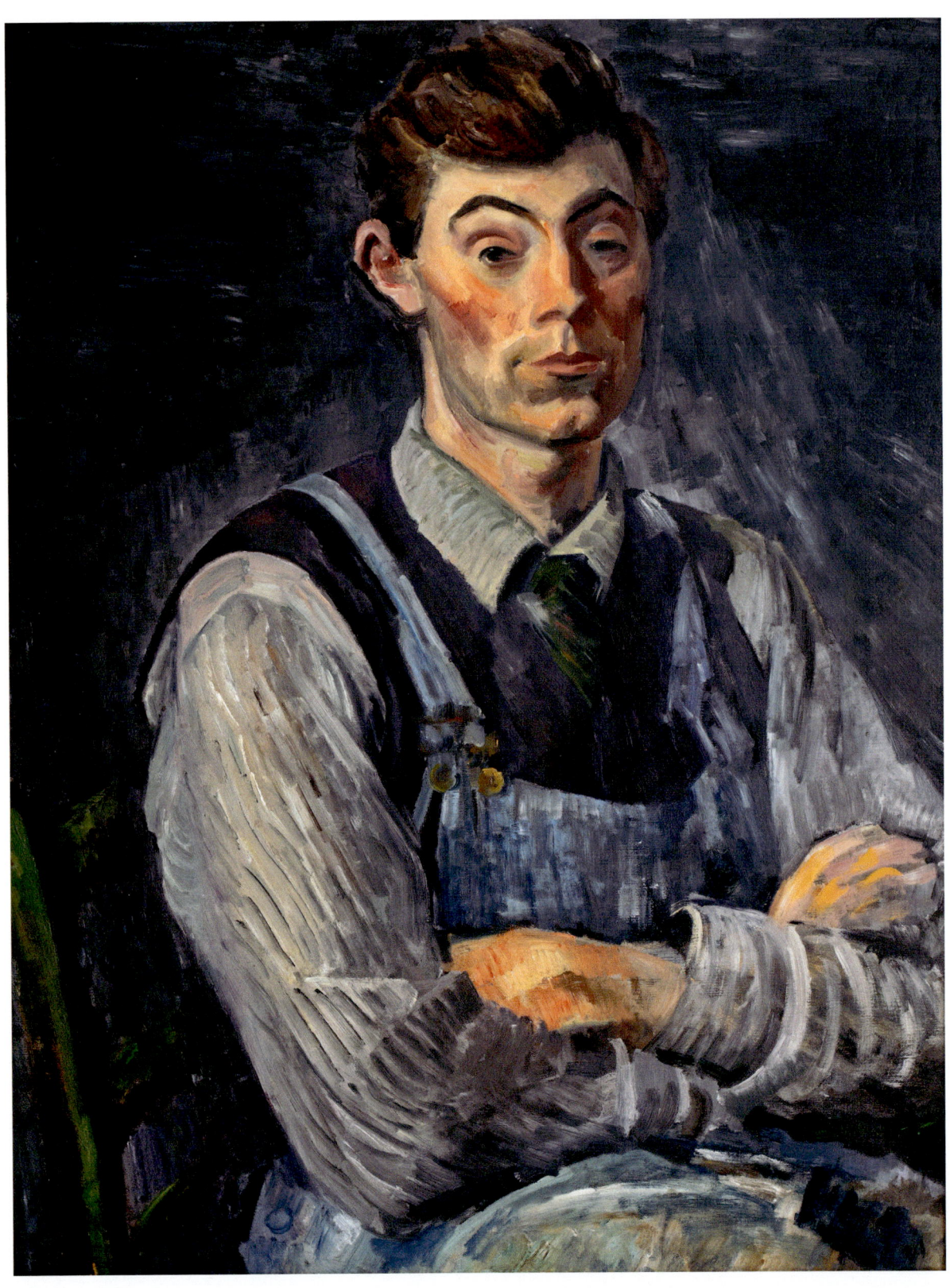

▲ Eugene Speicher (American, 1883–1962)
Farmer in Overalls, c. 1925
Oil on canvas

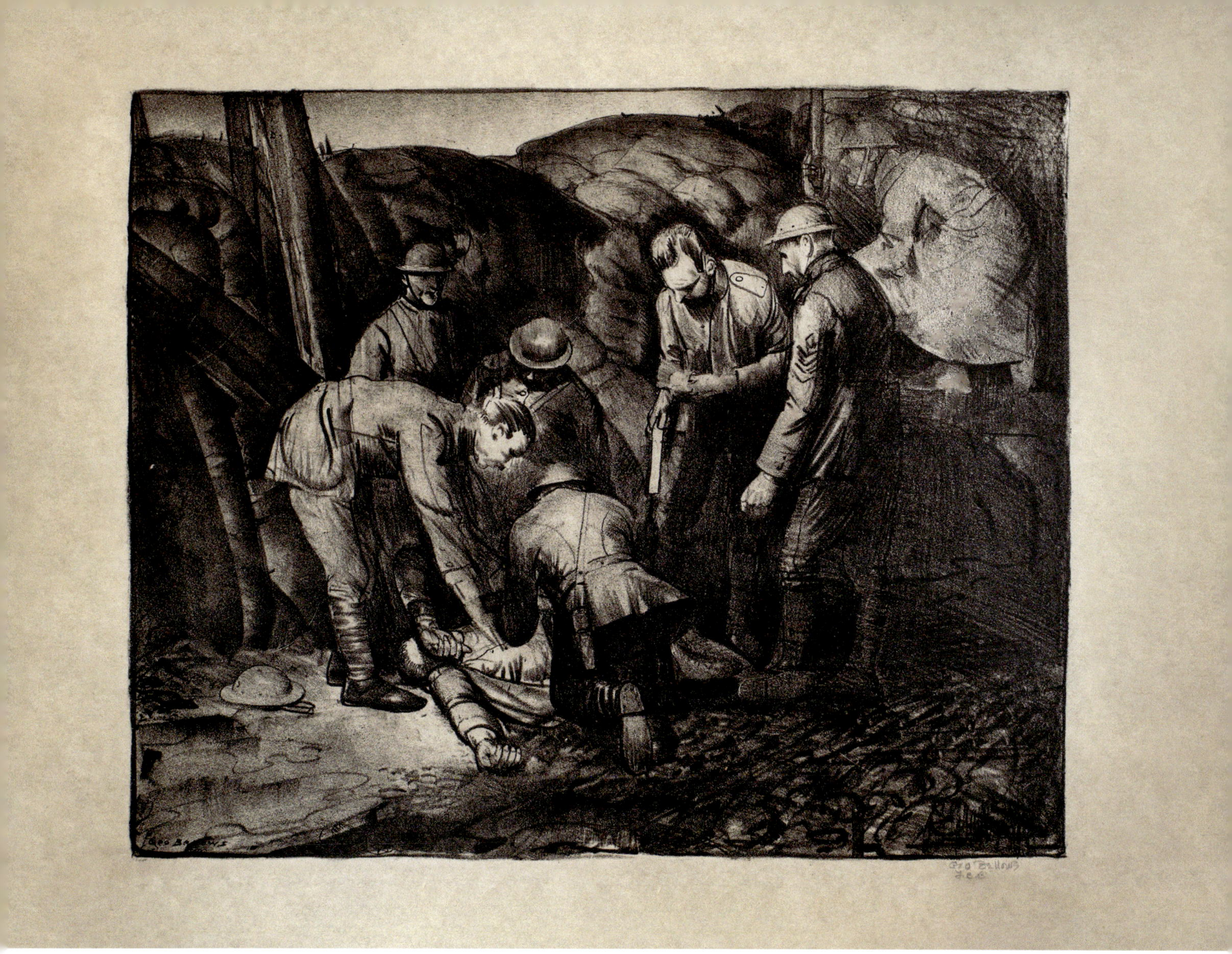

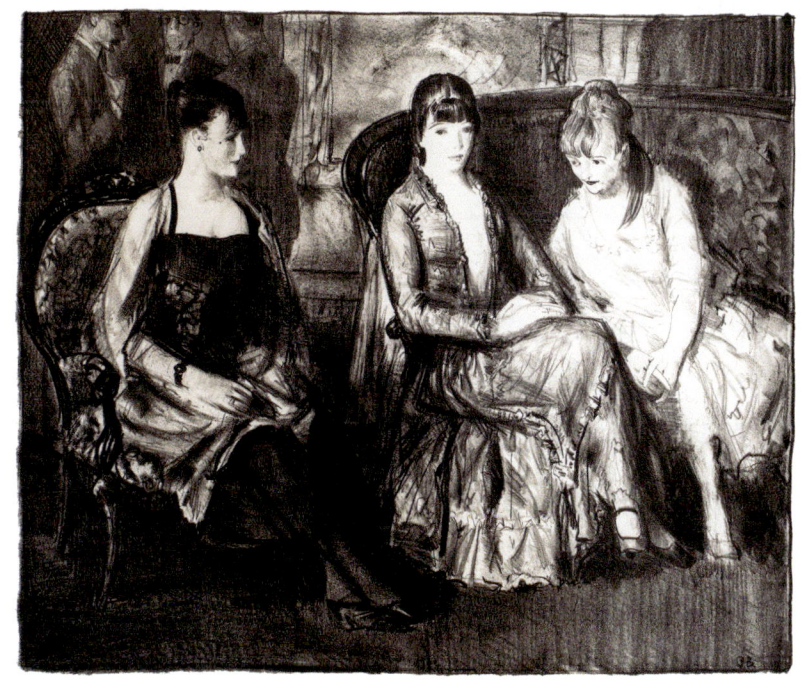

▲ George Bellows
(American, 1882–1925)
Sniped (War Series), 1918
Lithograph on paper

▶ George Bellows
(American, 1882–1925)
Elsie, Emma, and Marjorie, 1921
Lithograph on paper

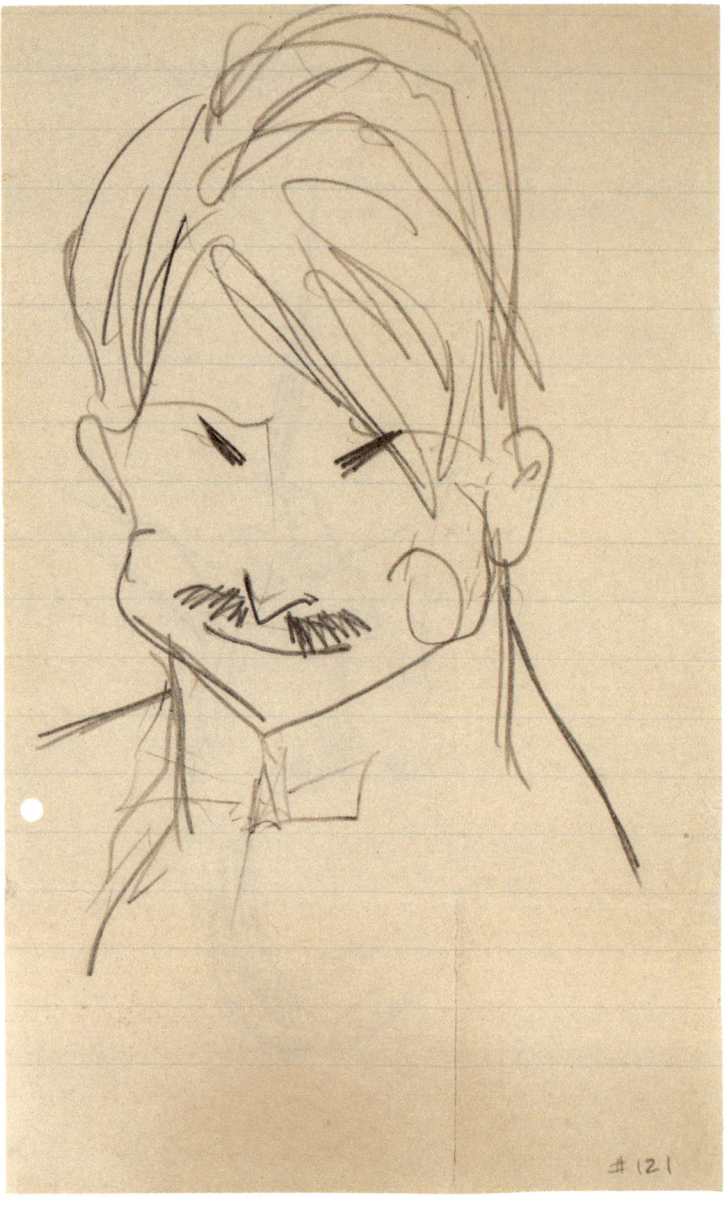

▶ Leon Kroll (American, 1884–1974)
Young Girl, c. 1930
Red chalk on paper

▼ Robert Henri (American, 1865–1929)
Three Studies, Madrid, 1906
Conte crayon on paper

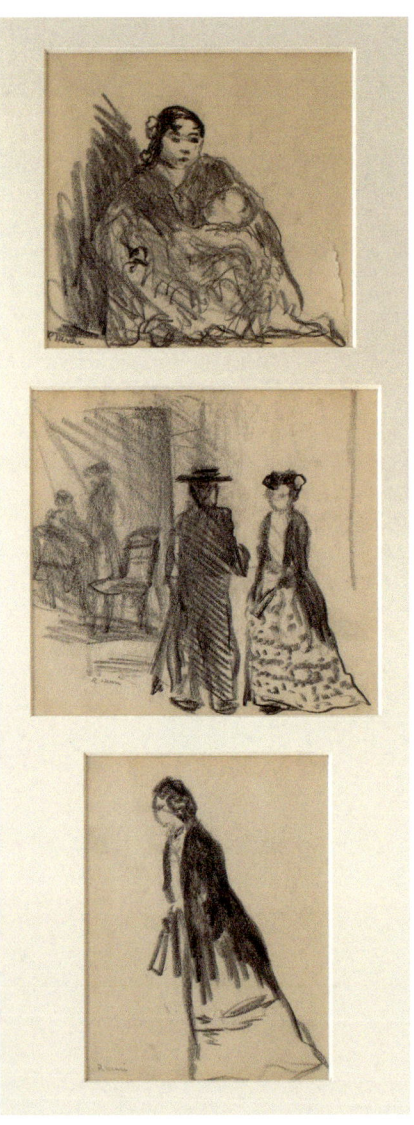

▲ George Bellows (American, 1882–1925)
Robert Henri, c. 1921
Graphite on paper

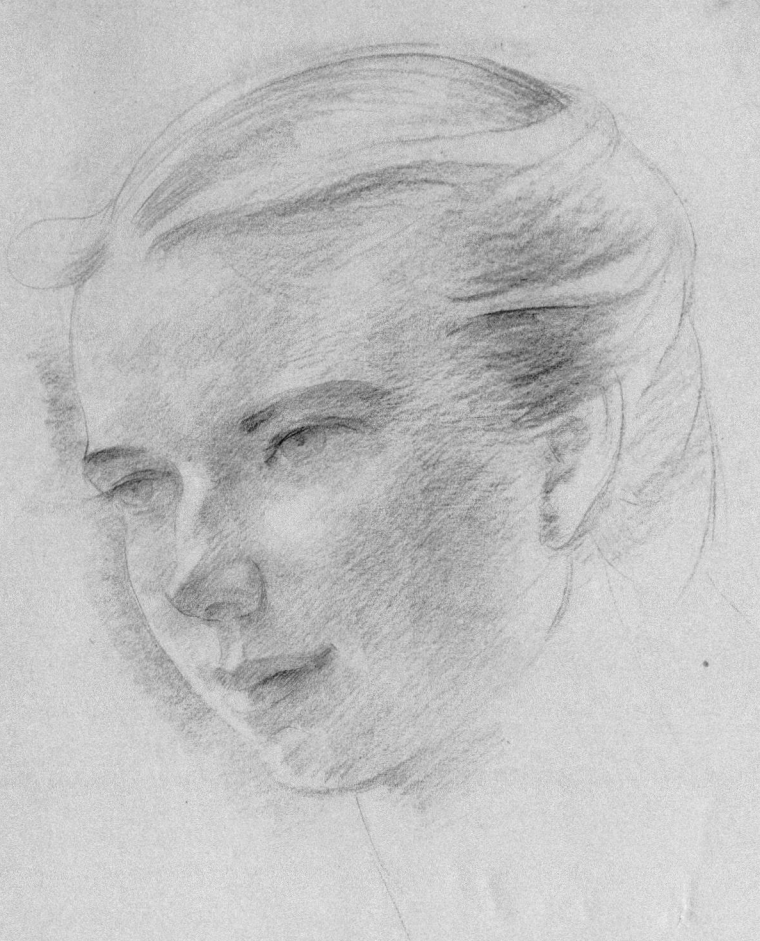

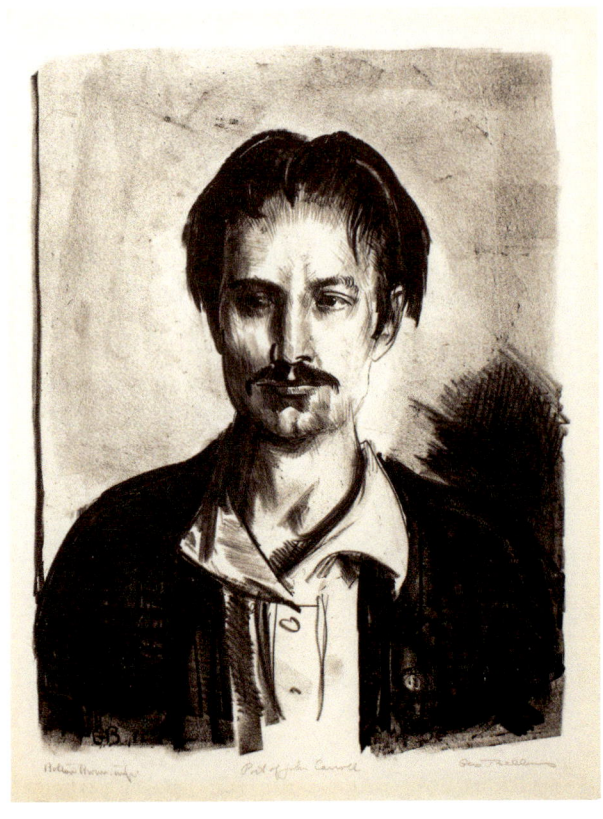

◄ George Bellows (American, 1882–1925)
Portrait of John Carroll, 1923
Lithograph on paper

► George Bellows (American, 1882–1925)
Charles Rosen, c. 1922
Conte crayon on paper

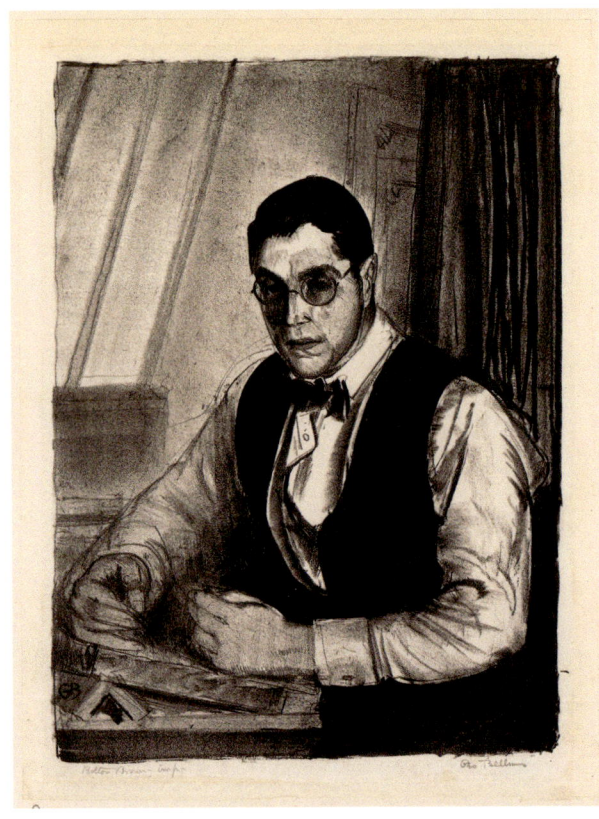

◄ George Bellows (American, 1882–1925)
Eugene Speicher Drawing on a Stone, 1921
Lithograph on paper

► George Bellows (American, 1882–1925)
Self Portrait, c. 1921
Conte crayon on paper

► George Bellows (American, 1882–1925)
Portrait of John Carroll, c. 1922
Conte crayon on paper

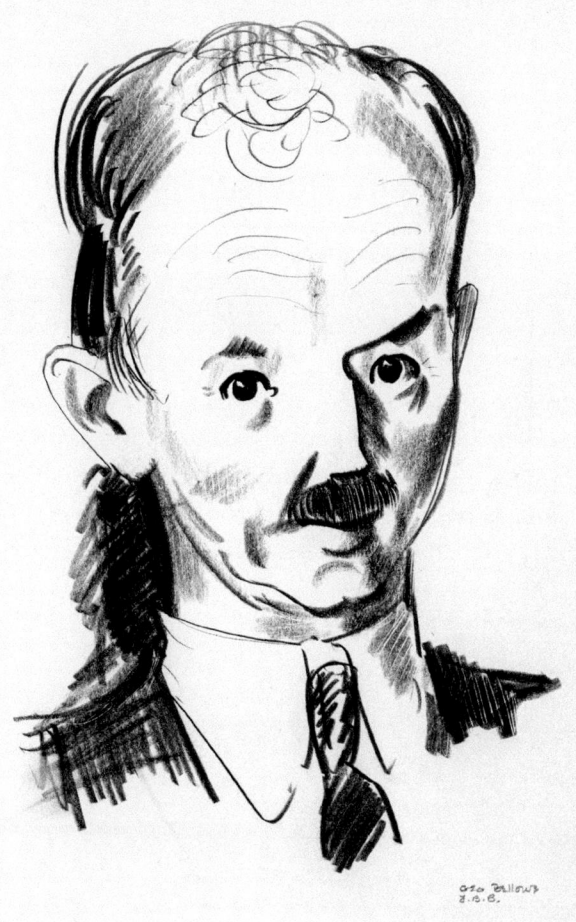

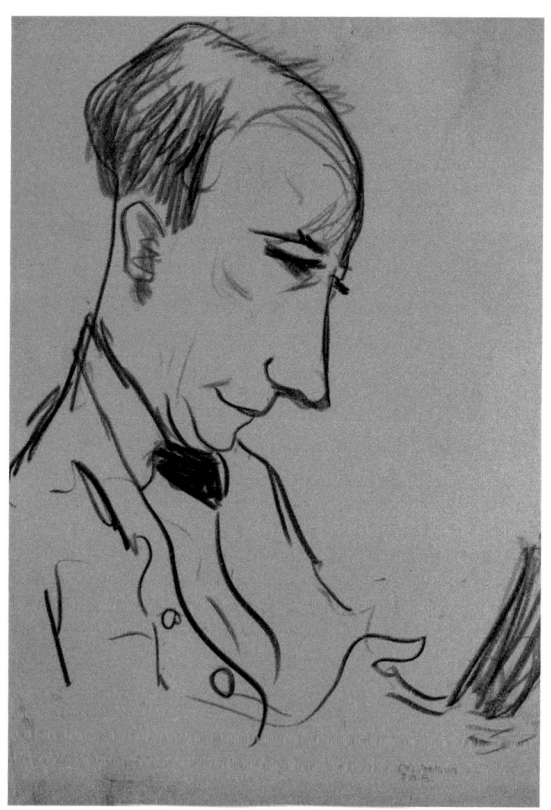

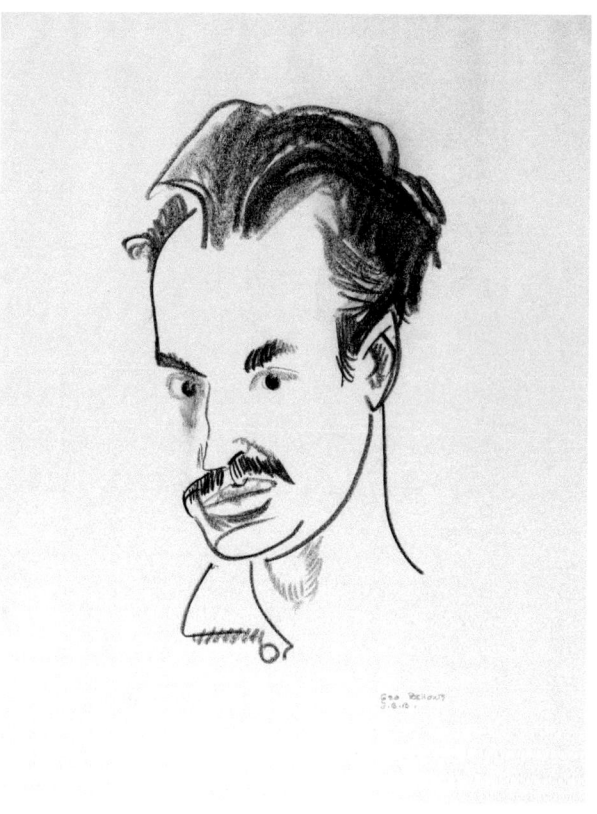

A RARE FRIENDSHIP

—— Marianne S. Kearney ——

George Bellows might never have lived and worked in Woodstock had not his friend and fellow artist, Eugene (Gene) Speicher, invited him to visit in the spring of 1920.[1] The two men spent every day painting out of doors, packing up Bellows's Buick, "Gertrude," and driving to various sketching locations in and around Woodstock. Before departing, George and his wife, Emma, rented the Shotwell House, a large summer residence not far from the Speichers', where there was enough room to accommodate a multitude of visiting artists, friends, and family. The summers that followed were halcyon days. At one time or another everyone close to Bellows was there, including immediate and extended family,[2] as well as artist friends Robert Henri, Gene Speicher, Leon Kroll, and a number of other artists and their families.[3]

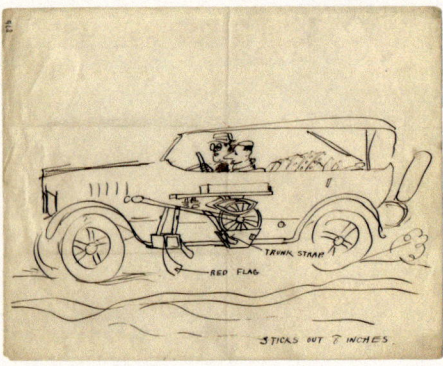

▲ George Bellows
Sketch of Bellows and Speicher in a Car (sketch in a letter to Robert Henri, November 5, 1920)
Pen & ink on paper

Robert Henri Papers (box 2, folder 27), Yale Collection of American Literature, Beinecke Rare Book and Manuscript Library

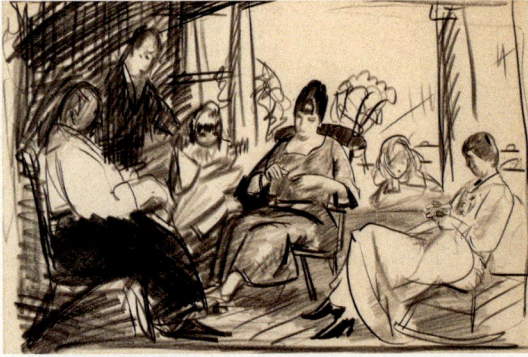

▲ George Bellows
The Reader, 1920 or 1921
Conte crayon on paper

L-R Anna "Grandma" Bellows, George Bellows, *Jean Bellows (the reader),* Emma Bellows, Anne Bellows, and Laura Bellows Monet

When autumn arrived, the Bellows children were packed off to the city in the care of their maternal grandparents while George, Emma, Gene, and his wife, Elsie, "renewed the charm and relaxation of the spring before, the same pattern of outdoor sketching and the type of cozy evening that only very close friends can know."[4] They would repeat this routine for the next four autumns, when the cooler weather and the sudden riot of color shifted their attention from the studio to the surrounding mountains, farms, and fields. Speicher had summered in Woodstock since 1908,[5] so it is surprising that Bellows did not take up residence sooner given the longevity and depth of their friendship, one that had grown since their 1907 meeting at the West 57th YMCA gym. According to Speicher, that chance meeting "was the beginning of a rare friendship."[6] In the years that followed they saw each other constantly, taking long walks all over New York, attending classes and late-night drawing sessions, challenging each other on the squash and tennis courts, critiquing each other's work, even marrying their respective sweethearts within months of each other.

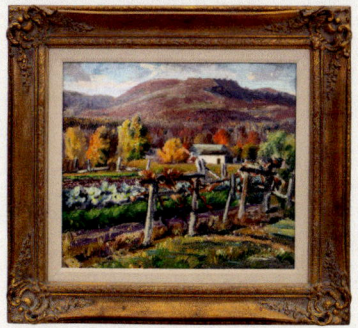

▲ Eugene Speicher
Kitchen Garden, n.d.
Oil on canvas

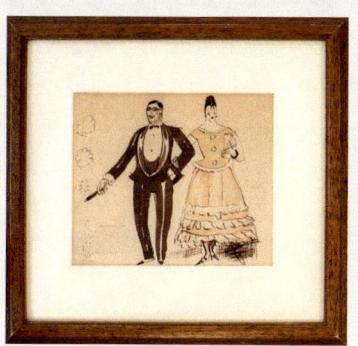

▲ George W. Bellows
Elsie & Gene Speicher, n.d.
Conte crayon on paper

The artists in Bellows's circle of friends often gifted small drawings to one another including this one given to Charlie Rosen.

The Speichers and the Bellowses were part of a group George happily christened the "The Society of Perfect Wives and Husbands."[7] The "Society" frequently gathered, first in New York City and later in Woodstock, to draw, dine, joke, play poker and discuss their work, art, books, politics, music, and theater. At various times and places the group swelled, but Will and Effie Glackens, Robert and Marjorie Henri, Gene and Elsie Speicher, George and Emma Bellows, Leon Kroll, and, when in Woodstock, Charlie and Mildred Rosen, were the constant core. "Their laughter echoed through the halls of our house," remembered Bellows's oldest daughter, Anne, "and made life exciting and interesting for two little girls sitting on the sidelines."[8]

On New Year's Eve 1924, the "Society" gathered at Henri's Gramercy Park studio. George "had discovered some costumes stashed away in the Henri studio…and had rigged himself up to resemble Queen Victoria… He had all present broken up with laughter."[9] It turned out to be the last carefree evening of Bellows's short life. He was ill the next day, then stricken on January 2nd with a ruptured appendix. He died six days later at the age of 42. Remembering that night Speicher reflected "there had never been a gayer evening with that crowd… It seemed later, to all of us, the most fitting spot and happy friendly atmosphere for that sudden and tragic farewell to have taken place."[10]

Outside of the immediate family, perhaps no one was more profoundly affected by George's death than Gene Speicher. Following the funeral, he wrote to Leon Kroll, who was teaching in Chicago, "The service they all say was impressive. To me, it was the longest twenty minutes I ever hope to put in. I saw no one, heard nothing, and then there was the trip through Brooklyn [to Greenwood Cemetery]."[11] Elsie Speicher also wrote to Kroll, "My Gene is hard hit & broke down completely."[12]

Speicher responded to what he called a "vast emptiness" with activity. He advised Emma as she took charge of inventories, collectors, exhibitions, dealers, and deals.[13] Although he served on the Metropolitan Museum's Committee on the Exhibition for the 1925 Bellows Memorial Exhibition,[14] it mostly fell to Emma to choose which works would be shown. She "measured her judgment with that of Henri and Speicher."[15] They also helped her compile a book of Bellows's lithographs to which Speicher added a concise introductory note.[16] The successful opening of Speicher's one-man exhibition at the Rehn Gallery, a first for a Woodstock artist, just one month after George's death must have been bittersweet.[17] He also continued to paint, but the ground had shifted under his feet.

In early 1926 the Speichers retreated to Europe[18] for the first time since their 1910 honeymoon, returning to Woodstock in June.[19] Later that summer Speicher wrote Frank Rehn that he had been hard at work and announced, "I have refused five portrait commissions, so you see how seriously I mean to be an artist."[20] Rejecting commissions that had brought him recognition and income was both risky and bold. The timing of this decision suggests that George's sudden death may have provoked Speicher to appraise and redirect his own career, an independent path he would follow until his own death in 1962.

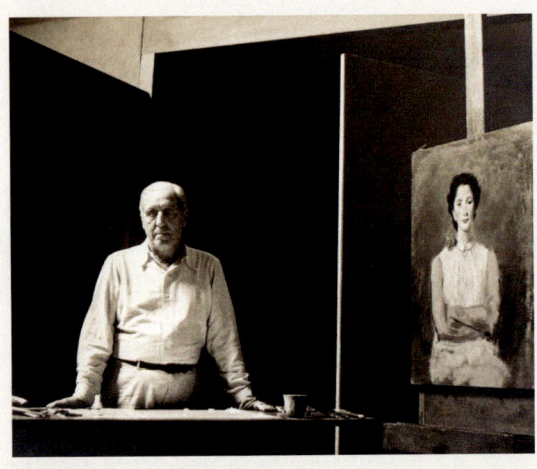

▲ Budd Studios, New York, NY
Eugene Speicher in his Studio, ca. 1957
Silver gelatin print

The Bellows family and the Speichers remained friends and Woodstock neighbors until the death of both Emma and Elsie in 1959. In those thirty-four summers, Speicher rarely deviated from his own disciplined routine. You could set your watch by his daily walk from home to the studio, home again for lunch, and return to the studio after.

Despite the difference in spelling, Bellows's second daughter, Jean, was Speicher's namesake. She modeled for him at least three times, first as a young girl a year or two after her father's death. When in 1937 Anne married in the garden of Bellows's Woodstock house, Speicher was "father of the bride." He reprised this role in 1949 when Jean wed in Bellows's New York City studio.

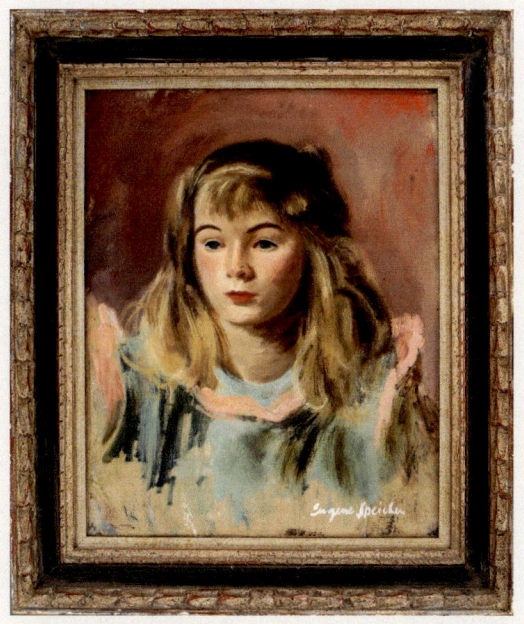

▲ Eugene Speicher
Portrait of a Young Girl (Jean Bellows), ca. 1926 or 1927
Oil on canvas

*Upon Speicher's death, his entire estate, excluding
his own artwork, was willed to Jean Bellows Booth.*

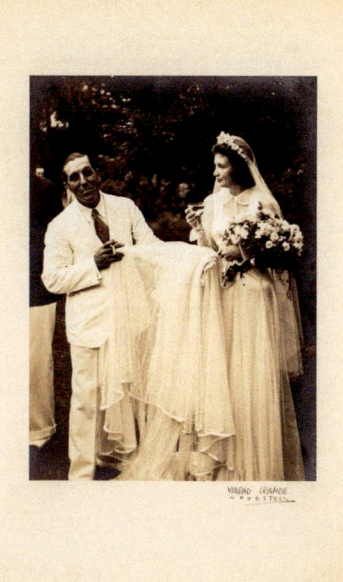

▲ Konrad Cramer
Untitled, Gene Speicher and Anne Bellows Kearney,
Woodstock, 1937
Silver gelatin print

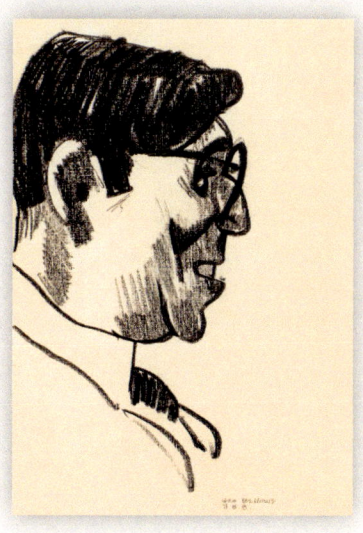

▲ *George Bellows
Portrait of Eugene Speicher –
Profile*, 1921
Conte crayon on paper

Neither Speicher nor Bellows ever completed an oil portrait of the other. The best Bellows could do was to produce caricatures, jokingly referred to as "poker drawings" (p. 44 and left), as well as at least one formal drawing,[21] four lithographs in which Speicher is the sole subject (p. 43), and four in which he is grouped with other friends (p. 37). Both attempted the challenge. Both destroyed the unsatisfactory results. According to Speicher, they failed because "we talked too much!"[22] Uncharacteristically, they allowed something to get in the way of their art, confirming that it was, indeed, a rare friendship. ■

1. Charles Morgan, *George Bellows: Painter of America* (New York: Reynal & Company, 1965), 235.

2. It is not known when or by whom this drawing of the Bellows family was titled. It came from the estate of artist Charles Rosen whose granddaughter believed the woman seated on the right was a visiting Christian Science reader, thus the title. The figure on the right is most likely Laura Bellows Monet, George's half-sister, who was not a Christian Scientist and is holding some kind of handwork, not a book. When the work was reproduced in the 2003 exhibition catalog *Leaving for the Country: George Bellows at Woodstock*, Memorial Art Gallery of the University of Rochester, the location was identified as a porch in Rhode Island, in 1919 (page 96). Yet, with the planked floor, solid wall on the left, double-hung window, and porch beyond, the drawing is consistent with the interior of the rented Shotwell House, Woodstock, thus dating the drawing to 1920 or 1921.

3. Morgan, *George Bellows*, 237. Bellows also connected with Bolton Brown, a seasoned hiker, artist, teacher, master printer, and cofounder of the Byrdcliffe Arts Colony, with whom he would, over the next four years, collaborate to create over 100 lithographs of which more than 50 portrayed friends and family.

4. Morgan, *George Bellows*, 238–239.

5. Anita M. Smith, *Woodstock History and Hearsay*, 2nd ed., (Woodstock: Woodstock Arts, 2006), 135.

6. Eugene Speicher, "A Personal Reminiscence," *George Bellows: Paintings, Drawings and Prints* (Chicago: The Art Institute of Chicago, 1946), 5. Exhibition catalog.

7. Anne Bellows Kearney, untitled public lecture about the life and work of her father, George W. Bellows (Transcript, Upper St. Clair, PA, ca. 1965), 9.

8. Kearney, untitled public lecture, 9.

9. Kearney, untitled public lecture, 9.

10. Speicher, "A Personal Reminiscence," 6.

11. Morgan, *George Bellows*, 288

12. Elsie Speicher, letter to Leon & Viette Kroll, 1925, Archives of American Art, Smithsonian Institution, Leon Kroll papers, circa 1900–1988, Box 4, Folder 28: Sp-Sw, 1927–1970. While hundreds attended Bellows's funeral, including Speicher and twenty-three other pallbearers, Elsie reported that only the Speichers, Sloans, Robertses, and Henris accompanied Emma Bellows to the burial in Greenwood Cemetery, Brooklyn, NY.

13. Eugene Speicher, letter to George Bellows, 1919 in George Wesley Bellows Papers (box 2, folder 12, Amherst College Archives and Special Collections, Amherst College Library). This newsy ca. 1919 letter from Speicher to Bellows in Chicago credits Emma with getting Leon Kroll a significant prize and sale and goes on to express his admiration for her grace and manners. It ends with imaginings of a world in which she would be at home "where the stress of life never permeates…where she would be judged by her intrinsic qualities." Fanciful musings aside, the deep respect he held for Emma would prove to be well placed in the months and years to come when she bravely and intelligently confronted the stresses of "life after George."

14. The Metropolitan Museum of Art, *Memorial Exhibition of the Works of George Bellows* (New York: The Metropolitan Museum of Art, 1925), 7. Exhibition catalog.

15. Morgan, *George Bellows*, 294.

16. Eugene Speicher, "Introductory Note," in Thomas Beer, *George W. Bellows: His Lithographs* (New York: Alfred A. Knopf, 1927), 33. Speicher ended this note saying, "He [Bellows] had wit, and never drew nor painted without it. He was human and humorous, adventurous and unafraid. He was idealistic, and not untouched by the romantic. Above all, he had a heart and used it at all times."

17. John Baker, *Henry Lee McFee and Formalist Realism in American Still Life*, 1923–1936 (Cranbury, NJ: Associated University Press, 1987), 56. Exhibition catalog.

18. David Dearinger, general editor, *Painting and Sculpture in the Collection of National Academy of Design (v.1)* (New York: Hudson Hill Press, 2004), 510.

19. Smith, *Woodstock*, 135.

20. Eugene Speicher, letter to Frank Rehn, 1926. Frank K.M. Rehn Galleries records, 1858–1969, bulk 1919–1968, Archives of American Art, Smithsonian Institution, (box 12: Speicher, Eugene and Elsie, 1923–1962, reel 5865, 299).

21. Charles Morgan, Introduction, *The Drawings of George Bellows* (Alhambra, CA: Borden Publishing Company, 1973).

22. Speicher, "A Personal Reminiscence," 6.

THE HISTORIC WOODSTOCK ART COLONY:
THE ARTHUR A. ANDERSON COLLECTION

Bolton Brown and Lithography

By 1915, Bolton Brown, a co-founder of Byrdcliffe, was immersed in lithography, a printmaking process using a stone plate. Although the process was invented at the end of the 18th century in Germany and used commercially and artistically throughout Europe and the United States in the 19th century, Brown is credited as the father of American lithography for his dedication to perfecting the medium scientifically and artistically. He experimented with and invented new processes, wrote on the subject, printed for other artists, and had an output of over 400 lithographs. His own work ranges in style and subject matter, exploiting the expressive possibilities of the process—from delicate, tonal landscapes to sharply delineated still lifes.

The popularity of lithography in Woodstock is evidenced by the number of artists who worked on the stone with seemingly limitless approaches and topics. Realist-inspired landscapes by Grant Arnold, Emil Ganso, and Rosella Hartman contrast with the modernism of Yasuo Kuniyoshi. Pele de Lappe captured some of the spirit of comraderie of Woodstock in *Picnic* (p. 55), depicting artists Doris and Russell Lee and Arnold and Lucile Blanch. Other genre subjects include the sketch-like *African-American Couple Playing Cards* (p. 56), by Albert Sterner, and John McClellan's humorous *Cat and Table* (p. 53).

▼ Rosella Hartman (American, 1895–1993)
Chickadees in the Snow, n.d.
Lithograph

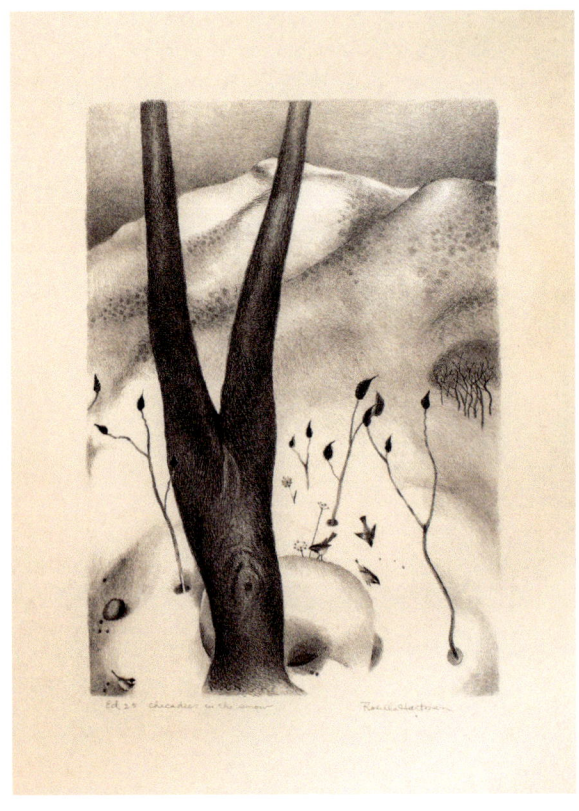

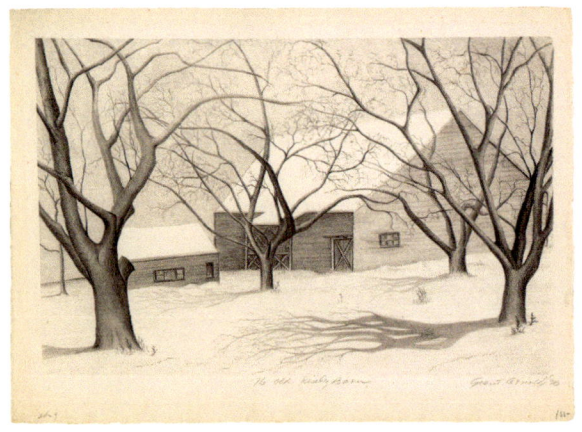

▶ Grant Arnold (American, 1904–1988)
Old Risely Barn, 1936
Lithograph on paper

▼ Rockwell Kent (American, 1882–1971)
Father and Son, 1920
Lithograph on paper

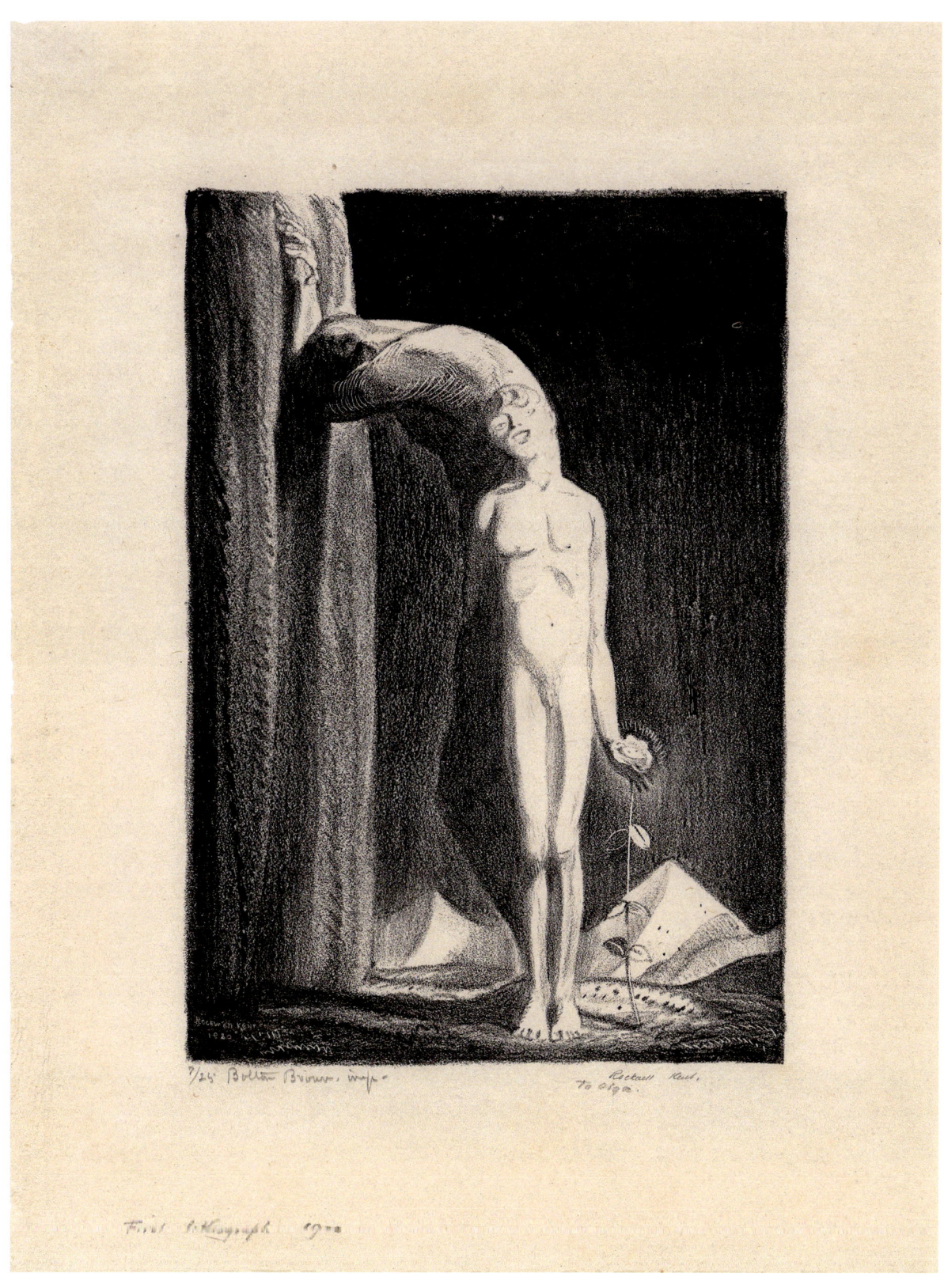

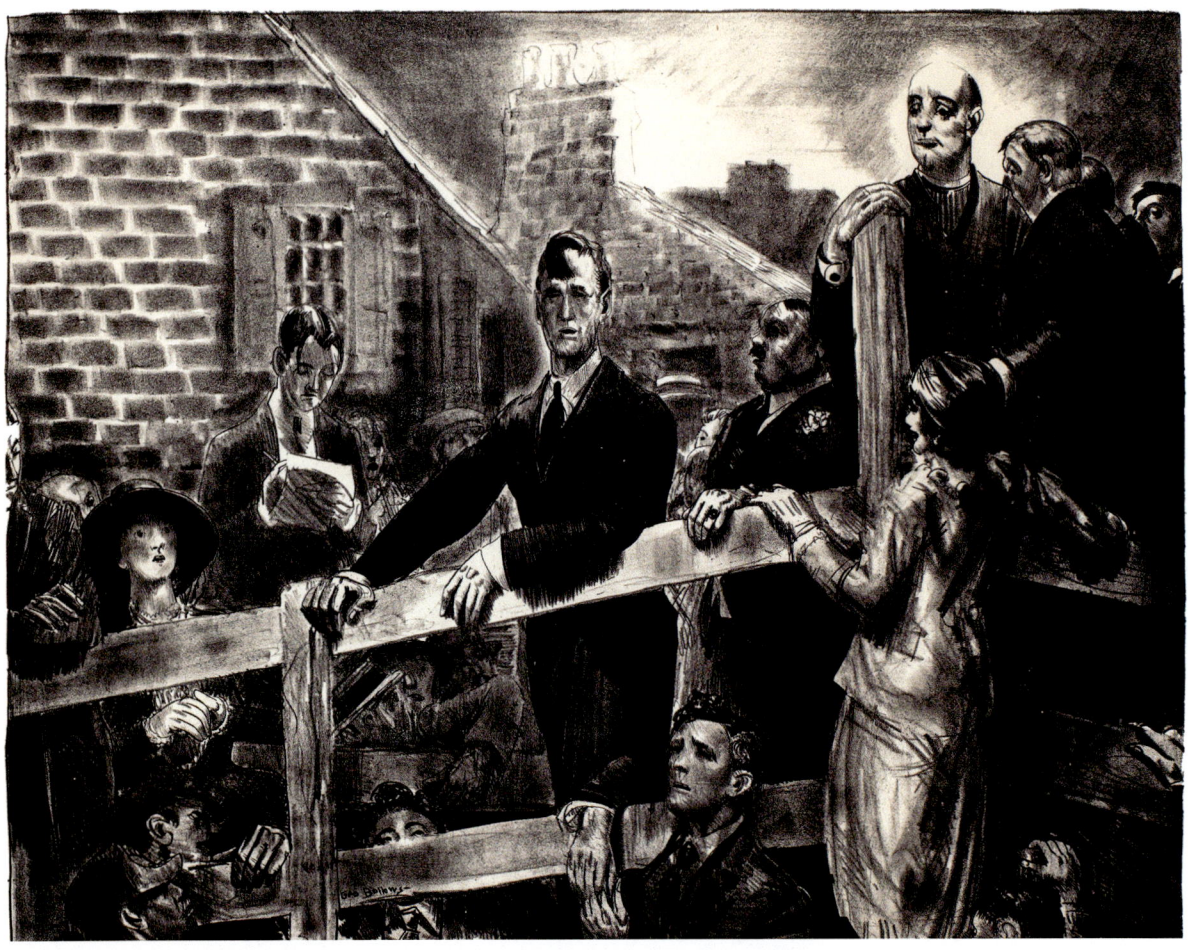

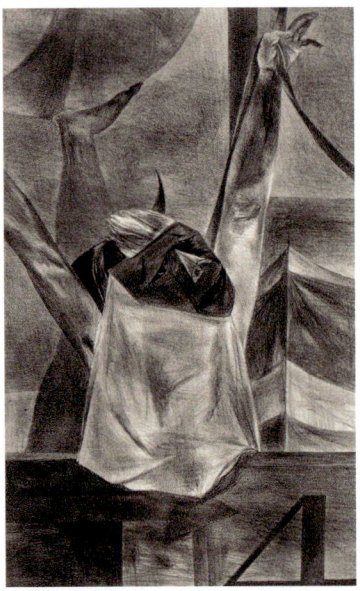

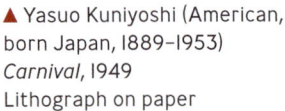

▲ Yasuo Kuniyoshi (American,
born Japan, 1889–1953)
Carnival, 1949
Lithograph on paper

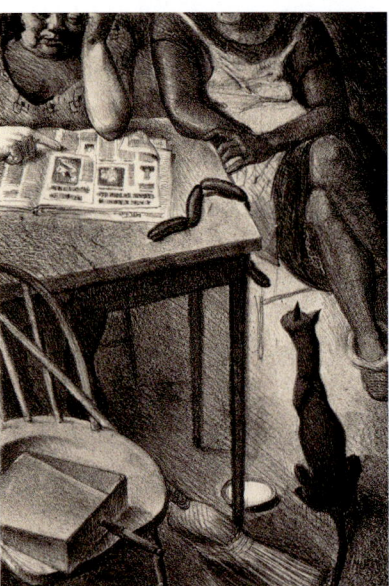

▲ George Bellows
(American, 1882–1925)
Appeal to the People, 1923
Lithograph on paper

◄ John McClellan
(American, born England, 1908–1986)
Cat and Table, 1939
Lithograph on paper

► Bolton Brown,
(American, 1864–1936)
Little A, 1915
Lithograph in sanguine ink on paper

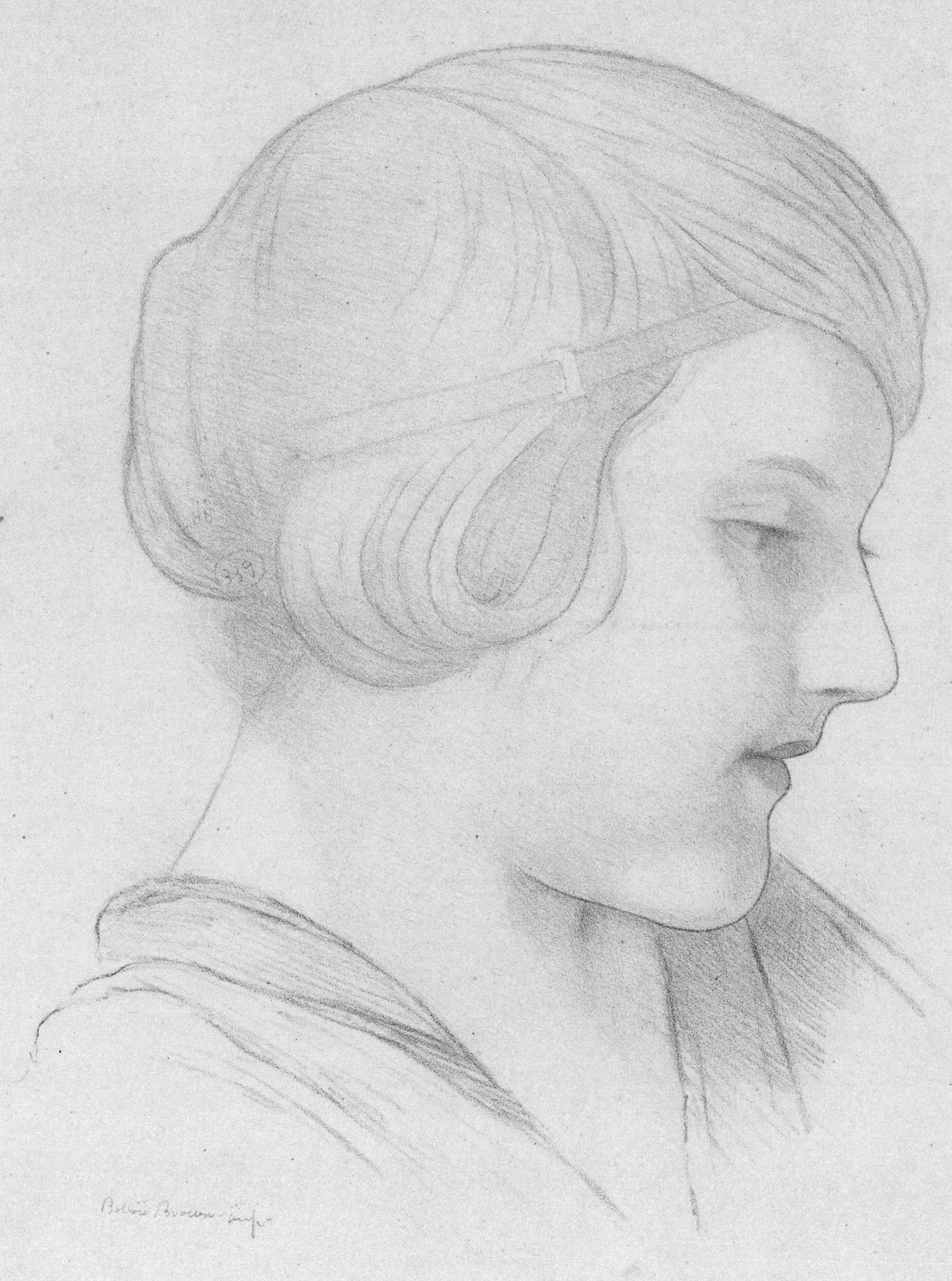

▼ Emil Ganso (American, born Germany, 1895–1941)
Spring, n.d.
Color lithograph on paper

▼ Bolton Brown (American, 1864–1936)
Storm, 1923
Lithograph on paper

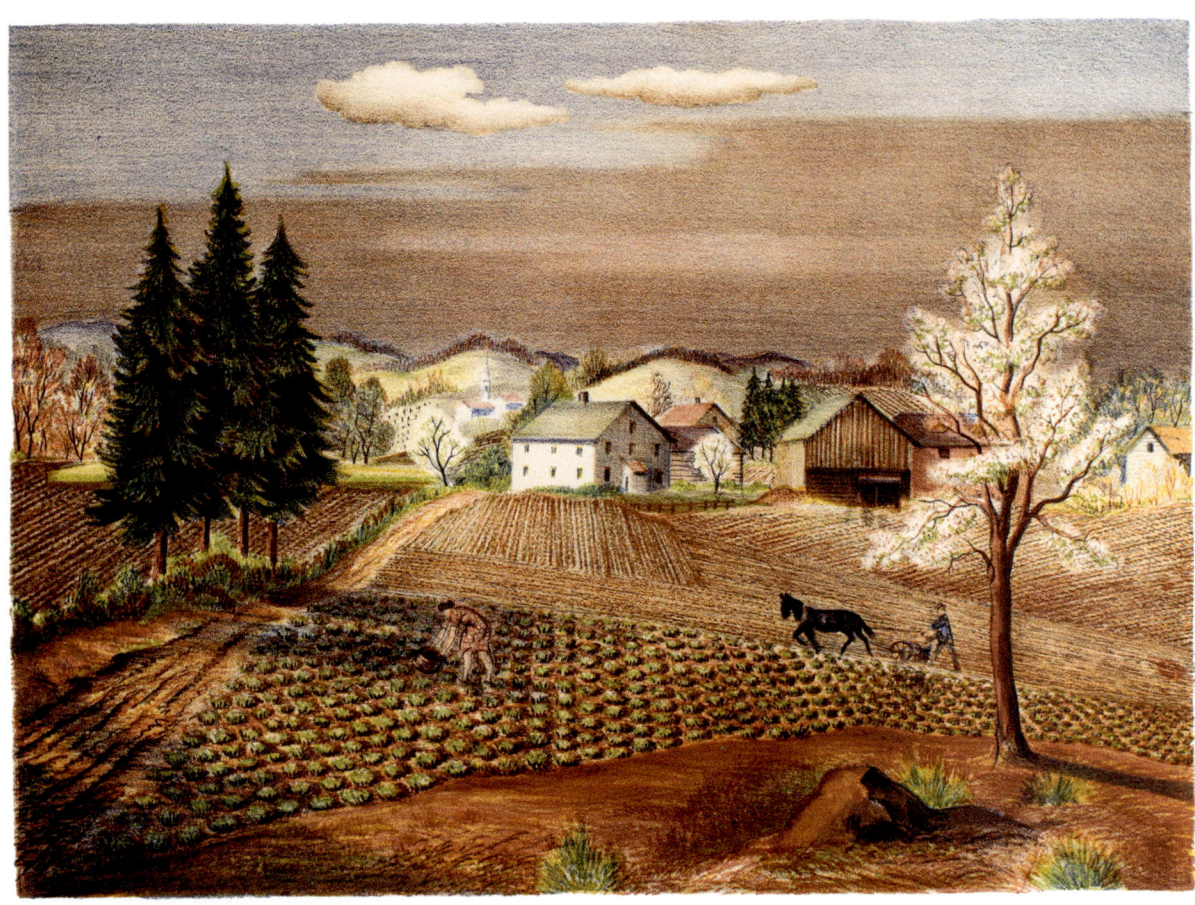

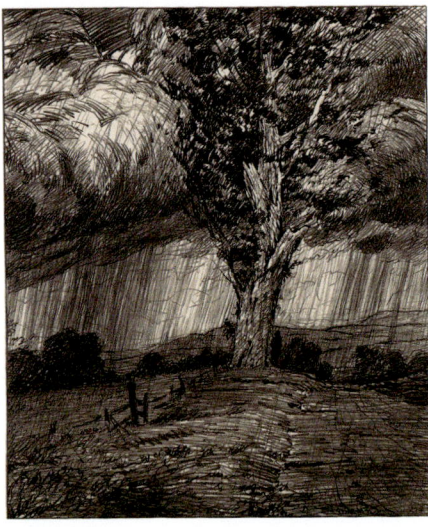

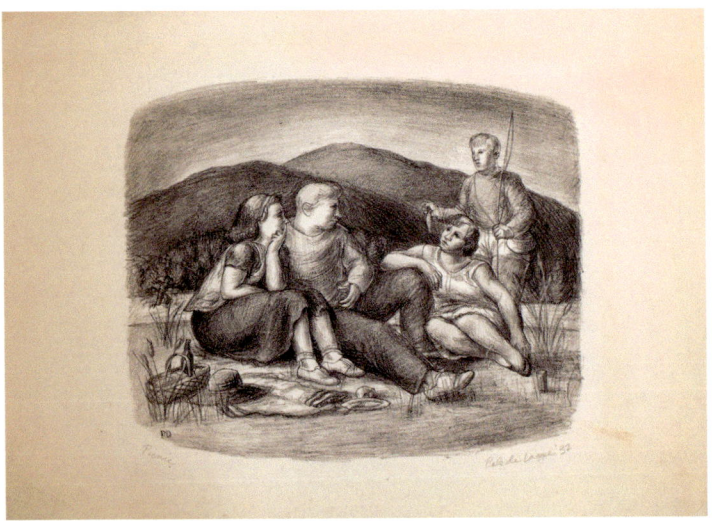

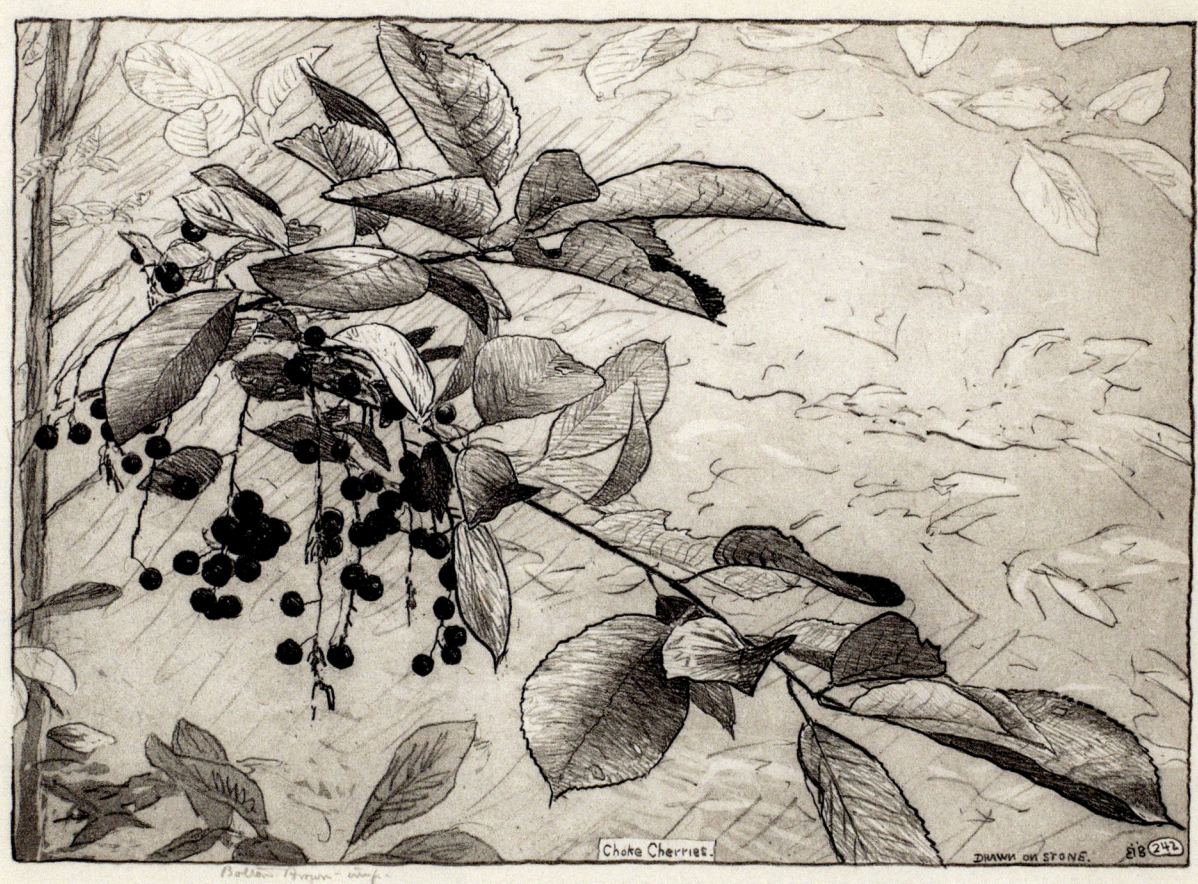

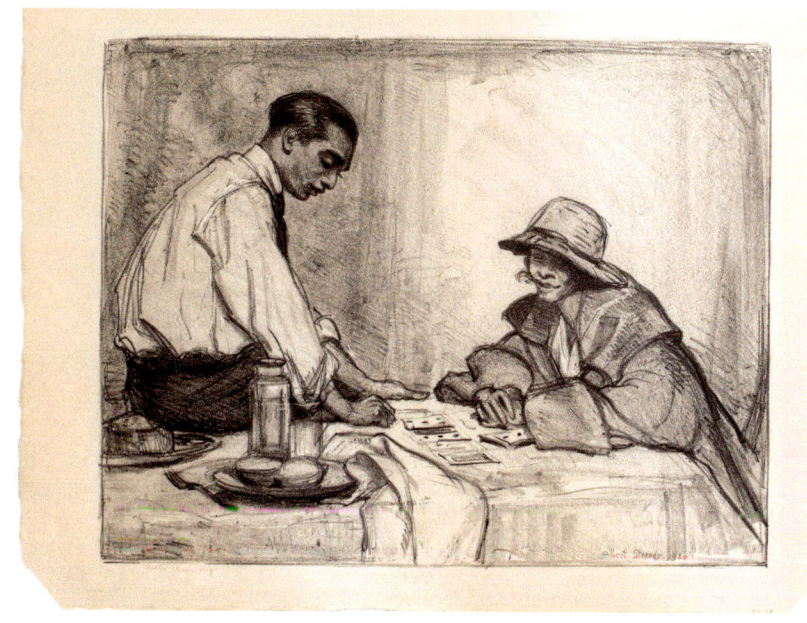

▲ Bolton Brown
(American, 1864–1936)
Choke Cherries, 1920
Lithograph on paper

◄ Pele deLappe
(American, 1916–2007)
Picnic, 1932
Lithograph on paper

► Albert Sterner (American,
born England, 1863–1946)
*African-American Couple
Playing Cards*, 1920
Lithograph on paper

THE HISTORIC WOODSTOCK ART COLONY: THE ARTHUR A. ANDERSON COLLECTION

Modernism in Woodstock

Works influenced by a number of European avant-garde movements also made their mark in Woodstock. Among those experimenting with varying degrees of abstraction were Konrad Cramer, Andrew Dasburg, and Henry Lee McFee, who were dubbed the "Rock City Rebels" after the part of Woodstock where they lived. Cramer, born in Germany, drew upon his experiences there with the radical art of Der Blaue Reiter, a group that used exaggerated forms and highly keyed colors to convey emotion. He experimented with different media as well as with styles ranging from the realistic to the abstract. Dasburg had visited France, where he met Henri Matisse, who emphasized color for its own sake—a style called Fauvism. In Paris, Dasburg also studied the work of Paul Cézanne and Cubism, perhaps the most influential of all modernist approaches, based on fragmented images seen from different viewpoints, and employed in work by Dasburg, Cramer, and McFee. Elements of all these styles are seen not only in the work of the Rock City Rebels but in that of other Woodstock artists as well, including Florence Ballin Cramer, Charles Rosen and Ernest Fiene. The multi-faceted Winold

Reiss, who opened a summer school in Woodstock, also promoted modernism through his graphic design, interior design, and portraiture.

Artists of all stylistic bents came together to establish the Woodstock Artists Association in 1919, a much-needed venue for exhibitions that remains active today as the Woodstock Artists Association and Museum.

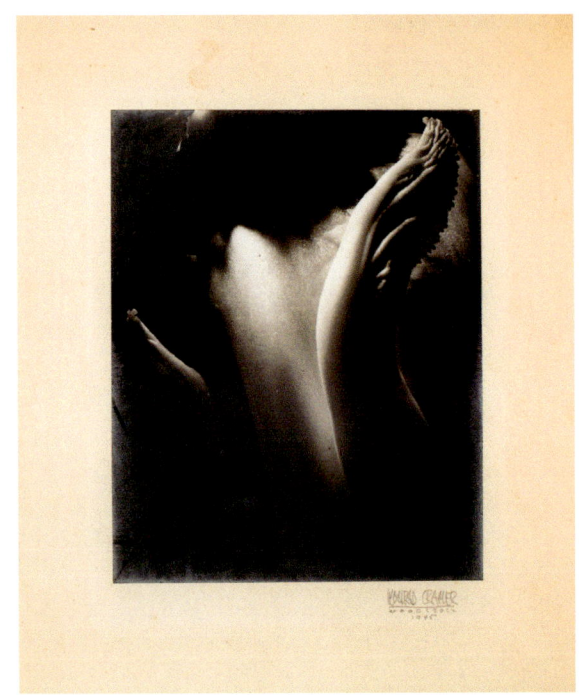

▶ Konrad Cramer
(American, born Germany, 1888–1963)
Abstraction, c. 1935
Photograph

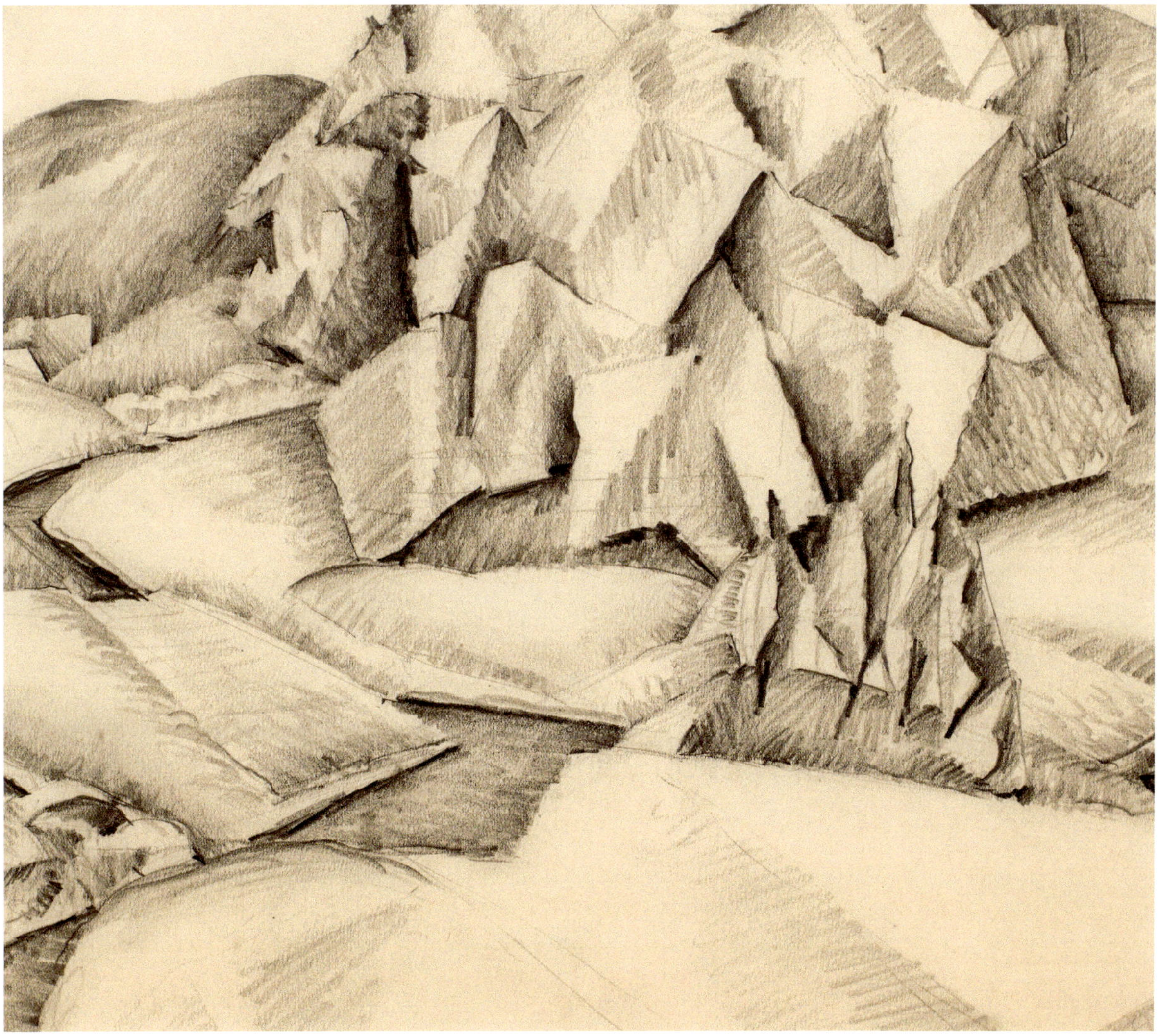

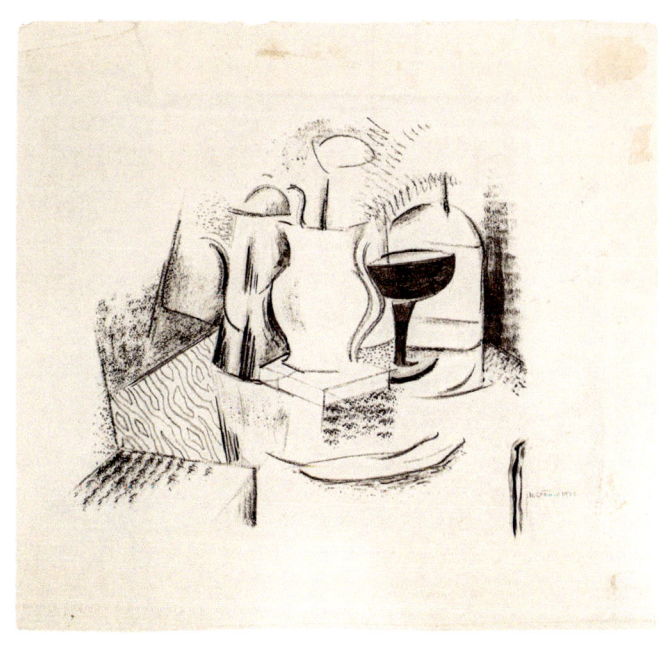

▲ Andrew Dasburg
(American, born France, 1887–1979)
Cubist Landscape, c. 1920
Graphite on paper

▶ Konrad Cramer
(American, born Germany, 1888–1963)
Still Life Abstraction #7, 1923
Lithograph on paper

▼ Charles Rosen (American, 1878–1950)
River Boat No. 2, Hudson River, 1939
Oil on canvas

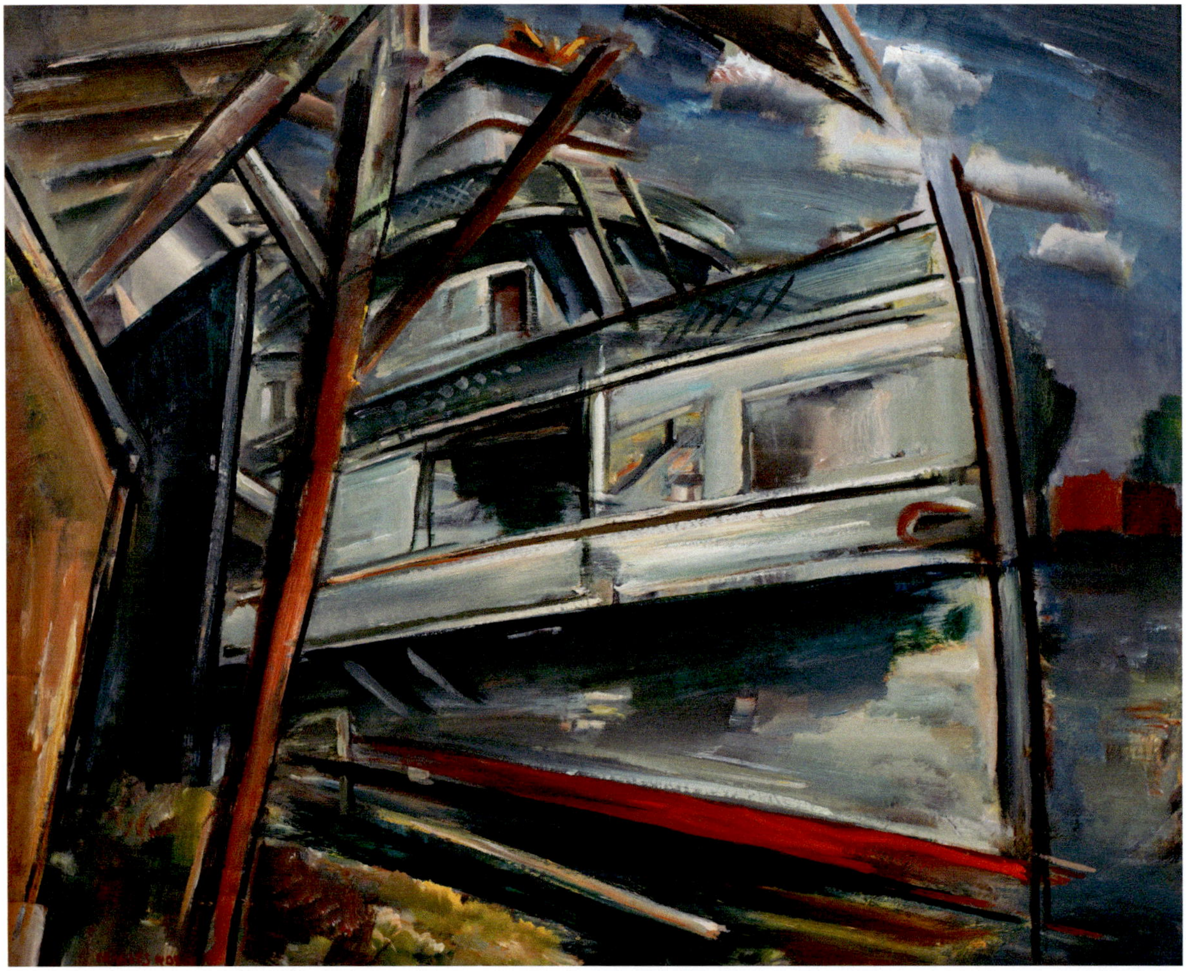

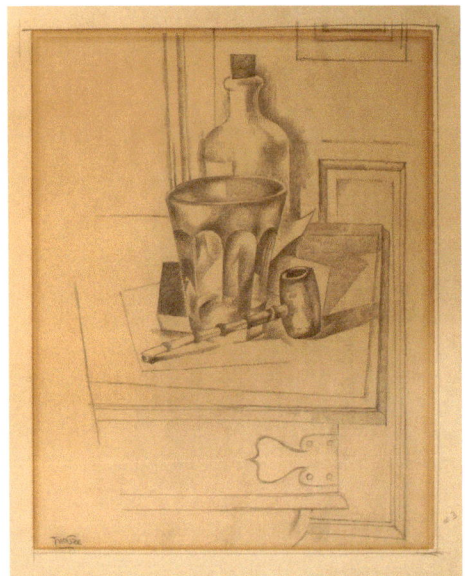

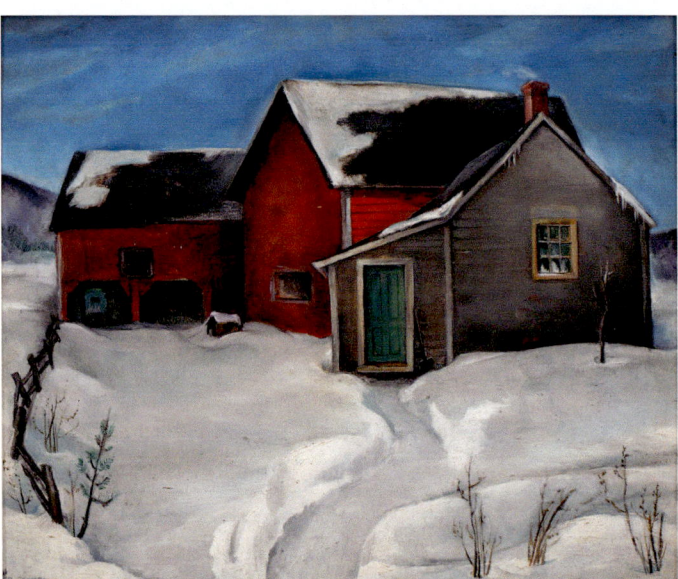

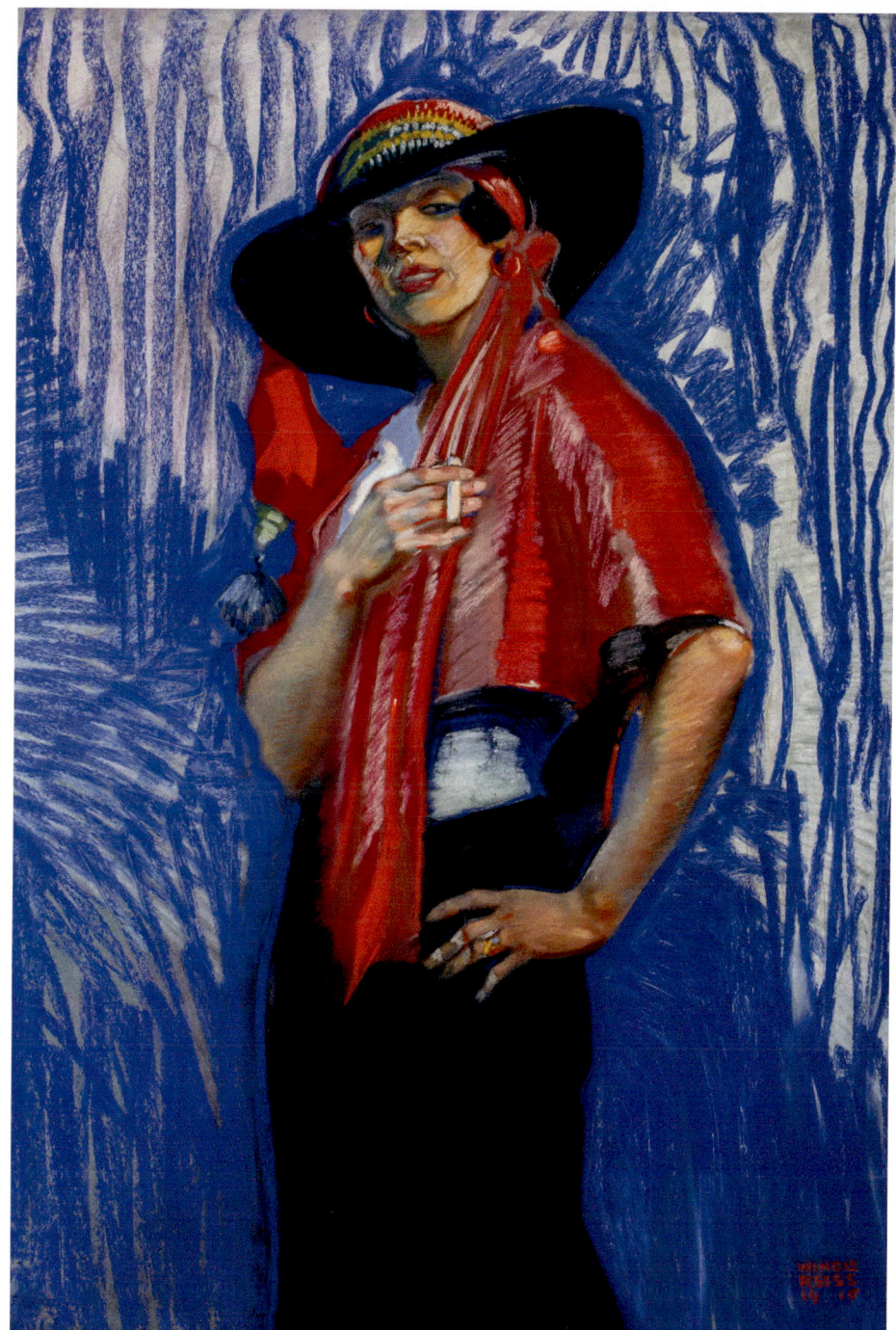

◄ Henry Lee McFee
(American, 1886–1953)
*Still Life with Glass
and Pipe*, c. 1919
Graphite on paper

◄ Florence Ballin Cramer
(American, 1884–1962)
*Cramer Homestead in
Winter*, 1926
Oil on board

► Winold Reiss (American,
born Germany, 1886–1953)
*Woman in Black Hat
with Cigarette*, 1917
Pastel on paper

▼ Henry Lee McFee (American, 1886–1953)
Portrait of Florence Ballin, c. 1916
Oil on panel

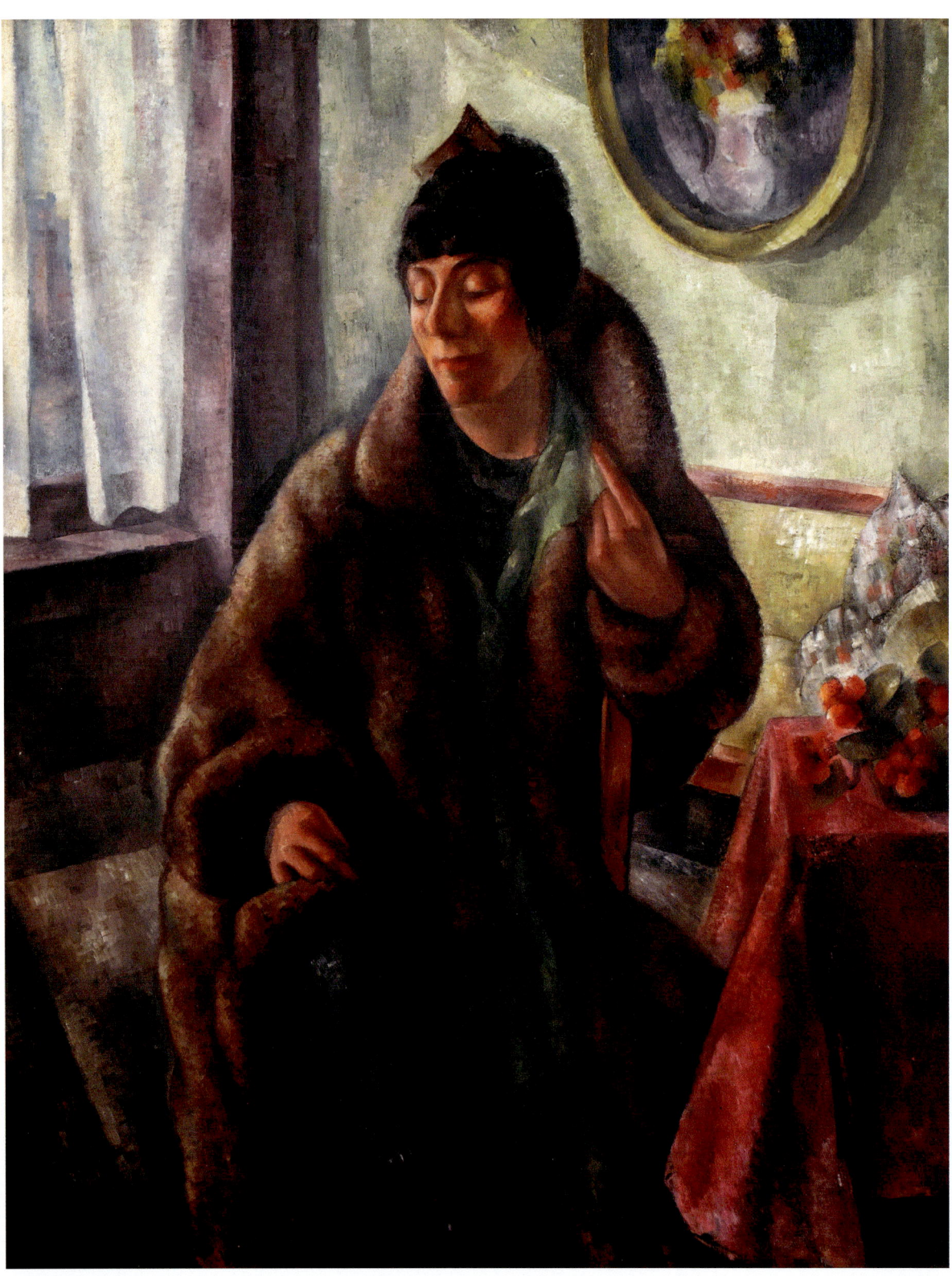

▼ Ernest Fiene (American, born Germany, 1894–1965)
Mountain Stream, 1938
Watercolor on paper

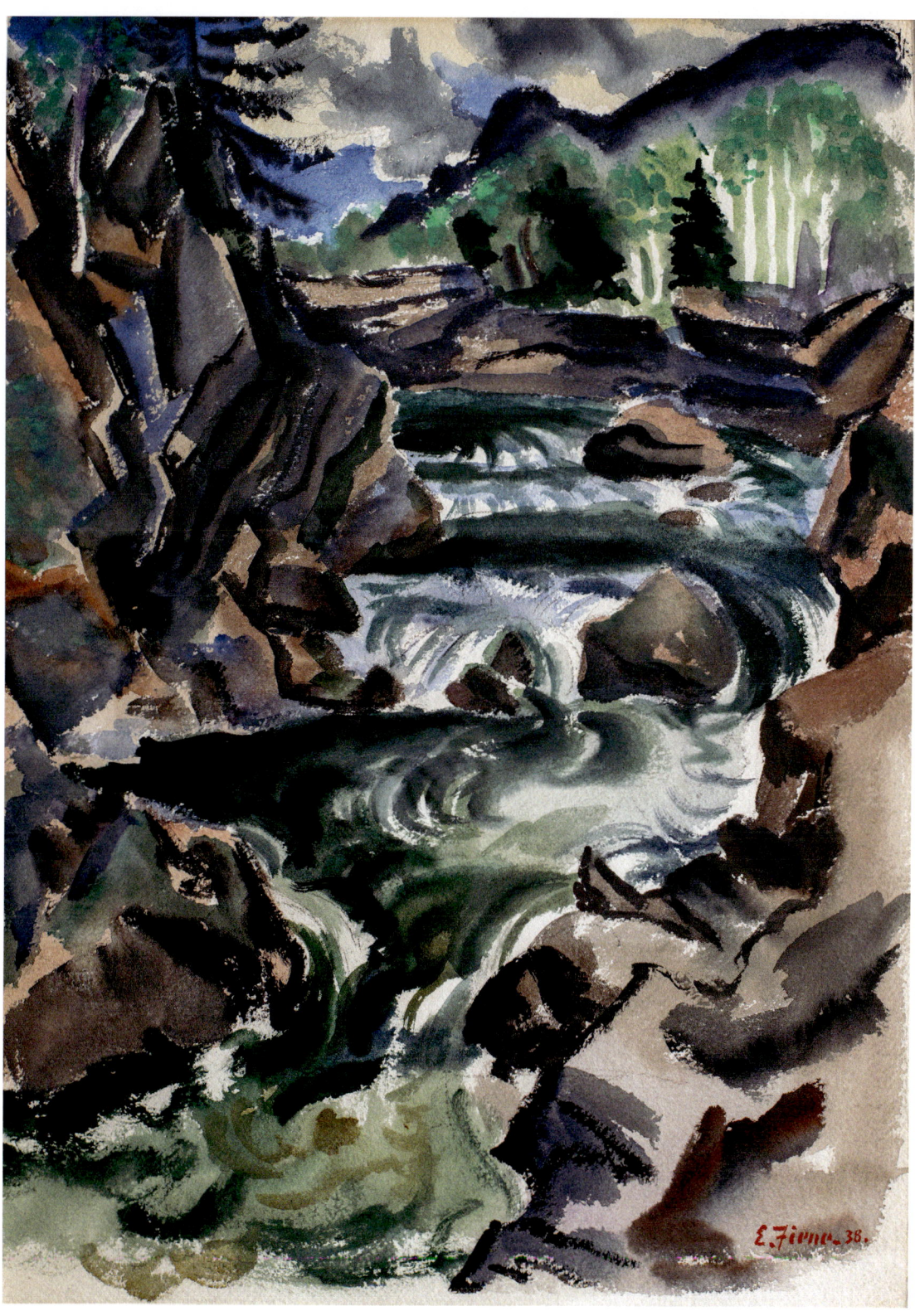

THE HISTORIC WOODSTOCK ART COLONY: THE ARTHUR A. ANDERSON COLLECTION

1930s and beyond

Although a wide range of artistic approaches in Woodstock continued in the 1930s, economic and social issues became more prevalent as subject matter with the onset of the Great Depression. Realism dominated much of the work, sometimes tinged with modernist elements, including abstraction. Various New Deal government programs—the Public Works of Art Project (1933–1934) and the Federal Art Project under the Works Progress Administration (1935–1943) —helped many Woodstock artists at this time. Some were commissioned to execute murals, and others to produce prints, easel paintings, sculpture, posters, crafts, and more. Ernest Fiene produced a design for a poster to sell war bonds, a complete turnaround in approach from his modernist work (p. 64). Charles Rosen's submission for a mural at the Poughkeepsie, New York, post office was chosen (pp. 65–66); Arnold Blanch's was not (pp. 67–68). Lithography continued to flourish in a wide range of styles and subjects from the realism of Margaret Lowengrund's *Coal Pickers* (p. 69) to Doris Lee's austere *Still Life with Fruit* (p. 70). Jenne Magafan used essentially the same composition in the print *Cornstalks* (p. 70) and the painting *Autumn Wind (Cornstalks)* (p. 70), adding birds in the sky and a crow in the foreground to the former.

After World War II, a new generation of artists arrived in Woodstock, joining those already established there. Interest in non-representational work rose with the development of Abstract Expressionism. Artists such as Rolph Scarlett, Karl Fortess, and Edward Chavez experimented with varieties of geometric abstraction, while Julio de Diego used biomorphic forms and Josef Presser favored a more expressive approach. Figurative subjects appealed to other artists, sometimes elegant and lyrical, like Mary Frank's *Figure with Deer* (p. 76), or more sturdy and powerful as those in sculptor David Smith's *Horses and Figure* (p. 75). The ink sketch is inscribed to Donovan Martin, son of artist Fletcher Martin, a friend of Smith, and may relate to Smith's lithograph titled *Don Quixote*.

Along with the continued success of the earlier institutions, the return of the Art Students League Summer School (1947– 1979) and annual events such as the Woodstock Art Conference (1947–1952) helped to ensure the enduring vitality of the colony, a vitality that carried through the end of the twentieth century and now into the twenty-first. The foresight of Arthur A. Anderson in forming the Historic Woodstock Art Colony Collection as a study collection and in giving it to the New York State Museum so that it will be accessible to a wide audience will also continue to guarantee the legacy of this special place.

▼ Ernest Fiene (American, born Germany, 1894–1965
War bonds poster, c. 1942
Print on paper

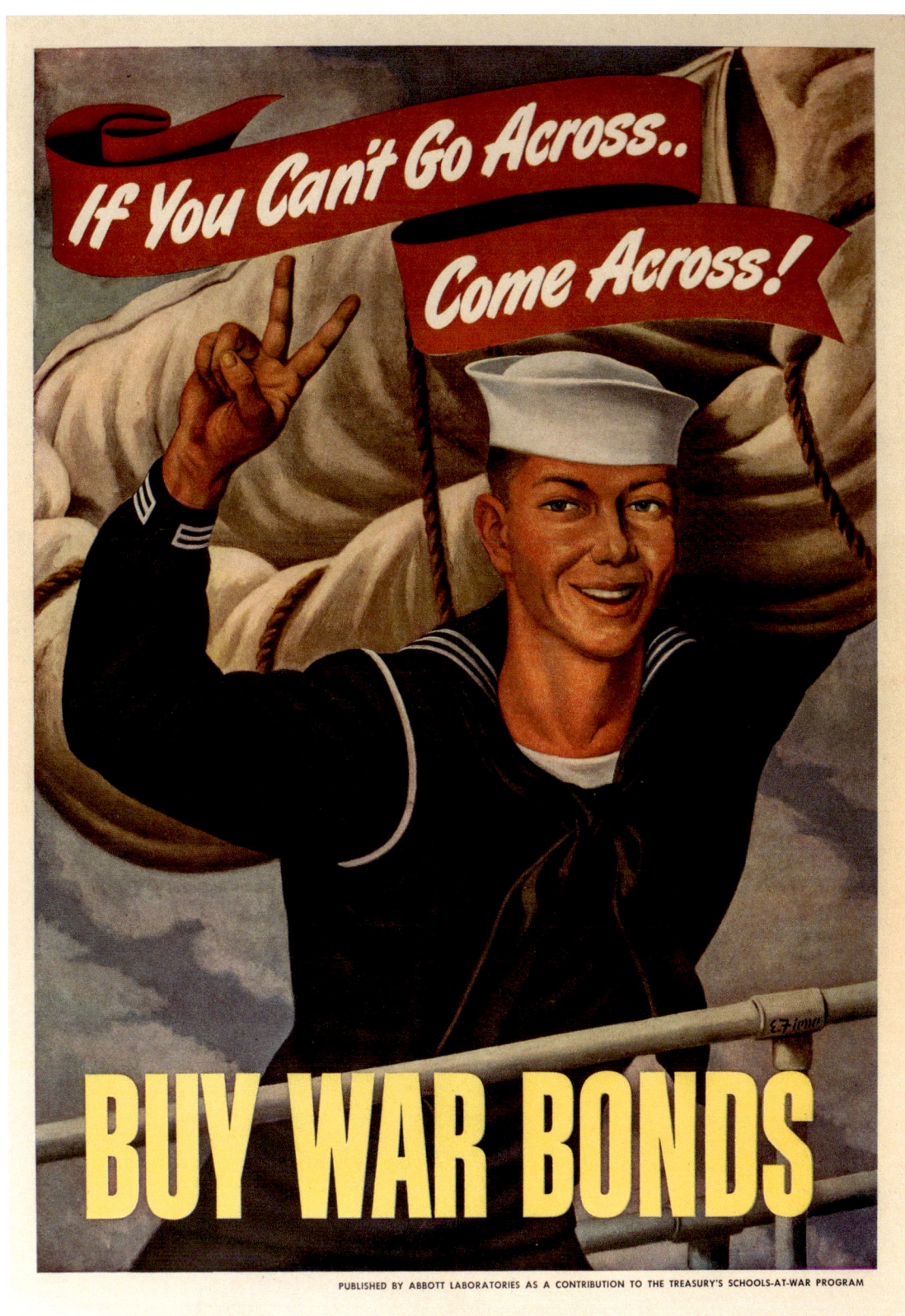

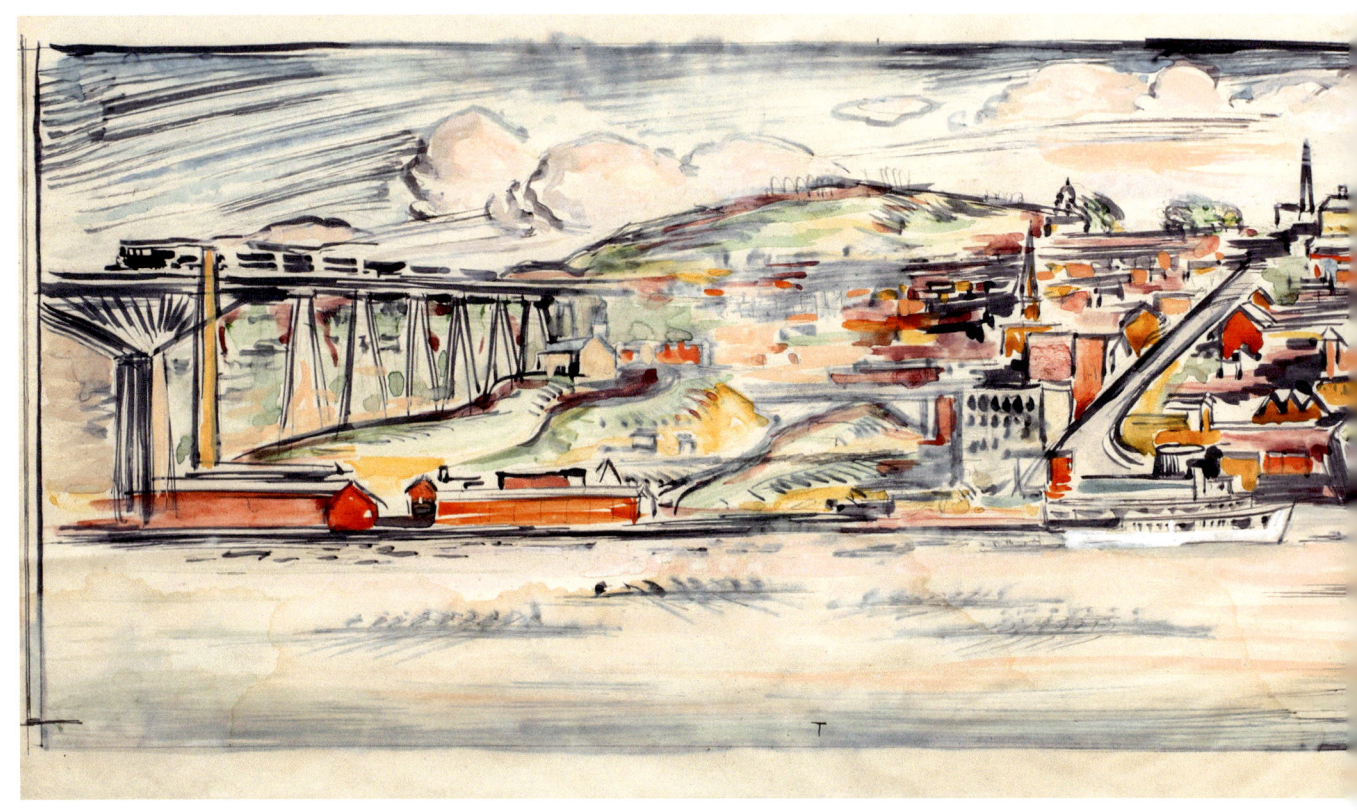

▲ Charles Rosen (American, 1878–1950)
WPA Mural Study for the Poughkeepsie Post Office, c. 1939
Gouache on paper

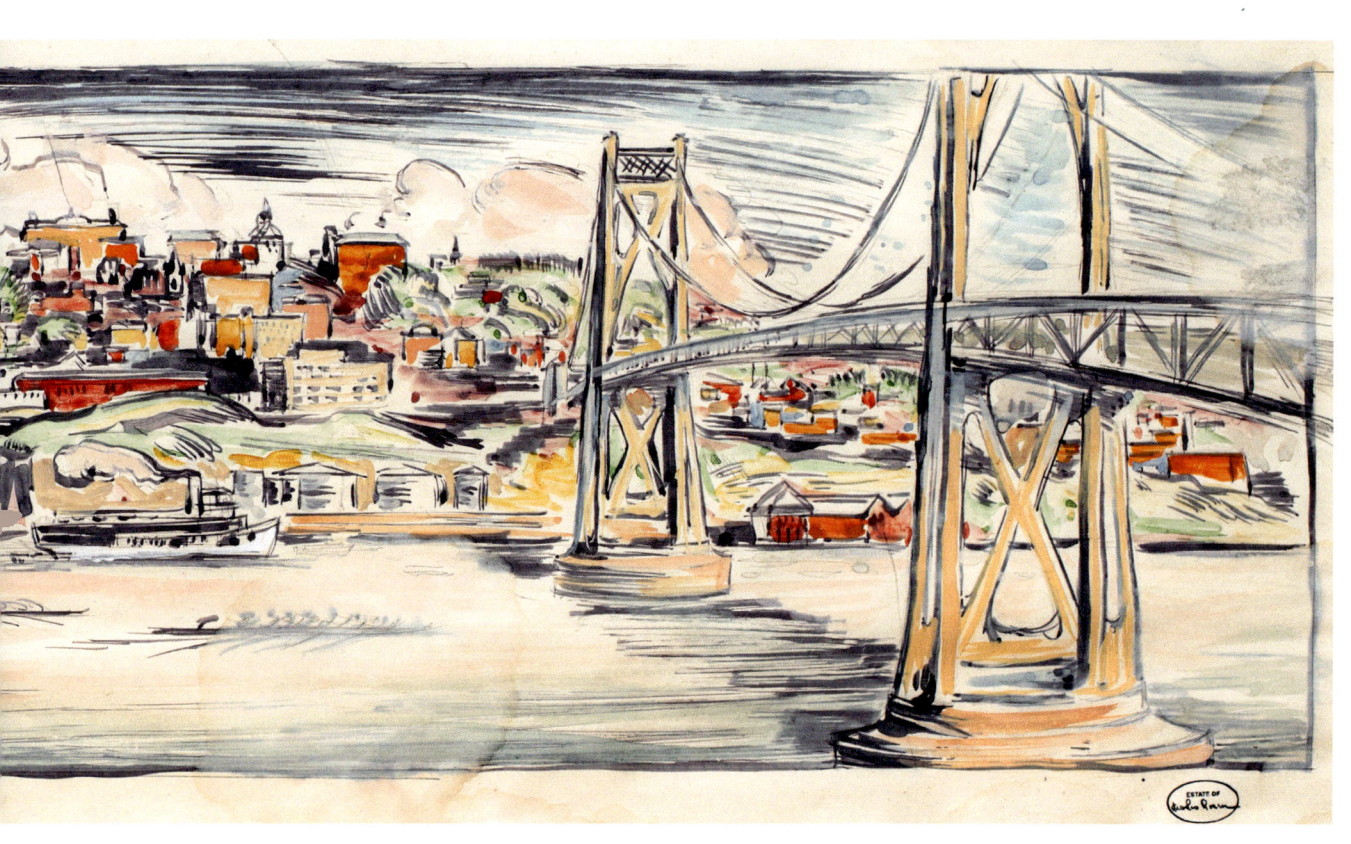

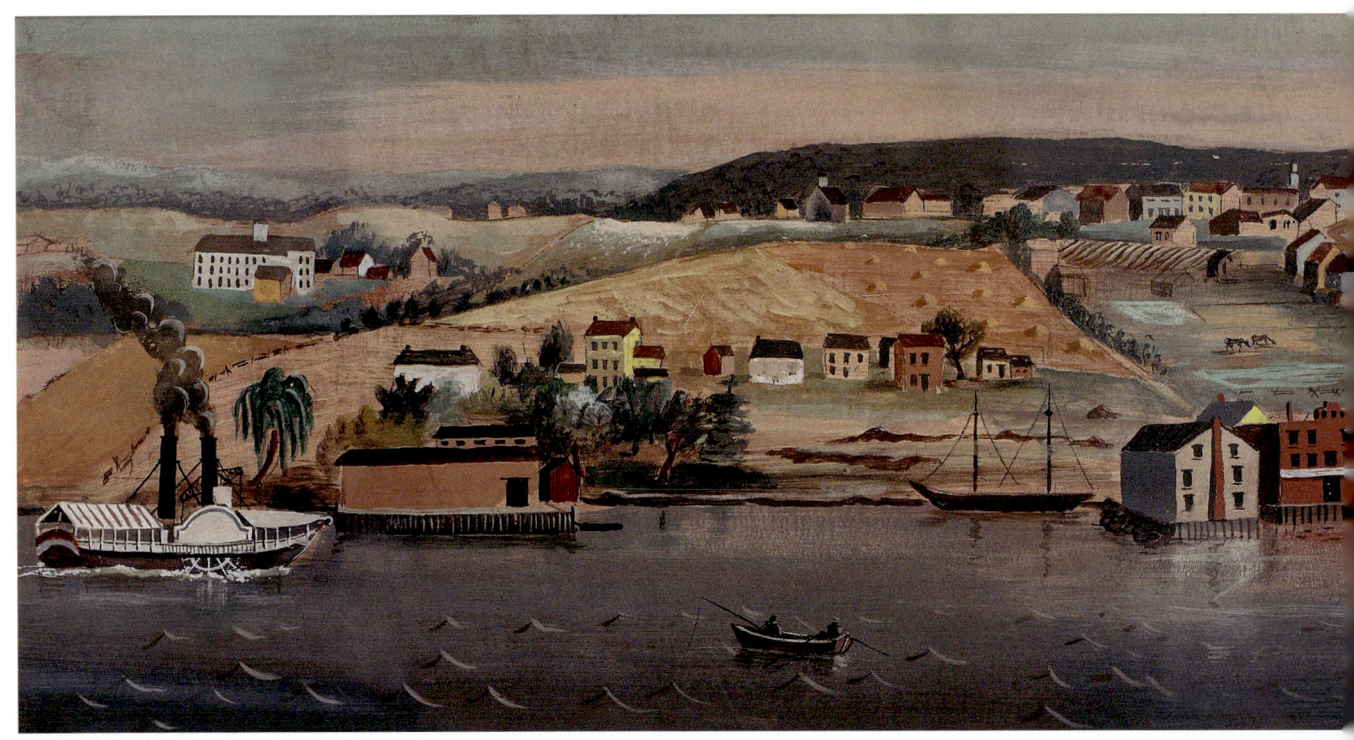

▲ Arnold Blanch (American, 1896–1968)
On the Hudson, c. 1930s
Tempera on panel

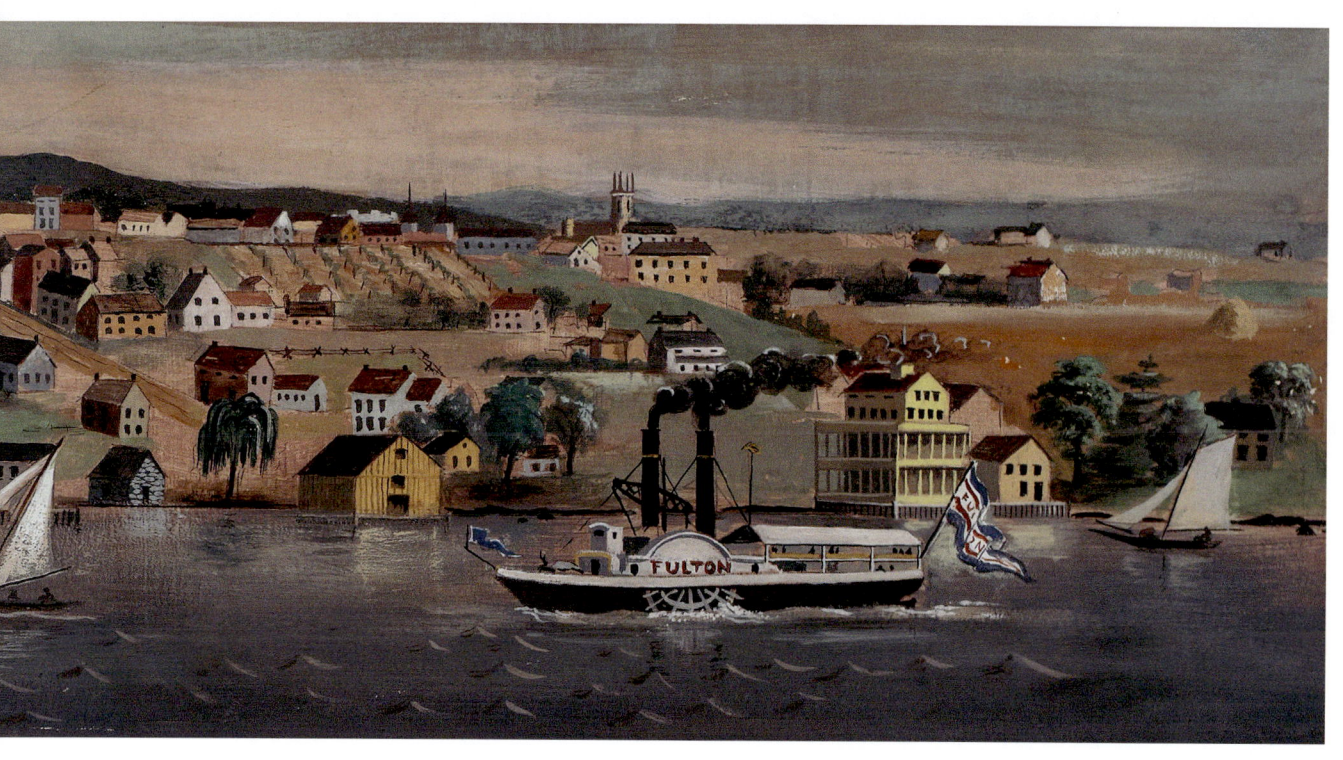

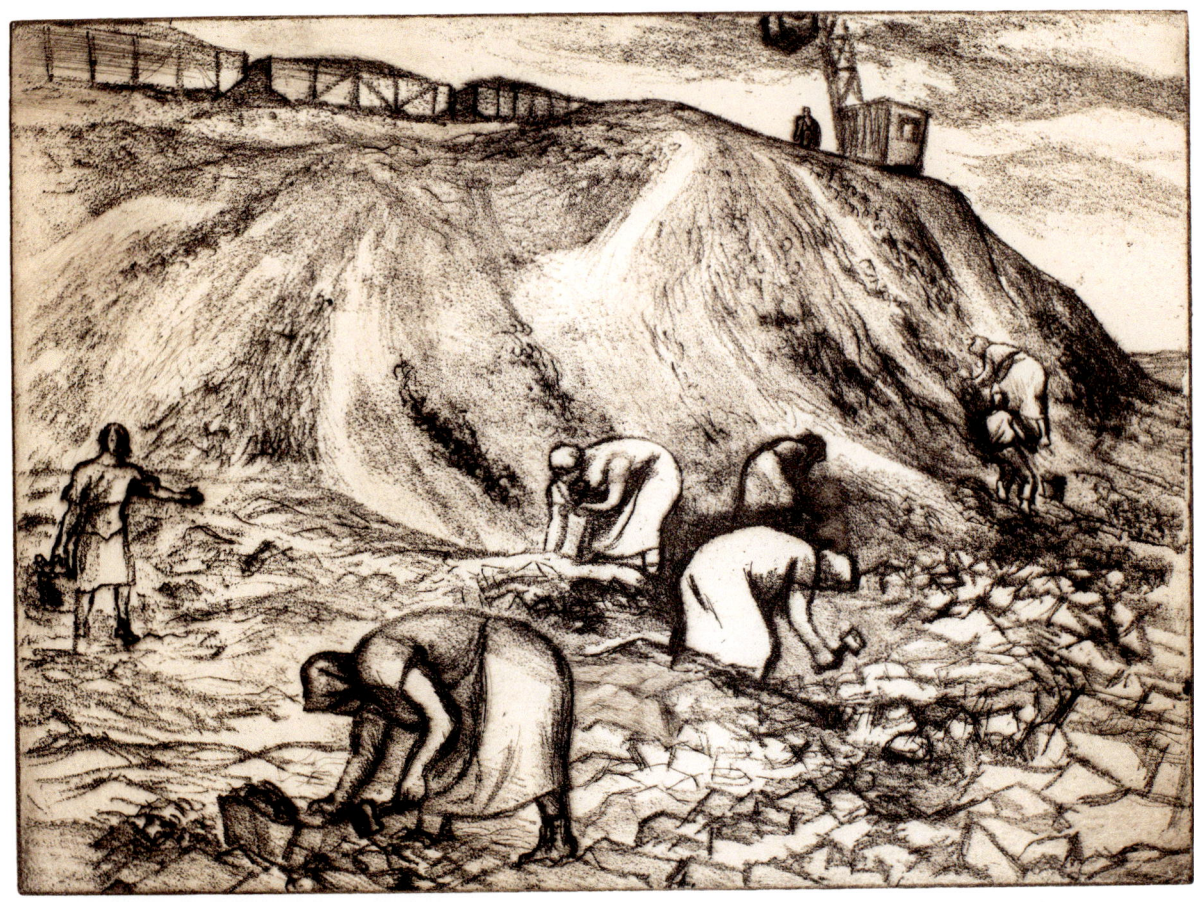

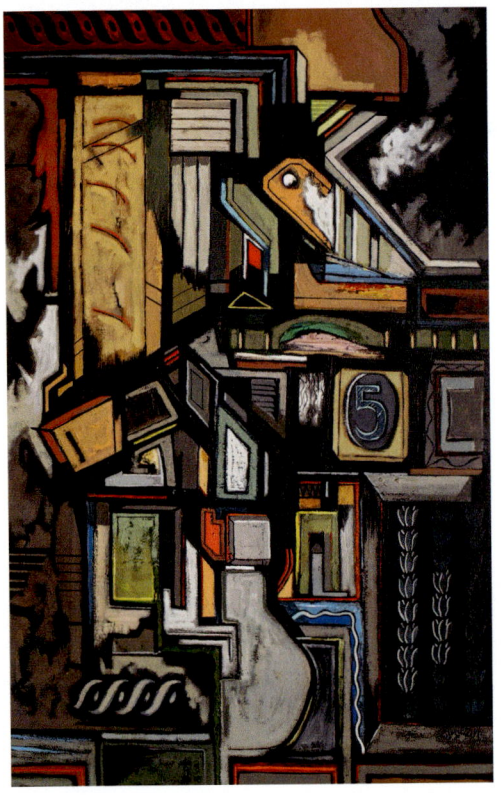

▲ Margaret Lowengrund (American, 1902–1957)
Coal Pickers, 1936
Lithograph on paper

◄ Karl Fortess (American, born Belgium, 1907–1993)
Abstraction No. 5, c. 1950
Oil on canvas

▶ Jenne Magafan (American, 1916–1952)
Cornstalks, 1942
Lithograph on paper

▶ Jenne Magafan (American, 1916–1952)
Autumn Wind (Cornstalks), 1942
Oil and tempera on board

▶ Doris Lee (American, 1905–1983)
Still Life with Fruit, c. 1945
Lithograph on paper

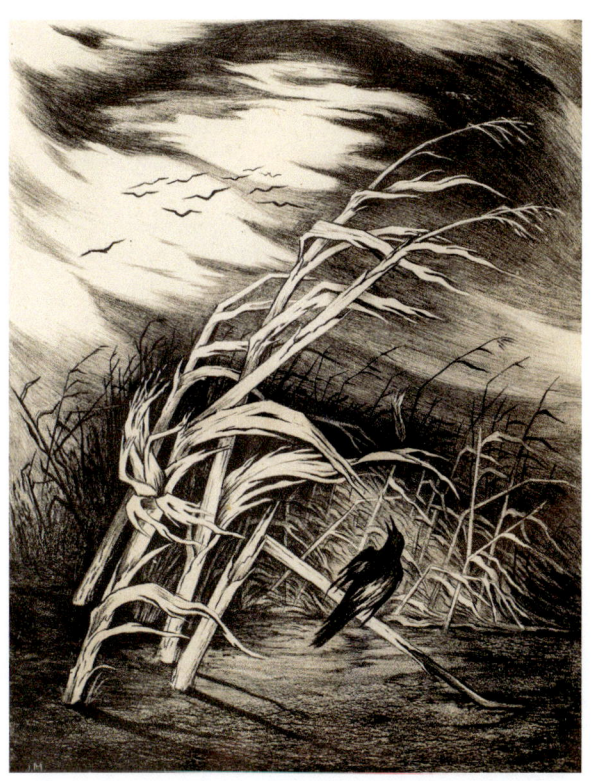

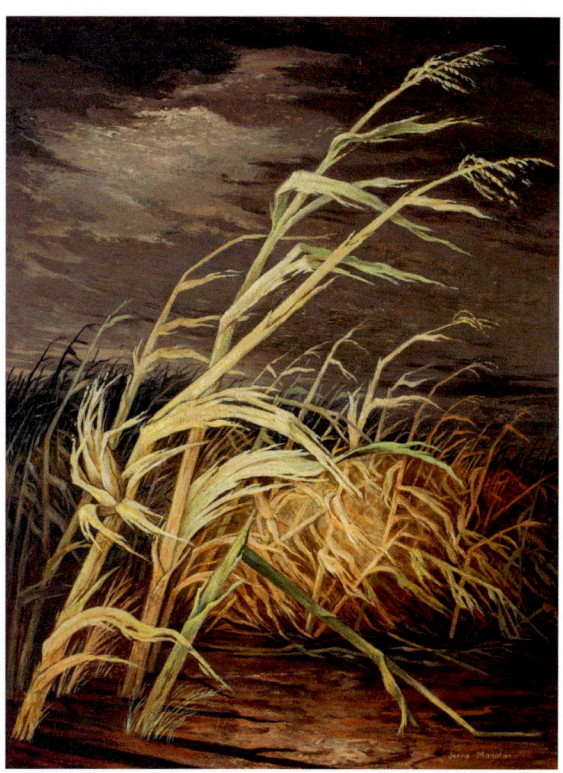

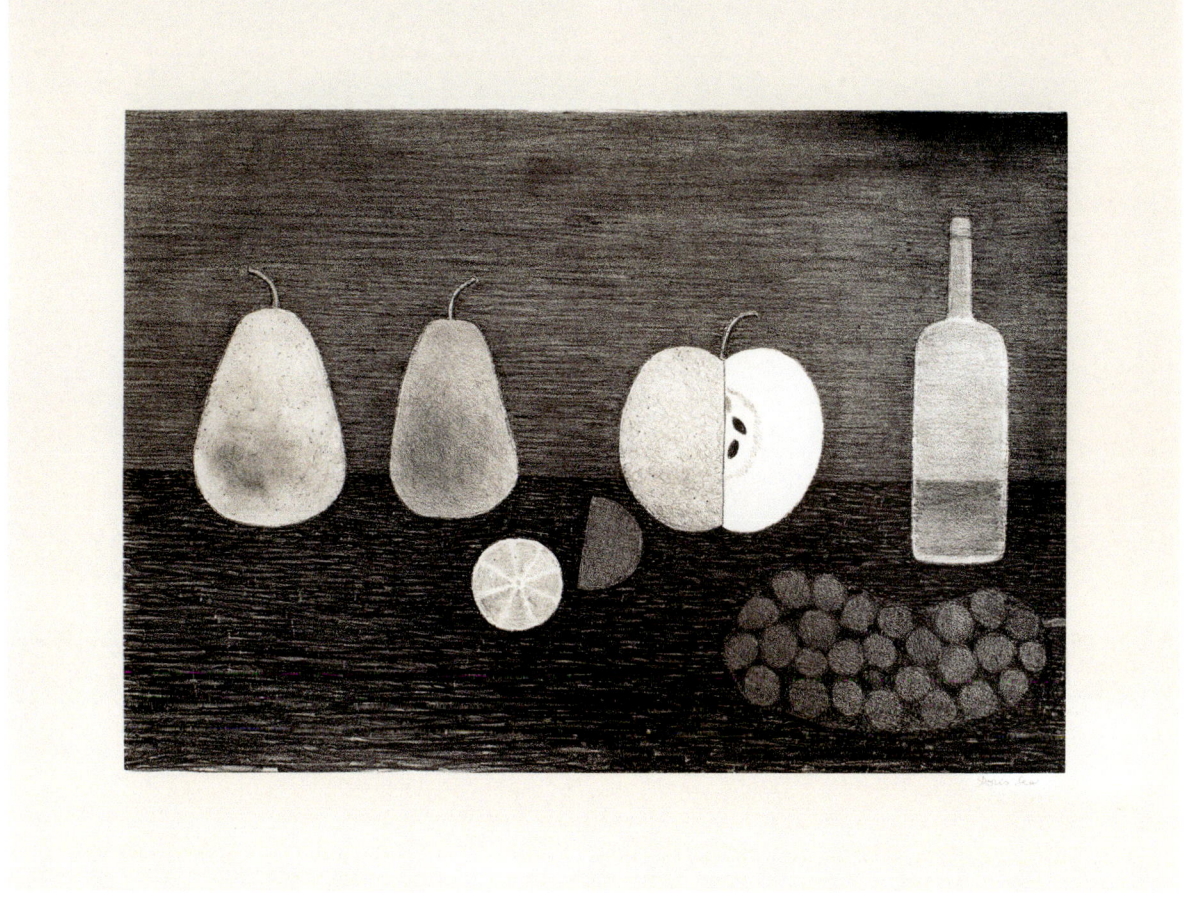

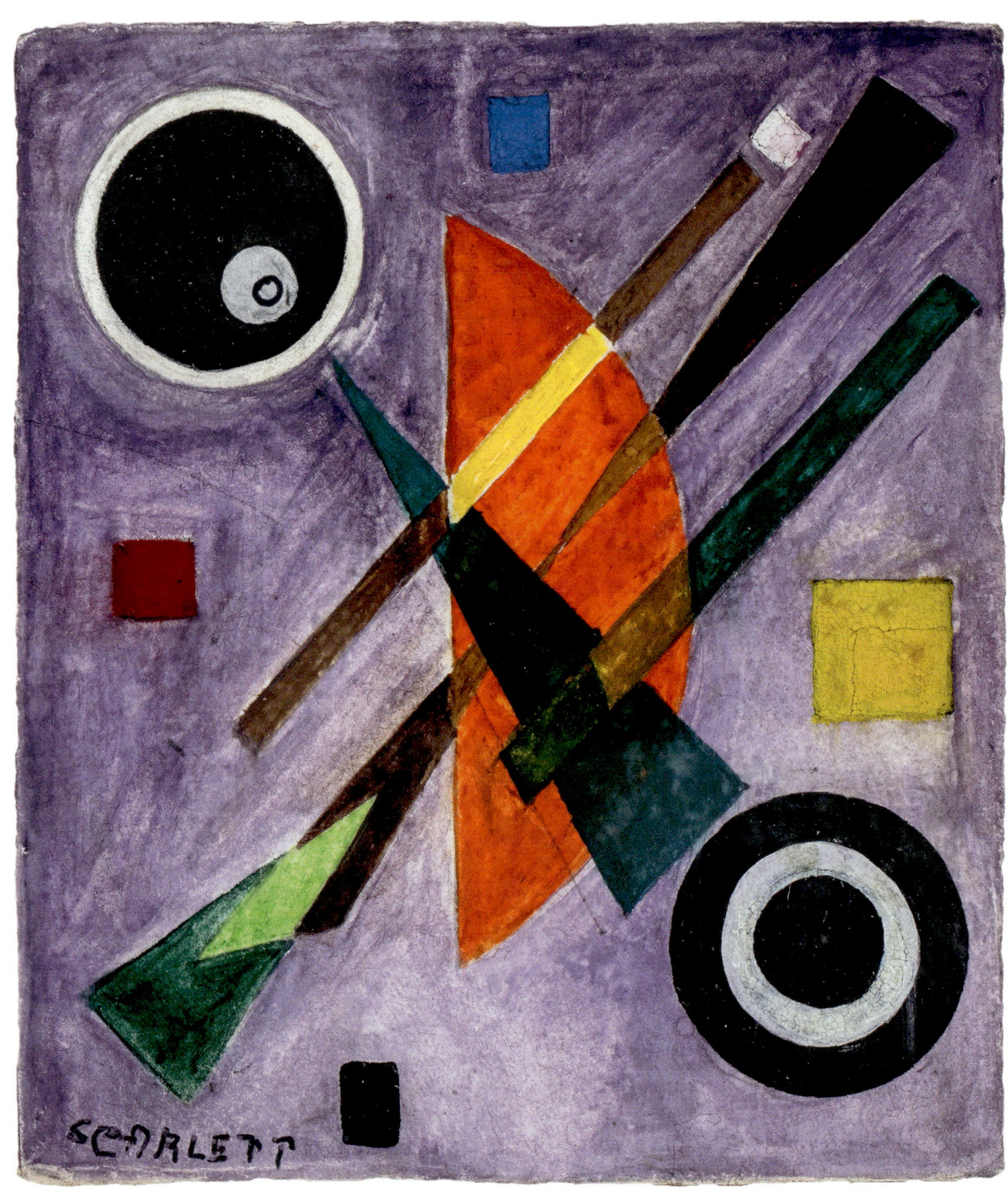

▲ Rolph Scarlett (American, born Canada, 1889–1984)
Abstract Composition, c. 1940
Gouache on paper

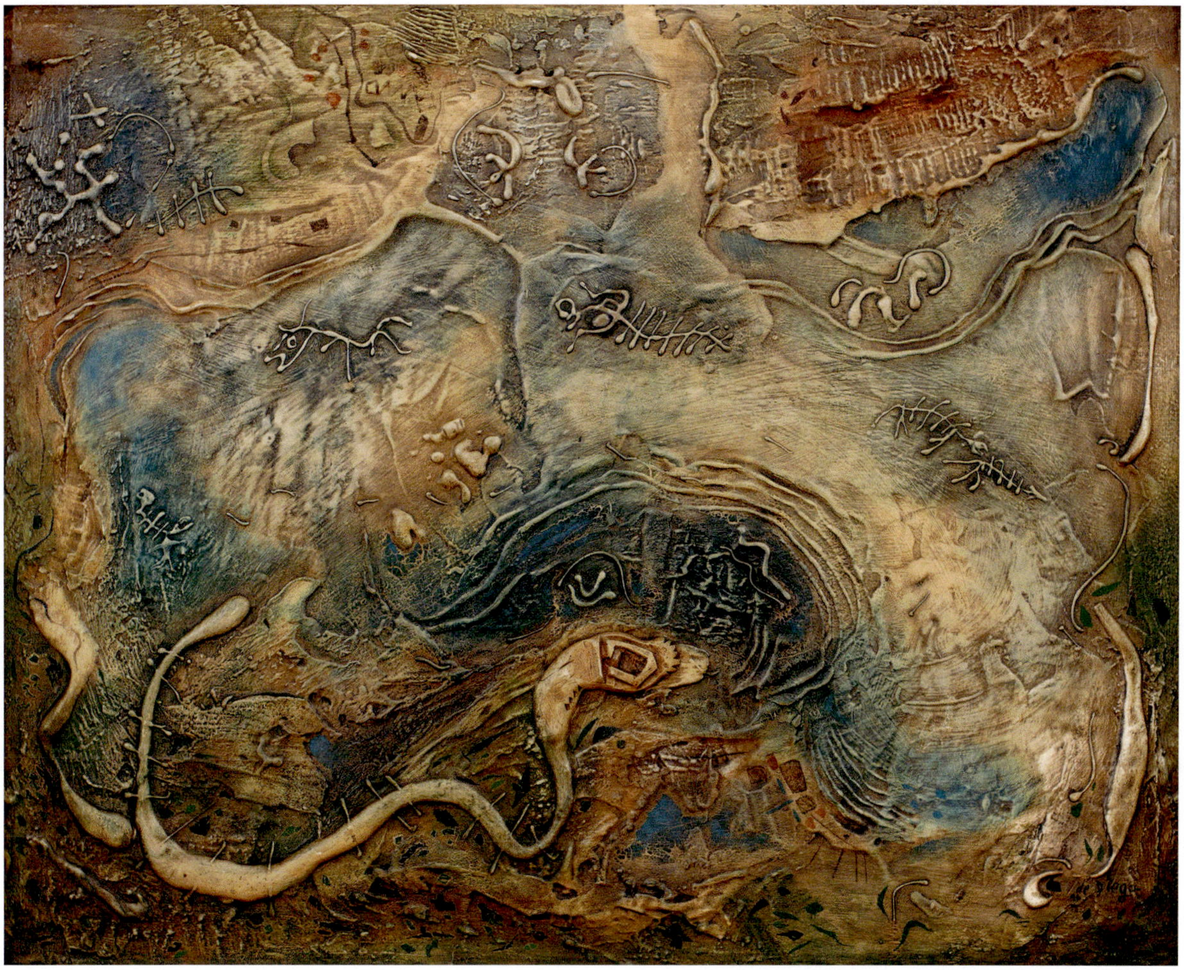

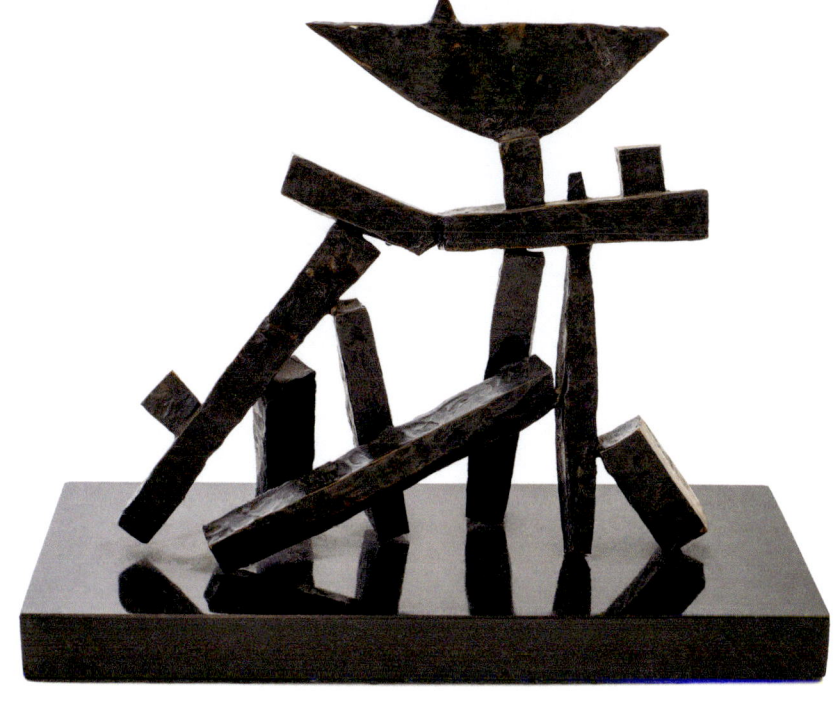

▲ Julio de Diego (American,
born Spain, 1900–1979)
Altitude 3000, 1946
Oil on board

▶ Edward Chavez
(American, 1917–1995)
Abstraction, n.d.
Bronze

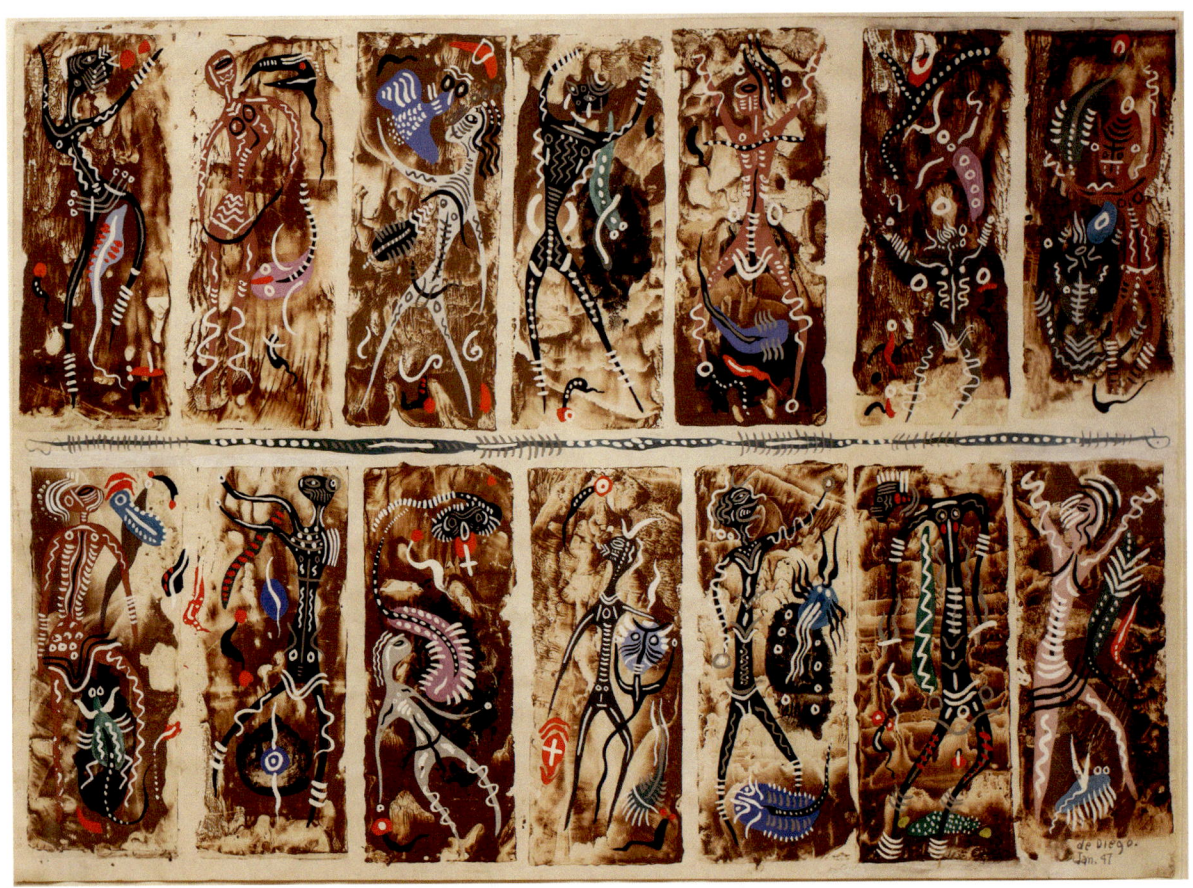

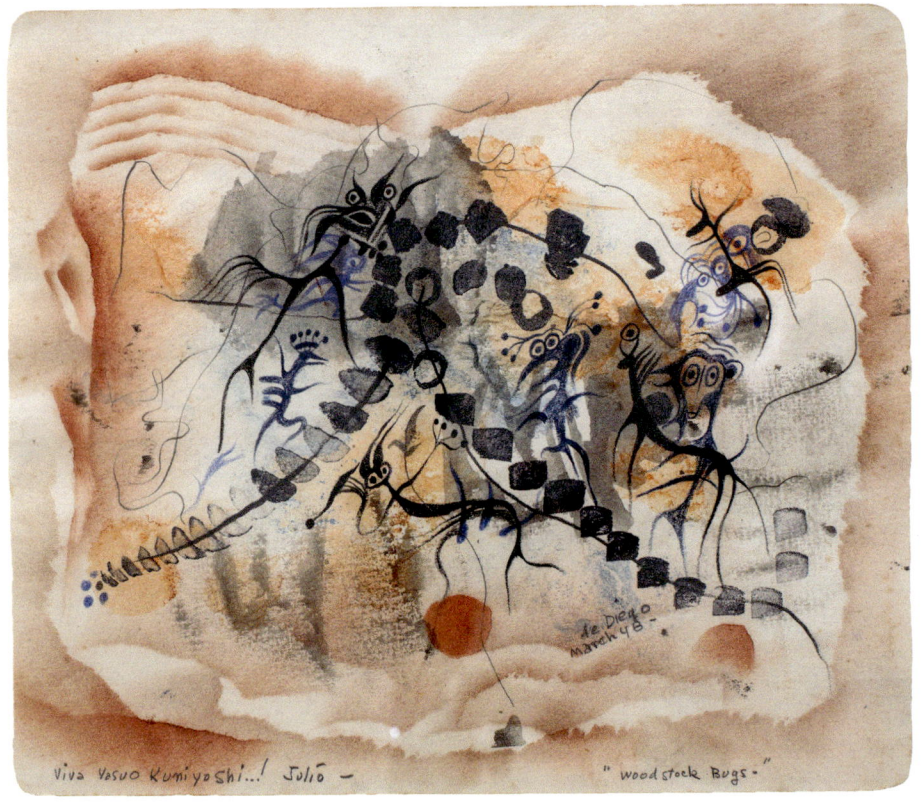

▲ Julio de Diego (American, born Spain, 1900–1979
Nichos No. 2, 1947
Tempera on paper

◄ Julio de Diego (American, born Spain, 1900–1979)
Woodstock Bugs, 1948
Watercolor on paper

▼ Josef Presser (American, born Poland, 1909–1967)
String Bass Player (Abstraction), c. 1945
Oil on canvas

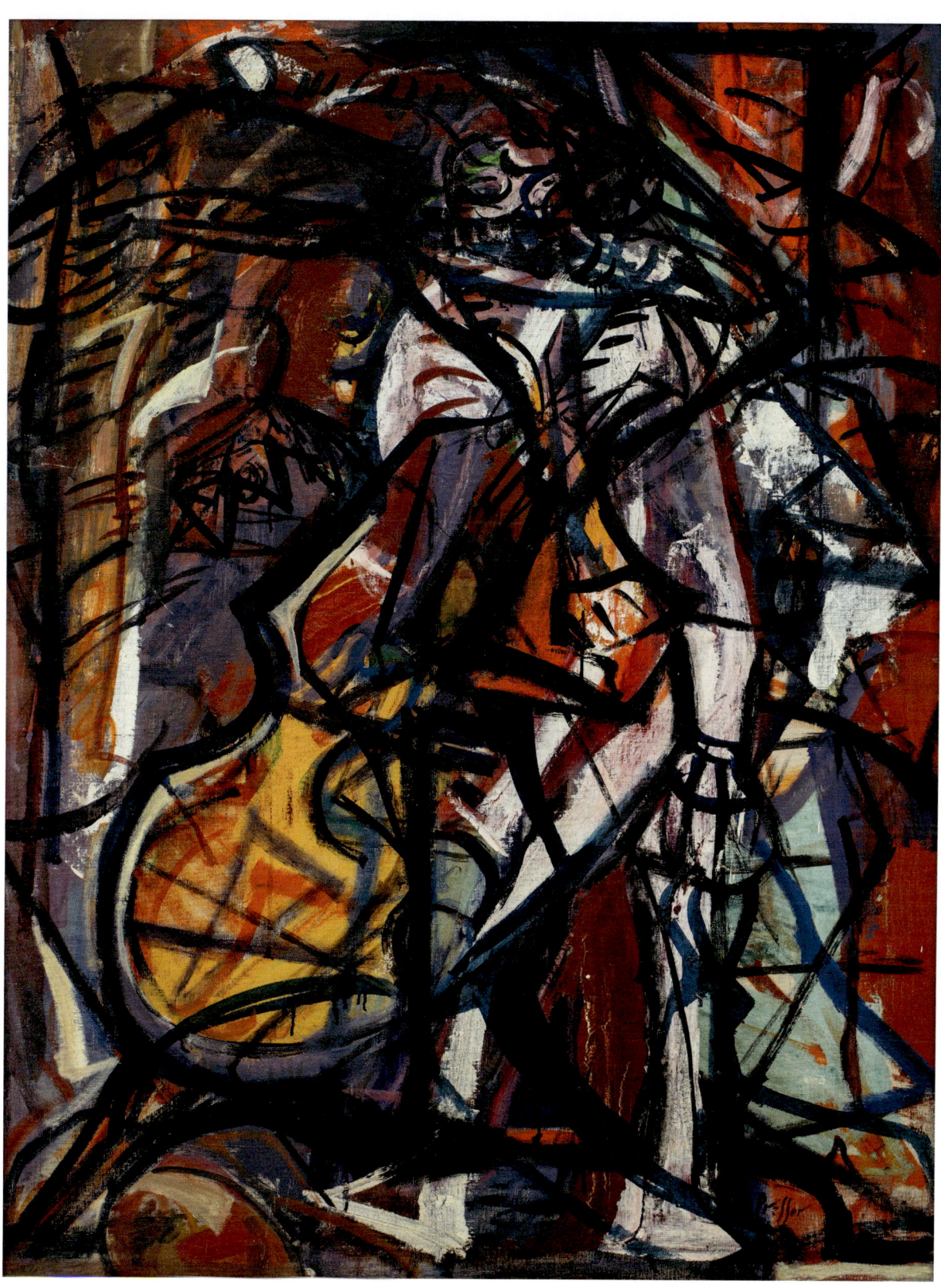

▼ Fletcher Martin (American, 1904–1979)
Far Off City, 1946
Oil on canvas

Martin was hired by *Life* magazine in 1943 as an artist correspondent. He covered World War II in Europe and North Africa, experiences which provided subjects for his work even after the war.

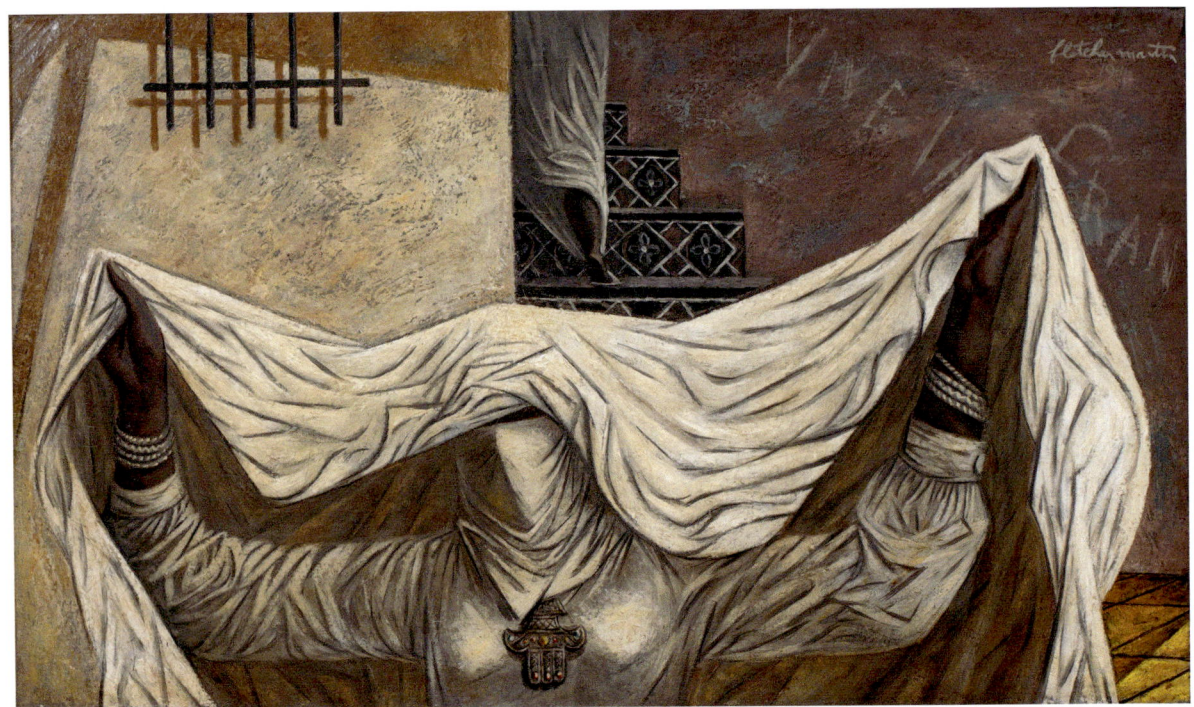

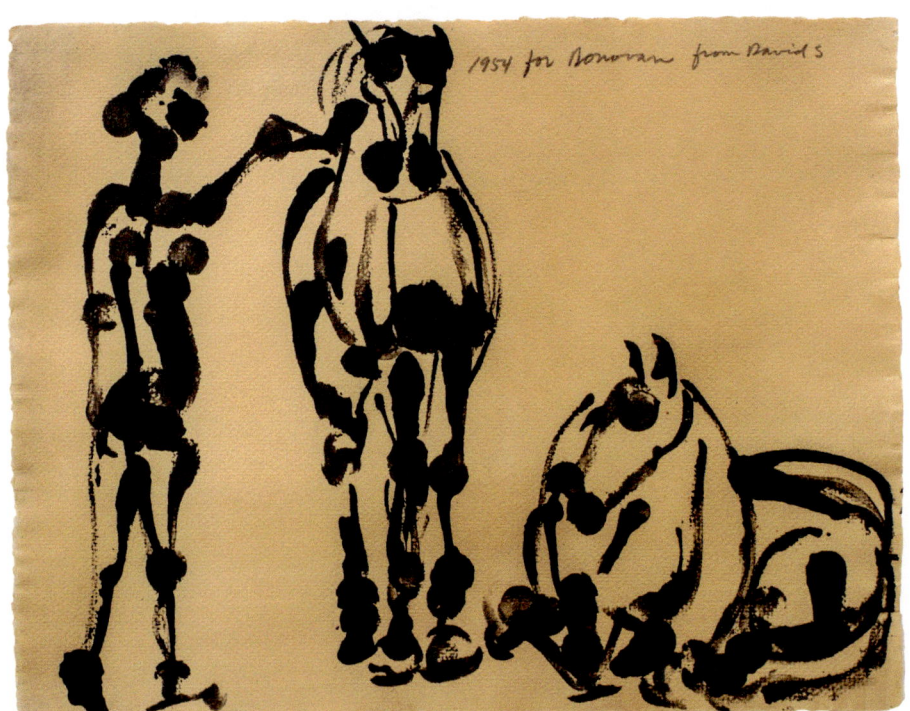

◀ David Smith (American, 1906–1965)
Horses and Figure (Don Quixote), 1954
Ink on paper

▶ Mary Frank (American, born England, 1933)
Figure with Deer, 1962
Ink on paper

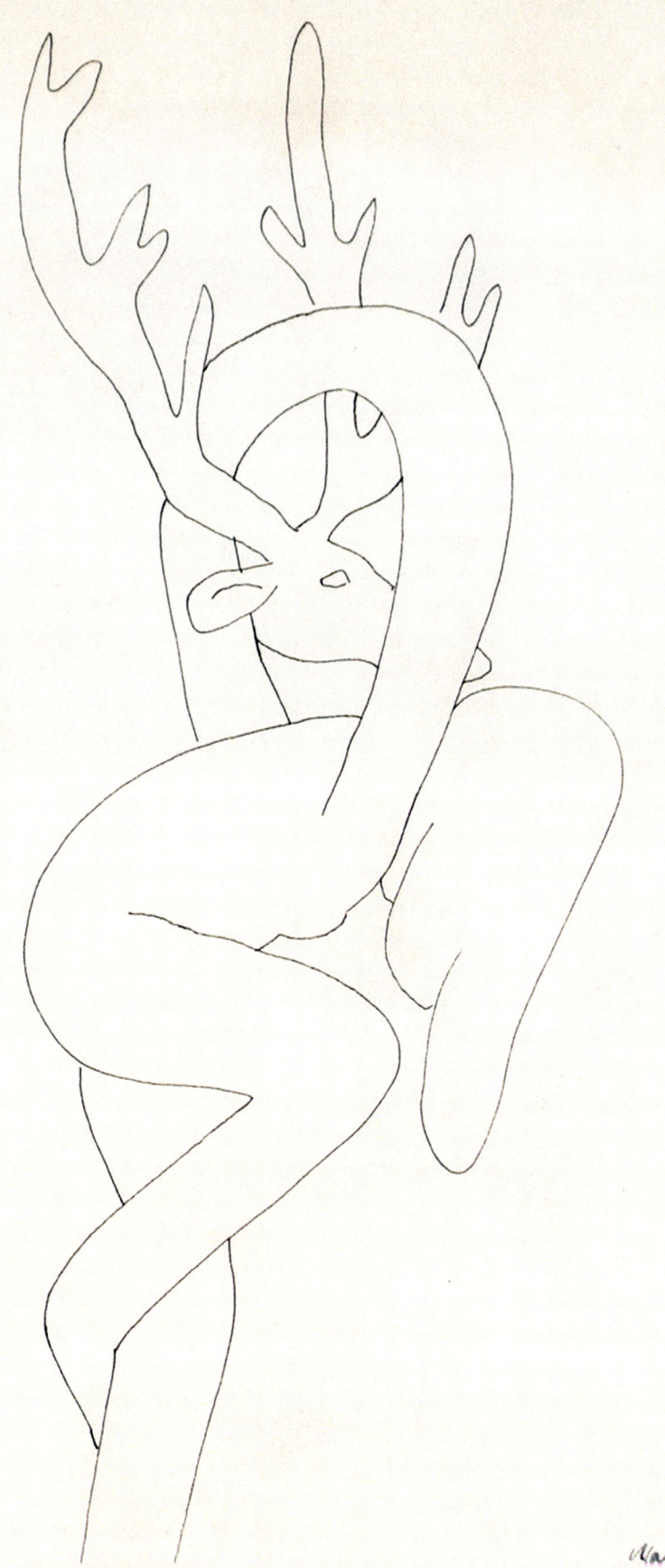

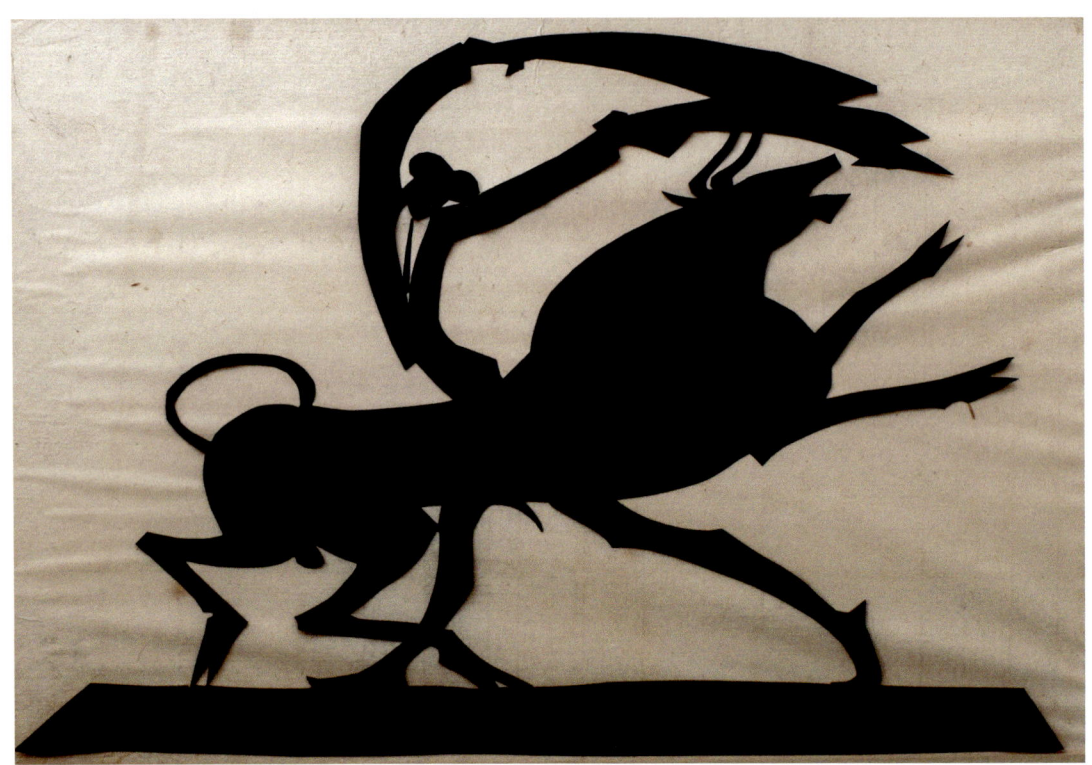

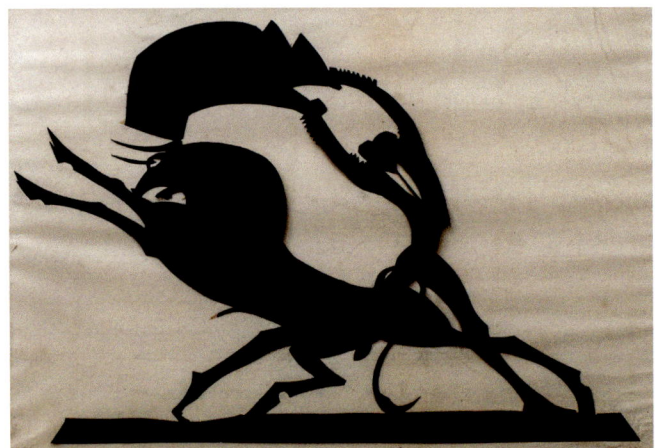

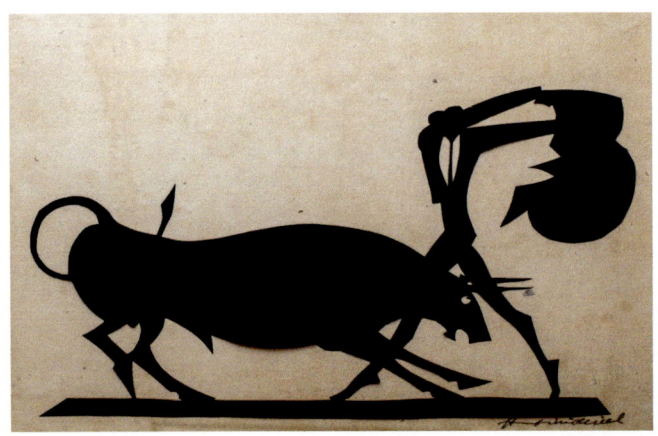

▲ William Hunt Diederich
(American, born Hungary, 1884–1953)
Bullfight Silhouette, c. 1930s
Cut paper silhouette

◄ William Hunt Diederich
(American, born Hungary, 1884–1953)
Bullfight Silhouette, c. 1930s
Cut paper silhouette

◄ William Hunt Diederich
(American, born Hungary, 1884–1953)
Bullfight Silhouette, c. 1930s
Cut paper silhouette

▼ Anton Refregier
(American, born Russia, 1905–1979)
Mural Study for 1939 World's Fair, 1939
Gouache on paper

▼ Marion Greenwood
(American, 1909–1970)
Study for Tennessee Mural, 1940s
Graphite on paper

▼ Mary Frank,
(American, born England, 1933)
Face and Hands, n.d.
Ceramic

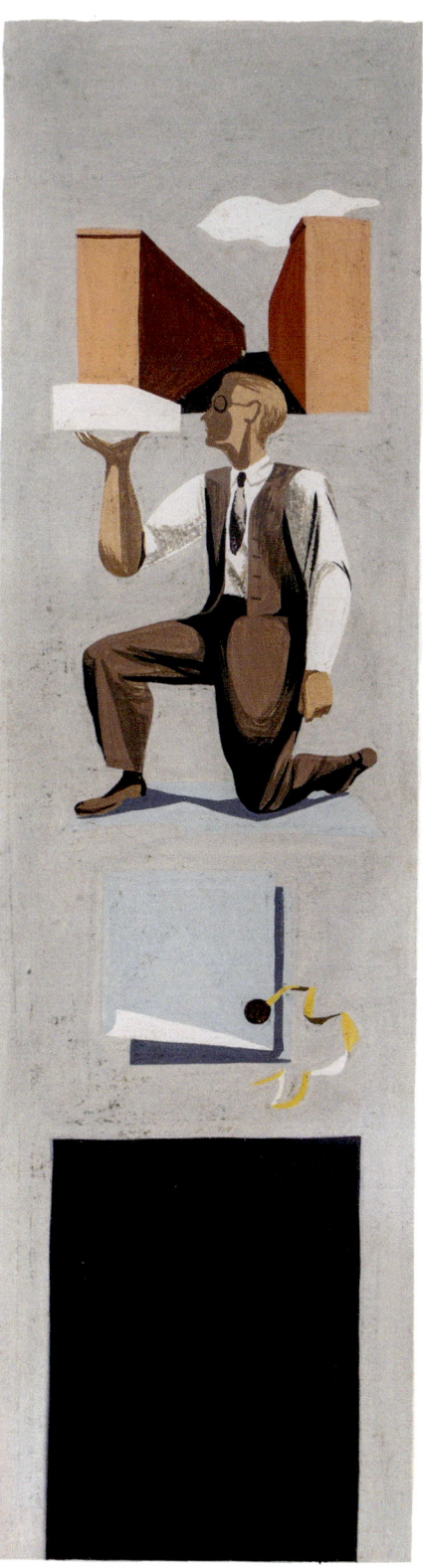

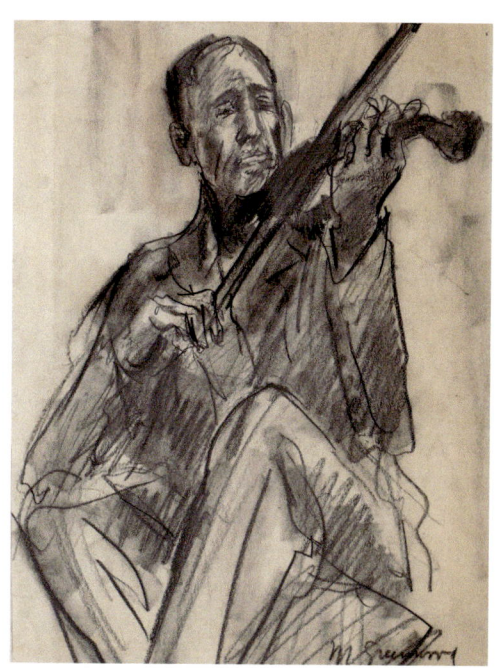

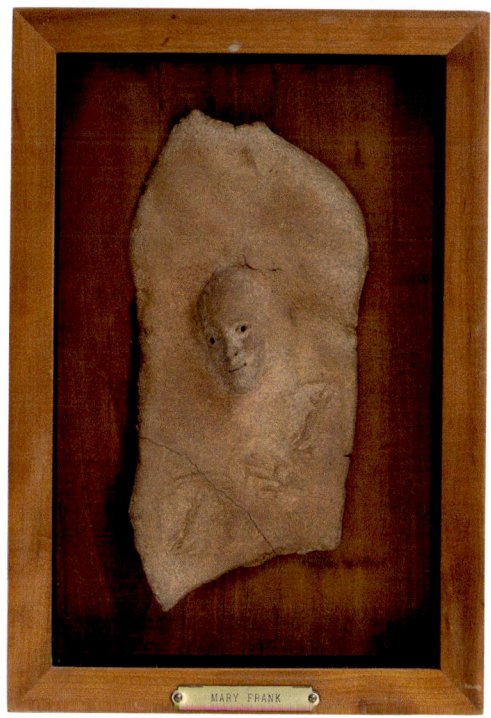

▼ Al Held (American, 1928–2005)
Stone Ridge #6, 1984
Colored etching on paper

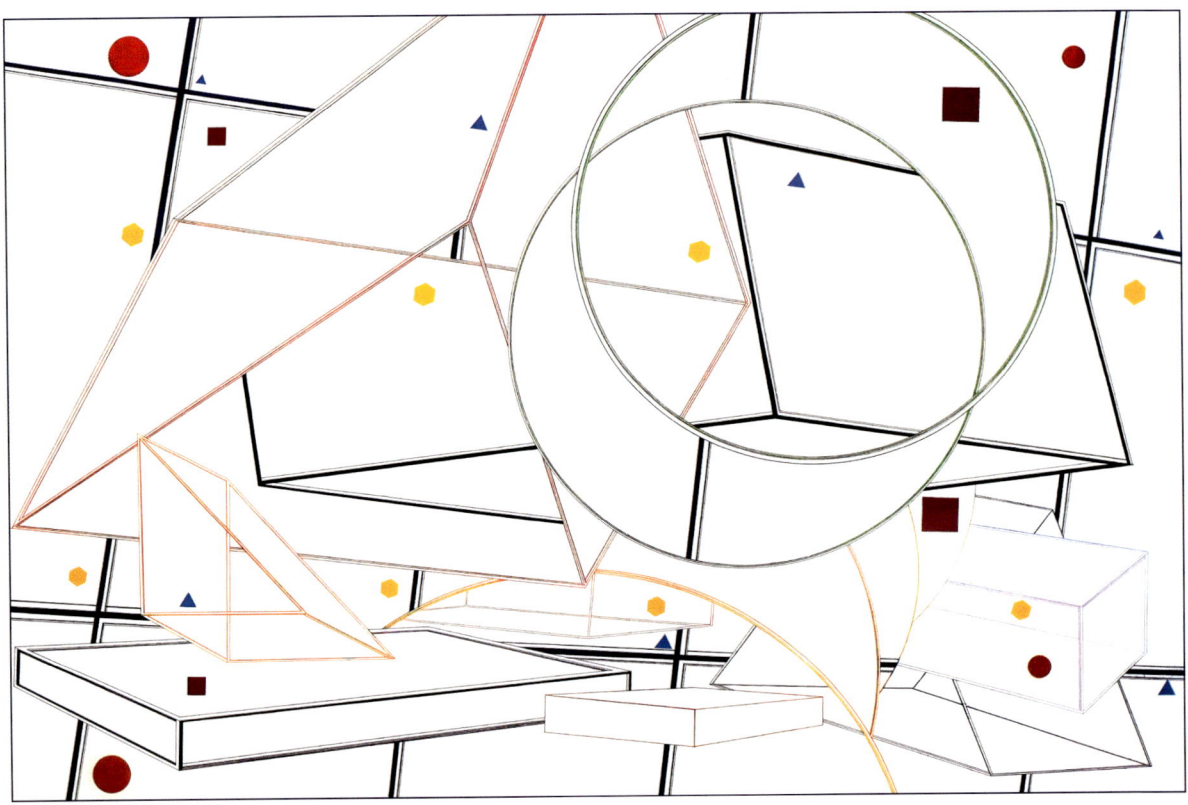

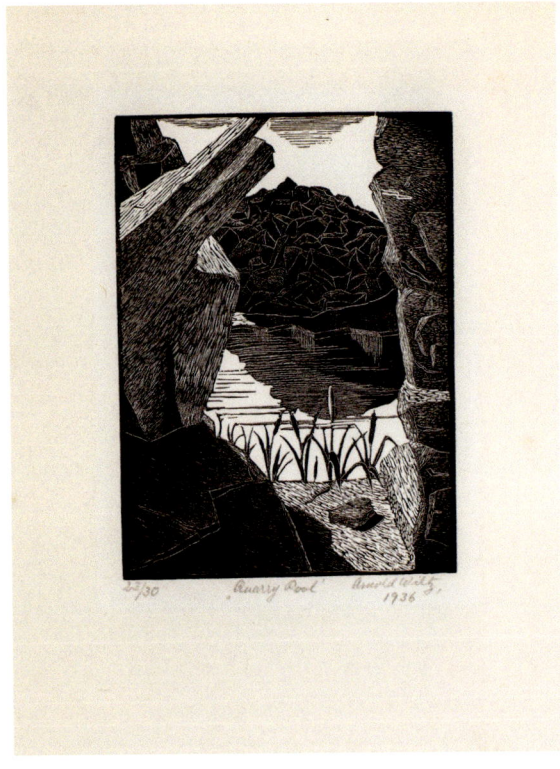

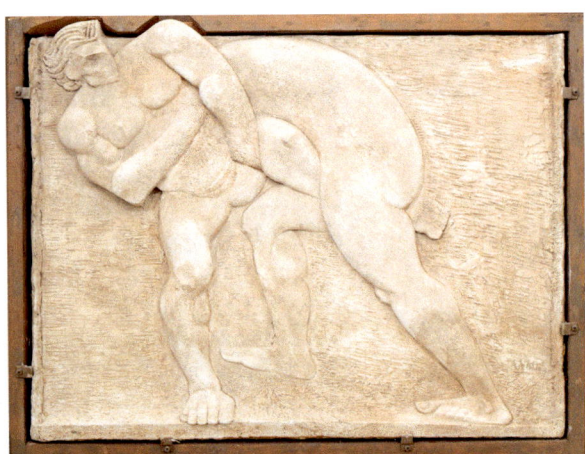

▲ Alfeo Faggi (American, born Italy, 1885–1966)
Greco Wrestlers, c. 1930
Terracotta

◄ Arnold Wiltz (American, born Germany, 1889–1937)
Quarry Pool, 1936
Wood engraving

Note

1. Birge Harrison, "The Woodstock School of Landscape Painting," *Art and Progress* 1, no. 11 (Sept. 1910): 322.

ARNOLD WILTZ: THE DREAMLIKE LANDSCAPE

John P. Murphy

Arnold Wiltz's bildungsroman could have been written by Joseph Conrad. Born in Berlin in 1889 to a painter father, he worked for nearly a decade as a sailor and deckhand on square riggers before landing in Argentina for a spell as an oil driller, railroad foreman, and cattle herder. At age twenty-five he arrived in New York where he remained at the outbreak of the First World War. He took night classes at the National Academy of Design while working odd jobs as a longshoreman, carpenter, and dishwasher. As early as 1921 a catalog for a group exhibition at the Corcoran Gallery in Washington, DC, listed Wiltz's hometown as Bearsville, New York, just outside Woodstock. He married fellow artist Eva Madeline Shiff in 1922 and they made the Hudson Valley their home.[1]

In 1926 the Richard Dudensing Galleries in New York gave Wiltz a one-person show, which received positive notice in *Arts & Decoration* for showcasing work "by a new recruit in the bright world of aesthetic promise."[2] Two years later Wiltz's travels in France exposed him to new currents in European art. He sojourned in Vence in southeastern France and made works inspired by the region's terraced hills and olive and almond trees. A critic for *The New Yorker* credited Wiltz's time abroad for rescuing him "from the academic average of his habitat" and argued that "Wiltz's great task has been to rid himself of Woodstock and the self-satisfaction of an art colony."[3] By this time Wiltz had developed a modern style that suggested the influence of Precisionism and the Neue Sachlichkeit in its cool geometry and crisp edges.

Other critics, however, noted the central importance of the Hudson Valley landscape to his practice. Eleanor Jewett detected in Wiltz's paintings marks of the "German primitive in its perfection and rigidity," and associated their "leisurely gait" with Wiltz's occupation as a farmer in Woodstock.[4] "No true farmer ever hurries," she wrote. "He waits upon nature and the seasons and thinks, plans, and moves in accordance with the gentle progress of the year." In Jewett's view, Wiltz's patient work expressed an attunement to natural cycles and seasonal rhythms.

A recurring motif in Wiltz's oeuvre is the Ashokan Reservoir, built in the early twentieth century to supply New York City with potable water. Citing eminent domain, New York state overrode local objections and began the legal displacement of nine communities in the Esopus Valley, ultimately clearing more than 12,000 acres and over 2,000 people. Construction continued until September 1913, when the Board of Water Supply stopped the flow of Esopus Creek, allowing water at the Ashokan Dam to accumulate up to more than 1.6 billion gallons of water.[5]

The artificial lake became a popular tourist attraction and inspiration to area artists. Wiltz painted *Spillway—Ashokan Dam* (1934) while employed by the Public Works of Art Project,

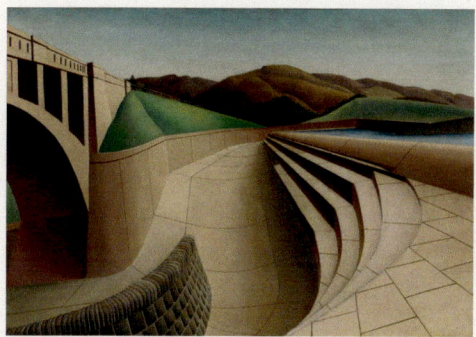

▲ Arnold Wiltz (German, 1889–1937)
American Landscape, 1936
Oil on canvas

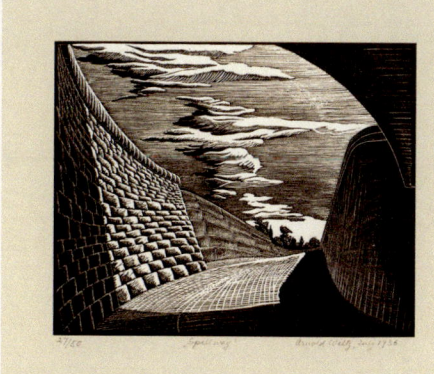

▲ Arnold Wiltz (German, 1889–1937)
Spillway—Ashokan Dam, 1936
Woodblock print on paper

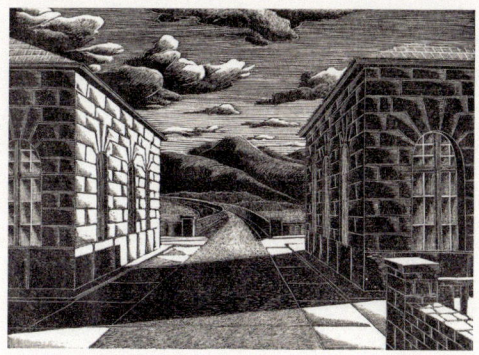

▲ Arnold Wiltz (German, 1889–1937)
The Causeway, 1936
Wood engraving on paper

the short-lived antecedent to the Federal Art Project (FAP) of the Works Progress Administration. The painting was featured in the National Exhibition of Art by the PWAP held April to May 1934, at the Corcoran Gallery in Washington, DC. The rhythmic patterns and eerie airlessness of *American Landscape* recall the landscapes of Grant Wood, but with an undercurrent of menace closer to proto-surrealist Giorgio de Chirico. The reservoir embodied the abstract power of the distant, faceless city, registered in Wiltz's prints and paintings as both monumental and forbidding.

Wiltz produced several wood engravings related to his Ashokan paintings while on the payroll of the Federal Art Project in the mid-1930s. The reservoir's spillway—a sluice for excess water from the dam—inspired the curving rhythms of a 1936 wood engraving, the massive manmade forms in tension with the feathery clouds and distant treeline. *The Causeway* depicts the two rusticated gatehouses flanking a concrete weir dividing the reservoir's eastern and western basins. Wiltz's wood engravings, like his paintings, portrayed the reservoir as monumental and alien in the natural surroundings.

Wiltz's sharp, linear aesthetic made wood engraving—a medium with a long history in German visual culture—well-suited to his favored landscapes and scenes of rural labor. *Wood Chopper* (p. 83) treats the eponymous figure as a heroic model of self-reliance, while *Quarry Pool* (p. 79) evokes the history of the bluestone industry in the area. These wood engravings were featured in an exhibition dedicated to the Ulster County Federal Art Project, which broke attendance records during its October 1936 run at the Woodstock Art Gallery.[6]

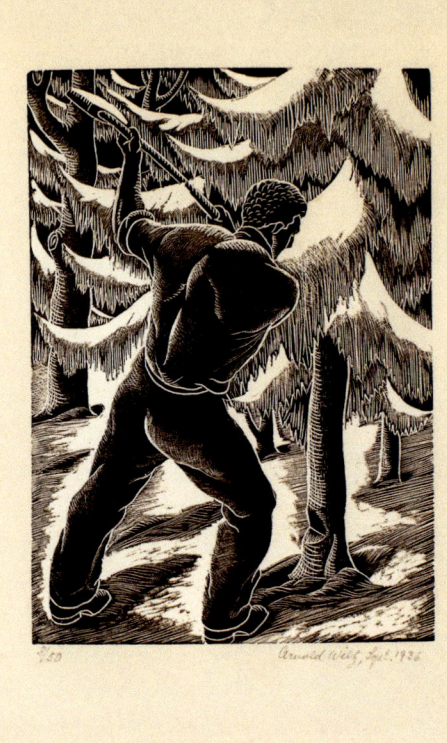

▲ Arnold Wiltz (German, 1889–1937)
Wood Chopper, 1936
Woodblock print on paper

Wiltz involved himself in the Woodstock community, serving as a board member of the Woodstock Friends of Art, established in 1933 to support struggling artists during the Depression. Along with fellow artist Konrad Cramer, Wiltz participated in the formation of the Winter Sports Association in 1936 and the creation of the toboggan run on Ohayo Mountain. An avid skier, Wiltz contributed his painting *Down Hill* for use in circulars advertising the Woodstock ski slopes.[7] Exposure may have contributed to the case of pneumonia Wiltz caught in the winter of 1937. He died in Kingston at the Benedictine Hospital, survived by his wife, Madeline, and their twelve-year-old son, Eric. The Woodstock Art Association (now the Woodstock Artists Association and Museum) honored Wiltz with a memorial exhibition that paid homage to his singular, visionary interpretation of the Woodstock landscape tradition. ■

Notes

1. A short biographical entry on Wiltz appeared in the *National Cyclopedia of American Biography: Index of Twentieth Century Artists 4*, no. 4 (January 1937): 383–84. See also Wiltz's obituary in the *New York Times*, 15 March, 1937, 23; and Robert Plate, "Arnold Wiltz," *Woodstock's Art Heritage: The Permanent Collection of the Woodstock Artists Association* (Woodstock, NY: Overlook Press, 1987): 144–45.

2. "Art's Spring Song," *Arts & Decoration* 26 (1926), 104.

3. "The Art Galleries," *New Yorker*, clipping in Arnold Wiltz file, Woodstock Artists Association and Museum (WAAM). My thanks to archivist Emily Jones for assistance in accessing the Wiltz material held by WAAM.

4. Eleanor Jewett, "Seasons' Flow Seems to Guide Artist Farmer," *Chicago Daily Tribune*, June 7, 1930, 16.

5. For more on the history and construction of the Ashokan Reservoir, see David Stradling, *Making Mountains: New York City and the Catskills* (Seattle, WA: University of Washington Press, 2010).

6. "WPA Art Exhibition Draws Crowds to Woodstock Gallery," *The Overlook*, October 23, 1936, clipping in Wiltz file, WAAM. See also Patricia Phagan, *Made In Woodstock: Printmaking from 1903 to 1945* (Poughkeepsie, NY: The Frances Lehman Loeb Art Center, Vassar College, 2002), 48–49.

7. "Winter Sports in Phoenicia and Woodstock is Doing All Sorts of Good for Business," *Stamford Mirror-Record*, 13 February 1936; "Catskill Winter Plans," *New York Times*, 14 November 1937.

Everything is hard work.
Everything I have done in the way
of creating has been painful—with
a tremendous amount of effort.

– Julio de Diego, Woodstock artist

JULIO DE DIEGO: A PICARESQUE JOURNEY IN ART

Susana Leval

Julio de Diego's audacious life as an artist was his greatest creation. It followed a picaresque[1] journey, creating works that delineated the impulsive ups and downs of his chosen vocation. De Diego's peripatetic life and work—roving from Madrid to Santa Fe, New York, Chicago, Woodstock, and Sarasota, and travel in Europe and the US—produced a rich, varied lifetime of work: paintings; murals; scenery for the Madrid Opera; prints and drawings; book and magazine illustrations; medical drawings; designs for jewelry, fabrics, costumes, theater productions, vaudeville shows, circus carnivals, shop windows, and even an erotic hotel laundry bag. At seventeen, he danced in *Scheherezade* and *Petrouchka* with Diaghilev's Ballet Russes, so well that he was offered a place in the company. He was a color consultant to Paramount Pictures in the late 1950s, and an extra in a 1958 movie with Yul Brynner. De Diego is a brilliant example of the creative power of artists whose talents enrich the world even when they remain largely unknown.

Julio de Diego was, first and foremost, a Spaniard. The parameters of his life—in art, in love, in good and bad times, flowed from his native country of Spain. At the beginning of his unpublished 1971 autobiography, he wrote, "With all my years away I cannot eliminate the background of being Spanish. I have all the influences, good or bad or indifferent of the Spanish man."[2] In *Self-Portrait with Pipe*, Julio presents himself as a mature Spaniard at the height of his intellectual and artistic powers. He was strikingly handsome; his stepson's vivid description matches this image perfectly: "Tall, dark, and sinewy, he wore his long hair combed straight back and had a gaunt face with strong features, lots of creases, and an intense, brooding expression that contrasted sharply with his flamboyant personality."[3]

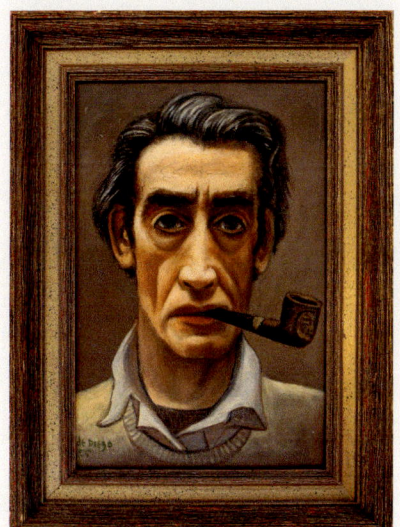

▲ Julio de Diego
Self-Portrait with Pipe, 1955
Oil on board

Born in 1900 in Madrid, near Puerta del Sol, the center of the cosmopolitan city, Julio loved the sounds of Madrid from his youth—of church bells and the cries of street sellers, as well as its smells of fresh bread, roasting coffee, and Valencia oranges. This hypersensitivity to urban sights and sounds presages the intensely passionate artist he would become. The youngest of four siblings, the boy grew up alone or unnoticed, playing fantastical games of war, "with things that I made."[4] His imagination was unbounded, fueled by the writings of Jules Verne, James Fenimore Cooper, and cowboy heroes like Buffalo Bill.

His conversion to life as an artist came early, at age six, while walking with his mother. They ran into a street painter, and Julio was transfixed: "When I got home, I started to do exactly what I saw this man do. I wanted to create that magic."[5] But his stern father disapproved of this life choice and destroyed all his works when Julio was fifteen. The picaresque Julio left home and never looked back.

Young Julio's intense interest in art found a limitless source in his own neighborhood, El Museo del Prado. There he discovered the work of two lifetime artist heroes: Hieronymus Bosch (1450–1516) from the Netherlands and Spaniard Francisco de Goya y Lucientes (1746–1828). With its human/animal hybrids in infinite forms of copulation, Bosch's extraordinary triptych, *the Garden of Earthly Delights*,[6] immediately caught Julio's imagination, feeding his early interest in alchemy and ancient erotic cults. He had a lifelong admiration for Goya as the first modern painter to record contemporary political events in "stop action."[7] He kept a copy of Goya's *Caprichos* in his library.

Every day on his way to school, Julio spent hours watching and learning from fine *madrileño* craftsmen: carpenters, upholsterers, shoemakers, jewelers, watchmakers, cork makers, frame makers, altar painters.[8] Julio, who wasted nothing he learned, used all he absorbed from these skilled craftsmen throughout his long artistic life.

If Julio's first love was art, his love of women was second. From age six, he developed a fascination with women's bodies, stirred by *Divine Leaf*, a Playboy-type magazine he found in a neighborhood shop, playing doctor with a little girlfriend under the huge dining table during Christmas dinner, and a few teenage encounters, worthy of Buñuel, with the family maids. His adoration of females also sprang from deep love and respect for his mother, as well as from an awe-inspiring experience at age ten, when he helped a peasant woman give birth in the middle of a field. In any case, Julio's "theatrical libido"[9] and natural curiosity led him to relish a life of joyous sexuality, a guilt-free participation in what he called the "orgiastic fiesta of man and woman."[10] His most successful partnership was a seven-year marriage to Gypsy Rose Lee, a famous vaudeville theater entertainer, stripper, author, film star, and radio and TV personality. Gypsy was a life force, a sexually liberated woman with a beautiful body, who matched him in intelligence and talent, and to whom he remained a devoted friend until her death in 1970.

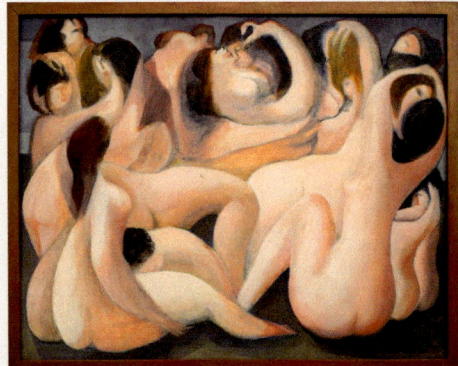

▲ Julio de Diego
Serraglio, 1948
Oil on canvas

Seraglio, inspired by Ingres's *Turkish Bath* of 1862, is one of Julio's many painted celebrations of the naked female body. Although expressionistically brushed rather than drawn

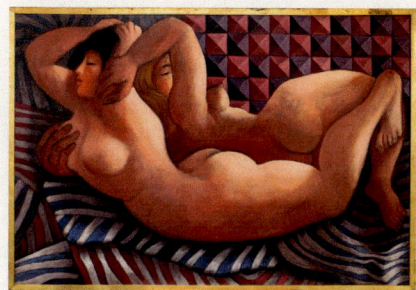

▲ Julio de Diego
Two Nudes with Hand, 1950
Oil on canvas

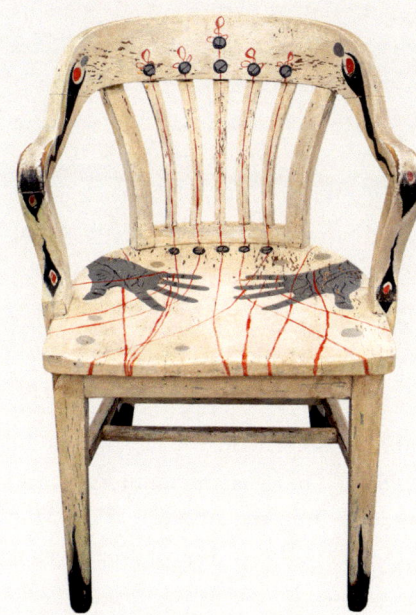

▲ Julio de Diego
Love Chair, n.d.
Painted wood

with neoclassical perfection, he conveys the sensuality in the hothouse of the communal bath, with adroit reference to Ingres. The tangle of fleshy limbs in languid poses conveys the nearness and weight of perfumed skin and erotic stimulus. *Two Nudes with Hand* recalls the monumentality of Matisse's *The Pink Nude* of 1935. Julio, however, squeezes not one, but two languorous bodies into a shallow space adorned by geometric patterns. He adds a homosexual dimension, and—could that be his large dark hand on her breast? The painted wooden *Love Chair* in his Woodstock home was a reminder of his uninhibited, humorous, at once romantic and matter-of-fact approach to lovemaking.

He was similarly alert to the contemporary artists and art movements of his time. Although he vigorously declared himself independent of any artist or art movement, Julio had a talent for distilling and absorbing stylistic elements from those who interested him. He emphatically declared he was not a Surrealist, yet he was invited to include a lithograph in *Surrealisme en 1947,* a collection of prints was published by André Breton, who had drafted the *Surrealist Manifesto* in 1924, and Marcel Duchamp. The small, powerful lithograph alternates biomorphic forms with richly inked cloudlike patches, anchored by abstract fan forms and undulating plant-like ribbons. A series of abstract works from 1947–48, titled *Altitude 3000* (p. 72), attracted much critical attention at the Passedoit Gallery in New York.[11] The illustrated piece relates to Surrealism by its second title, *Biomorphic Abstraction from Airplane,* and fascinating technique. Despite its dense oil and encaustic medium, it recalls the organic fluidity of forms in André Masson's "automatic" sand paintings[12] of the 1920s and follows Breton's "pure psychic automatism"[13] techniques, developed to best capture the unconscious workings of the mind.

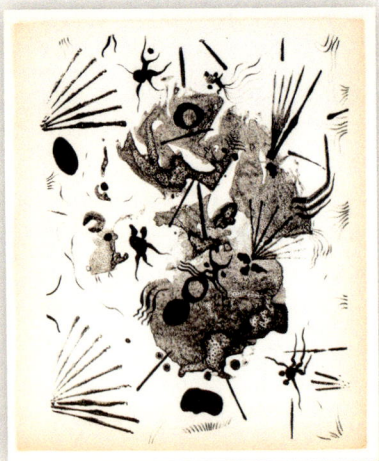

▲ Julio de Diego
Spring Fantasia from
Surréalisme en 1947
Lithograph on paper

Julio's interest in Surrealism took an unexpected turn during his visits to Mexico in 1939–41, where he made a lifelong friendship with Carlos Mérida, a Guatemalan artist of Mayan Hispanic origin. Julio was deeply struck by Mérida's blend of "Indian culture with the Spanish,"[14] which sparked a lifetime interest. Mérida's unique fusion of modernist forms, Aztec myths, and Mayan petroglyphs exerted a strong influence on him, clearly seen in his 1947 *Nichos No. 2* (p. 73), inspired by Mayan codices. In 1954 Julio would retake this inspiration for *Hieroglyphics*, an award-winning fabric design for Associated American Artists.

De Diego's floating, surrealist manner resurfaces in a lighthearted work on paper of 1948, *Woodstock Bugs* (p. 73), a playful spoof of natural history with curving centipedes, crowned reptiles, and prancing creatures. Inscribed "Viva Yasuo Kuniyoshi...", Julio dedicated it to his artist friend from Woodstock, New York, where he lived, among kindred spirits, from 1954 to 1977.[15] Julio's notorious parties there, during which he cooked *paellas* in an upended wheelbarrow, earned an article in a *Life en Español* issue of 1956.[16]

In 1954 de Diego succeeded Kuniyoshi as president of the Artists Equity Association, a late chapter in his lifelong engagement with political and social causes. He had been born into a liberal Spanish home that held strongly Republican, anti-clerical, anti-monarchic values. But by the time Generalissimo Francisco Franco became the tyrannical dictator of Spain in 1936, Julio had long been in Paris, since 1921 (where one of his myriad odd jobs was cleaning Picasso's studio). Three years later, he left for the United States, where he was naturalized and lived a lifetime in self-imposed exile. Throughout, he remained actively engaged in pro-Spanish causes, as well as in broader antiwar and social justice movements.[17]

Enraged and frustrated by medical rejection from military service during World War II, Julio vowed to himself to fight his own war.[18] During two frenzied months in 1943, he painted an extraordinary series of twenty-nine war pictures, shown at the Nierendorf Gallery in a show titled *Desastres del Alma (Disasters of the Soul)*, after Goya. *Art News* voted it one of the ten best exhibitions in New York, and *New Yorker* critic Robert Coates praised it as "the closest approach to truly great interpretation this war has so far produced."[19]

In 1988, a small, somber exhibition at the Museum of Contemporary Hispanic Art (MoCHA) in New York reunited eleven of those works, capturing the artist's glimpses of the horrors of war.[20] Painted in a fury, the works' staccato rhythms echoed war reports and communiqués of the day, and gave the works their titles.

The Latest Advance Officially Reported offers a panoramic view of an arid, charred landscape where two armies lay siege to an exploding city. Julio extends the terrifying crisscross of gunfire into the picture frame. No one is safe. He catches the random explosions in eerie white phosphorescent accents, achieved through tempera underpainting beneath multiple layers of oil glazes, an Old Master technique he learned in Madrid. In other works, these accents are extended by semi-automatic techniques the Surrealists favored: stencils, decalcomania, image transfers, and automatic writing. These created a seemingly random, organic matrix from which the artist's imagination would elaborate further marks. The "armies" in the painting are disturbing for their abstract featurelessness, described in *Life* magazine as "impersonal as purposeful insects, their human-like qualities obliterated in a hopeless atmosphere of regimentation and mechanization."[21] Their depiction shows the continuing influences of Bosch's fish hybrids and Mérida's Mayan mask profiles.

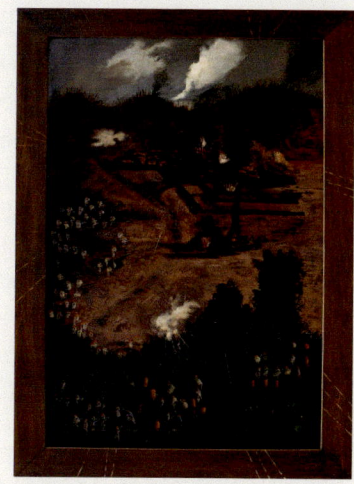

▲ Julio de Diego
The Latest Advance Officially Reported, 1942
Oil on board

Julio later said of the War Series, "I felt the War very deeply. I worked in the solitude of my studio thinking of man converted into a machine to destroy."[22] Many of the war pictures showed cities under siege, no doubt bringing back the rage and pain he felt during the Spanish Civil War as Madrid was bombed into submission by Franco. In 2022, we tragically continued to witness similar inhuman devastation wreaked on Ukraine by the Russian army.

This brief review of Julio de Diego's work ends on a light note, with a drawn 1949 pictographic letter to Duke Wilson, manager of "Royal American Shows," traveling carnival shows featuring Gypsy Rose Lee, for which Julio designed sets and costumes.[23] The letter's images swap his and Wilson's roles and captures the

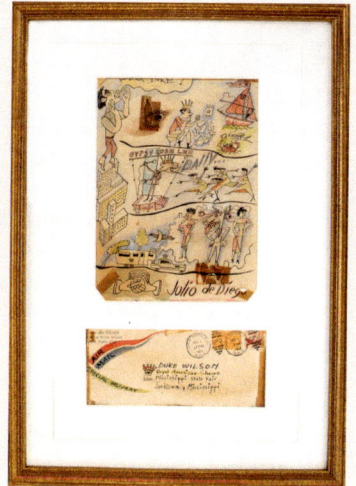

▲ Julio de Diego to Duke Wilson,
Letter, 1949
Mixed media on paper

picaresque journey of Julio's life and work. From his "barker" role atop a New York City skyscraper, he charms his way backstage, surrounded by beautiful chorus girls, finds adventure at sea, performs onstage—all with the madcap speed, gaudy style, and chaotic merriment of life on the road.

Despite the jollity, two details are dead serious in the image, emblematic of Julio's life and artistic career: the penetrating, Picassoid eye of the artist, upper left, and, below, next to his signature, the closed circle of a strong handshake.[24] Despite his flamboyant life and personality, life as an artist was uncompromising for Julio. He believed that "everything is hard work. Everything I have done in the way of creating has been painful —with a tremendous amount of effort."[25] His gift for friendship and humane, delightful qualities were reasons his artist friends loved and trusted him.[26] The emblem of that gift, next to his signature, is the handshake of a Spanish gentleman, Julio de Diego. ■

Notes

1. The *pícaro* is a distinctly Spanish anti-hero: a roguish, inventive character who lives an adventurous life by the seat of his pants, using his sharp wit and prodigious capacity to seize opportunity anywhere and everywhere.

2. Julio de Diego, *A Kind of Curious Thing: An Autobiography by Julio de Diego as Told to Marcia Corbino* (Sarasota, FL, 1971), 5. Unpublished manuscript transcript, Julio de Diego Archive, private collection.

3. Erik Lee Preminger, *My G-String Mother: At Home and Backstage with Gypsy Rose Lee* (Berkeley, CA: Frog, 2004), 205. Julio was a loving stepfather to Erik during his marriage to Gypsy Rose Lee.

4. de Diego, *A Kind of Curious Thing*, 5.

5. de Diego, *A Kind of Curious Thing*, 14.

6. de Diego, *A Kind of Curious Thing*, 34. Hieronymus Bosch's *The Garden of Earthly Delights*, (1500–1505), entered the Prado Collection in 1939. Julio describes his fascination with the painting: "I've always been attracted to mischievous things in painting. Even when I was a child…There are lots of naked girls and they are doing all kinds of mischievous things and that attracted me very much. It is what we would call today surrealism."

7. Julio de Diego, undated, unpublished notes for a lecture, ca. 1951, on the treasures of the Prado, highlighting Goya, whom he described as a "humanist…a man of humor and of the tragic sense of life" who used his art to expose the hypocrisy of the clergy and upper classes of Spain. Julio de Diego Archive, private collection.

8. de Diego, *A Kind of Curious Thing*, 30 "I owe everything that I know to curiosity." 3..

9. Erik Lee Preminger, (writer, actor, and producer), phone interview with Susana Leval, October 19, 2022. He holds lovely memories of his stepfather: "He had a gusto for life, an embracing warmth, and an ability to transform the ordinary into the magical that made him one of the most captivating people I have ever known." Preminger, *My G-String Mother*, 206.

10. de Diego, lecture notes. In the feminist, post Me Too movement, and contemporary US culture, it is perhaps impossible not to feel discomfort with such emphatic sexual freedom from a powerful male figure. Julio de Diego Archive, private collection.

11. Chronology of Julio de Diego's life, unpublished, edited by Arthur Anderson. Entry for 1947, p.17, quote from New York critic Ralph Parson: "These paintings are unique…highly significant." Entry for 1947, p.27, art historian Katherine Kuh described "The magic of de Diego's unusual textural approach to painting." Julio de Diego Archive, private collection.

12. William Rubin, *Dada, Surrealism and Their Heritage* (New York: Museum of Modern Art, 1968), 72. According to art historian William Rubin, André Masson "let the pen travel quickly, in 'mediumistic' fashion, over the paper, in visual free-association untrammeled by esthetic censorship." André Breton, Excerpt from Manifesto of Surrealism, 1924, as quoted in "André Breton, "What is Surrealism? 1934," in Herschel B. Chipp, *Theories of Modern Art: A Source Book by Artists and Critics* (Berkeley, Los Angeles and London: University of California Press, 1968), 412.

13. de Diego, *A Kind of Curious Thing*, 113.

14. Anderson, Chronology, 39.

15. "El Pintor Julio y sus Paellas," *Life en Español*, December 3, 1956, 91–95.

16. Spanish Child Welfare Association of America, 1939; Post Civil War committees to send aid to Spain; Joint Anti-Fascist Refuge Committee, 1946; President of Artists Equity Organization, 1954, succeeding Yasuo Kuniyoshi, its first president. A loyal friend to artists in need, he gave parties to raise funds for impoverished artists like his reclusive friend Joseph Cornell.

17. Susana Torruella Leval, "Julio de Diego 1900–1979," in *Woodstock's Art Heritage: The Permanent Collection of the Woodstock Artists Association* (Woodstock: The Overlook Press, 1987), 79. I was first captivated in the 1980s by one of de Diego's war pictures in the Woodstock Artists Association and Museum's permanent collection. It is my best hope, in highlighting this artist among the many fine artists in *The Historic Art Colony: The Arthur A. Anderson Collection*, that the next generation of young scholars will find Julio de Diego a proper place in a future, revised canon of "American" art.

18. Robert Coates, "The Art Galleries: The Artists and the War", *The New Yorker*, May 8, 1943.

19. *Julio de Diego: The War Series or Los Desastres del Alma, January 21–February 28, 1988*, (New York: Museum of Contemporary Hispanic Art, 1988), 2. Published in conjunction with an exhibition of the same name, curated by Susana Torruella Leval at MoCHA with the generous help of Julio's daughter, Kiriki Metzo. Exhibition catalog.

20. "Julio de Diego: Paints Weird War and Peace." *Life*, March 11, 1946, 80.

21. MoCHA, exhibition catalog, 6.

22. Julio de Diego, letter to Duke Wilson, 1949, Julio de Diego Archive, private collection.

23. de Diego, letter to Wilson.

24. de Diego, *A Kind of Curious Thing*, 13.

25. Anderson, Chronology, 23. The list of Julio's lifelong artist friends and acquaintances in the US is impressive: it included Yul Brynner, Alexander Calder, Edward Chavez, Minna Citron, Joseph Cornell, José de Creeft, Marcel Duchamp, Buckminster Fuller, Philip Guston, June Havoc, Yasuo Kuniyoshi, Jacob Lawrence, Robert Motherwell, Louise Nevelson, Gypsy Rose Lee, Gordon Parks, Cornelia Otis Skinner, Dong Kinmann, Mitchell Siporin, Carlos Mérida, and Esther Williams.

WOODSTOCK AND KINDRED SPIRITS

James Cox

In 1990, I made the decision to leave my position as director of the Grand Central Art Galleries in New York City and move with my wife, Mary Anna Goetz, a landscape painter, and our two children to a new territory. I hoped to find an affordable place to live and open a full-service gallery that would cater to museums and collectors. Woodstock, the famous art colony, located just two hours north of Manhattan, was a consideration.

Through a family connection, I was introduced to Aileen Cramer, a town activist, and daughter of German-born artist/photographer Konrad Cramer, who moved to Woodstock in 1912 with his artist wife, Florence Ballin. We first met Aileen at the Woodstock Artists Association where she and two other women, Lillian Fortess and Betty Sturgis, had recently raised funds to build a major addition to the historic building. The new gallery, named the Phoebe and Belmont Tobin Wing, would house a growing collection of art and archives.

This encounter proved to be a pivotal one for me. Aileen generously took it upon herself to show me and my family all of the colony's attractions and resources, including galleries, studios, theaters, churches, and historic sites. She also introduced me to many of the town's movers and shakers. Of special note were Alice Lewis, Jean Gaede, Kay Warner, Andrée Ruellan, and Jane Van De Bogart. Ann Blanch generously offered to host a welcoming party to augment our gallery's grand opening. It seemed as if the whole town turned out.

Another momentous connection to my Woodstock journey is my friendship with Arthur Anderson, which began more than two decades ago. Early on a certain comradery developed due to our similar Midwestern origins and experience with some of the movers and shakers in Indiana, where I was raised, and Michigan, Arthur's home state. In the Hudson Valley we were involved with art organizations in Woodstock and New Paltz. Importantly, we both knew Neil Trager, Director of the SUNY New Paltz College Art Gallery.

Neil was a man with a vision who dreamed of building a first-class art museum on the college campus. He brought together a small group including Alice Chandler, the college president, philanthropists Mary and James Ottaway, Samuel Dorsky, a New York businessman and his family, and Arthur and me, among others. Together we formed what would become the founders of an important regional art museum.

During this period Arthur, the consummate host, held gatherings at his beautiful home and studio on Moonhaw Road in West Shokan, just a few miles from our Woodstock gallery. Arthur and I also collaborated with the board and staff of the Woodstock Artists Association and Museum (WAAM) to create a series of fundraising events, mostly fine art auctions that raised substantial funds for artists' programs and the venerable organization's newly formed permanent art collection.

Along the way Arthur and I became close friends and shared our mutual enthusiasm for historic Woodstock art. As an art gallery owner, I had access to many local artists' estates and private collections from which I was able to draw examples that complimented Arthur's growing collection. These included prime examples by first-rate artists including Andrew Dasburg, Rolph Scarlett, George Bellows, Georgina Klitgaard and Rudolf and Margaret Wetterau, the latter two creators of an historic map of Woodstock Artists' studios which is now part of Arthur's collection (p. 2).

It is a true pleasure to witness Arthur's philanthropy, the generous gift of over fifteen hundred works of art from his collection to the New York State Museum for the education and enjoyment of citizens of New York and beyond. Being a part of Arthur's fascinating story and seeing his ongoing promotion of the cultural role of Woodstock has been, and will continue to be, an honor for me. ■

▶ Margaret Wetterau
(American, 20th century)
*Woodstock Gallery
Opening*, c. 1950
Ink on paper

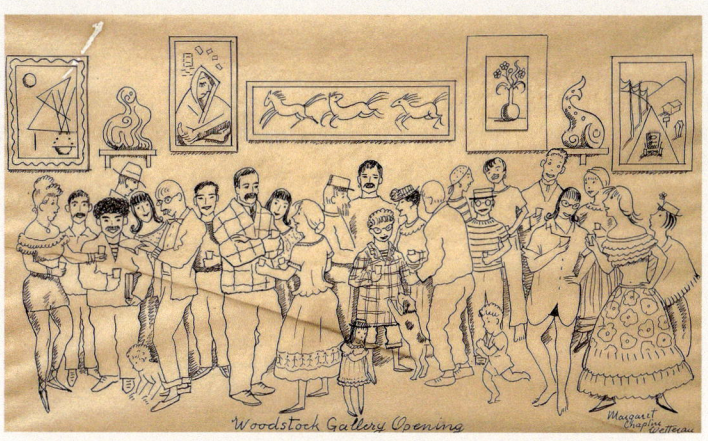

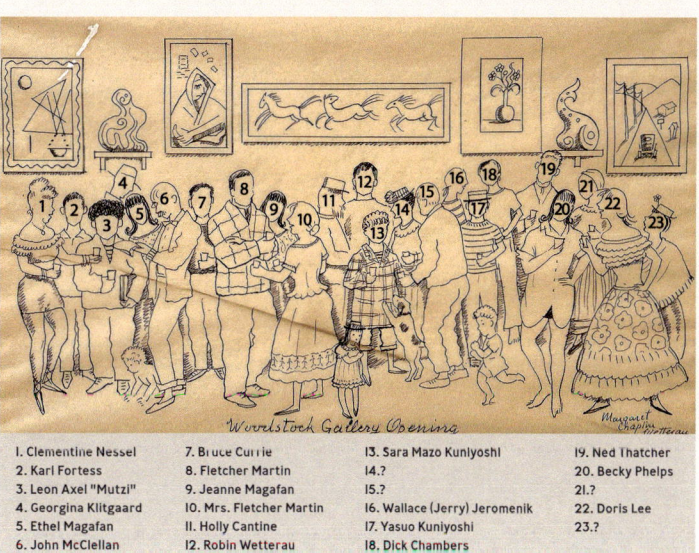

I. Clementine Nessel	7. Bruce Currie	13. Sara Mazo Kuniyoshi	19. Ned Thatcher
2. Karl Fortess	8. Fletcher Martin	14.?	20. Becky Phelps
3. Leon Axel "Mutzi"	9. Jeanne Magafan	15.?	21.?
4. Georgina Klitgaard	10. Mrs. Fletcher Martin	16. Wallace (Jerry) Jeromenik	22. Doris Lee
5. Ethel Magafan	II. Holly Cantine	17. Yasuo Kuniyoshi	23.?
6. John McClellan	12. Robin Wetterau	18. Dick Chambers	

> The desire is to develop a
> number of individual painters
> and not to develop a 'school.'
>
> – Birge Harrison, Woodstock artist

BIBLIOGRAPHY

The background information in this book draws upon numerous publications on Woodstock including:

Bloodgood, Josephine and Tom Wolf, *The Maverick: Hervey White's Colony of the Arts* (Woodstock, New York: Woodstock Artists Association and Museum, 2006).

Evers, Alf, *Woodstock: History of an American Town* (New York: Harry N. Abrams, 1987).

Green, Nancy, Cheryl Robertson, et al, *Byrdcliffe: An American Art Colony* (Ithaca, New York: Cornell University Press, 2004).

La Motta, Janice, Tom Wolf, and Bruce Weber, *Woodstock Artists Association: One Hundred Years of Community and Art* (Woodstock, New York: Woodstock Artists Association, 2019).

Searle, Marjorie B., et al. *Leaving for the Country: George Bellows in Woodstock* (Rochester, New York: Memorial Art Gallery of the University of Rochester, 2003).

Wolf, Tom, *Woodstock's Art Heritage: The Permanent Collection of the Woodstock Artists Association* (Woodstock, New York: Overlook Press, 1987).

The individual institutions in Woodstock including the Woodstock Artists Association and Museum, the Woodstock-Byrdcliffe Guild, the Historical Society of Woodstock, and the Center for Photography at Woodstock all exhibit and publish on specific artists and themes.

NOTES

Born or Died "NYC"
New York City (including boroughs)

Born or Died "NYS"
New York State
(excluding NYC and Woodstock)

Died "Woodstock"
Woodstock and environs

Died with no locale stated
He/she died outside Woodstock,
NYC, or NYS

"WAC"
Interred Woodstock Artists
Cemetery (circa 1929–2022)

**With great appreciation to
Katherine McKenna and the
Woodstock Artists Cemetery.**

SUMMARY

183	total artists
0	born in Woodstock
18%	born in NYC (including boroughs)
5%	born in NY State (excluding NYC and Woodstock)
45%	born in USA excluding NYS and NYC
32%	born outside the USA
40%	died Woodstock
38%	interred Woodstock Artists Cemetery

ARTISTS

Allen, Willard
(b. 1860 Ohio – d. 1933)

Angeloch, Robert
(b. 1922 NYC – 2011 Woodstock)
WAC

Arms, John Taylor
(b. 1887 DC – d. 1953 NYC)

Arndt, Paul Wesley
(b. 1881 Illinois – d. 1978
Woodstock)

Arnold, Grant
(b. 1904 NYC – d. 1988 NYS)

Auerbach –Levy, William
(b. 1889 Russia – d. 1964 NYS)

Ault, George
(b. 1891 Ohio – d. 1948 Woodstock)

Avery, March
(b. 1932 NYC –

Avery, Milton
(b. 1885 NYS – d. 1965 NYC) **WAC**

Avery, Sally Michel
(b. 1902 NYC – d. 2003 NYC) **WAC**

Bacon, Peggy
(b. 1895 Connecticut – d. 1987)

Ballin, Florence (Cramer)
(b. 1884 NYC – d. 1962 Woodstock)

Barker, Albert W.
(b. 1874 Illinois – d. 1947)

Bellows, George
(b. 1882 Ohio – d. 1925 NYC)

Benda, Władysław Theoder
(b. 1873 Poland – d. 1948)

Benn, Ben
(b. 1884 Russia – d. 1983 NYC)

Benney, Robert
(b. 1904 Romania – d. 2001)

Bentley, John William
(b. 1880 New Jersey – d. 1951
Woodstock)

Bierhals, Otto
(b. 1879 Germany – d. 1944
Woodstock)

Billings, Henry
(b. 1901 NYS – d. 1985 NYS)

Blanch, Lucile
(b. 1895 Minnesota – d. 1981) **WAC**

Blanch, Arnold
(b. 1896 Minnesota – d. 1968
Woodstock) **WAC**

Bouche, Louis
(b. 1896 NYC – d. 1969)

Brace, Reeves
(b. 1898 Virginia – d. 1932 NYC)

Brinley, Daniel Putnam
(b. 1879 Rhode Island – d. 1963)

Bromberg, Manuel
(b. 1917 Iowa – d. 2022 Woodstock)
WAC

Brook, Alexander
(b. 1898 NYC – d. 1980 NYS)

Brown, Bolton Coit
(b. 1864 NYS – d. 1936 Woodstock)
WAC

Burlin, Paul
(b. 1886 NYC – d. 1969 NYC)

Bush, Elizabeth (Woiceske)
(b. 1883 Pennsylvania – d. 1958
Woodstock)

Cabot, Petra
(b. 1907 Pennsylvania – d. 2006
Woodstock) **WAC**

Carlson, John Fabian
(b. 1874 Sweden – d. 1945 NYC)
WAC

Carroll, John
(b. 1892 Kansas – d. 1959 NYS)

Caruso, Enrico
(b. 1873 Italy– d. 1921)

Chanler, Robert
(b. 1872 NYC – d. 1930 Woodstock)

Chase, Frank Swift
(b. 1886 Missouri – d. 1958
Woodstock) **WAC**

Chavez, Edward
(b. 1917 New Mexico – d. 1995
Woodstock) **WAC**

Chichester, Cecil
(b. 1891 NYC – d. 1948) **WAC**

Cochran, Allen
(b. 1888 Ohio – d. 1971 Woodstock)
WAC

Cramer, Konrad
(1888 Germany – d. 1963
Woodstock)

Currie, Bruce
(b. 1911 Iowa – d. 2011 Woodstock)
WAC

Dasburg, Andrew
(b. 1887 France – d. 1979)

de Diego, Julio
(b. 1900 Spain – d. 1979)

Dehn, Adolf
(b. 1895 Minnesota – d. 1968 NYC)

deLappe, Pele
(b. 1916 California – d. 2007)

Dodds, Peggy
(b. 1900 New Jersey – d. 1987)

Dow, Arthur Wesley
(b. 1857 Massachusetts – d. 1922
NYS)

Edie, Stuart
(b. 1908 Texas – d. 1974)

Edwards, Emmet
(b. 1906 Iowa – d. 1981 Woodstock)
WAC

Ellis, Vernon
(b. 1885 Pennsylvania – d. 1944)

Ernst, John
(b. 1923 Brazil – d. 1995) **WAC**

Evergood, Phillip
(b. 1901 NYC – d. 1973)

Evers, Alf
(b. 1905 NYC – d. 2004
Woodstock)

Evers, Ivar Elis
(b. 1866 Sweden – d. 1955 NYS)

Faggi, Alfeo
(b. 1885 Italy – d. 1966 Woodstock)
WAC

Fenton, John
(b. 1912 NYS – d. 1977 Woodstock)
WAC

Fenton, Sophie
(b. 1916 – d. 2005 Woodstock)
WAC

Fiene, Ernest
(b. 1894 Germany – d. 1965)

Fiene, Paul
(b. 1899 Germany – d. 1949
Woodstock)

Fischer, Anton Otto
(b. 1882 Germany – d. 1962
Woodstock)

Fishburne, St. Julian
(b. 1927 NYC – d. 2011 Woodstock)

Flannagan, John
(b. 1895 North Dakota – d. 1942
NYC)

Fortess, Karl
(b. 1907 Belgium – d. 1993
Woodstock) **WAC**

Frank, Mary
(b. 1933 England

Fruhauf, Aline
(b. 1907 NYC – d. 1978)

Ganso, Emil
(b. 1895 Germany – d. 1941) **WAC**

Gershoy, Eugenie (Gottlieb)
(b. 1901 Russia – d. 1983 NYC) **WAC**

Gottlieb, Harry
(b. 1895 Romania – d. 1993 NYC)

Greenwood, Marion (Plate)
(b. 1909 NYC – d. 1970 Woodstock)
WAC

Gropper, William
(b. 1897 NYC – d. 1977 NYS)

Gruppe, Charles P.
(b. 1860 Canada. – d. 1940 NYC)

Gruppe, Emil
(b. 1890 NYS – d. 1928)

Guston, Philip
(b. 1913 Canada – d. 1980
Woodstock) **WAC**

Haeberlin, Carolyn
(b. 1913 Illinois – d. 2000)

Handell, Albert
(b. 1937 NYC –)

Harrison, Birge
(b. 1854 Pennsylvania – d. 1929
Woodstock)

Hart, Agnes
(b. 1912 Connecticut – d. 1979
Woodstock) **WAC**

Hartman, Rosella (Fiene)
(1894 Kansas – d. 1984
Woodstock)

Heckman, Albert
(b. 1893 Pennsylvania – d. 1971
Woodstock) **WAC**

Henri, Robert
(b. 1865 Ohio – d. 1929 NYC)

Heermann, Norbert
(b. 1891 Germany – d. 1966
Woodstock) **WAC**

Hervey, Wilna
(b. 1894 California – d. 1979) **WAC**

Howe, Gurdon
(b. 1903 – d. 1984)

Hutty, Alfred
(b. 1877 Michigan – d. 1954
Woodstock) **WAC**

Ives, Neil
(b. 1892 Missouri – d. 1946
Woodstock) **WAC**

Johnson, Grace Mott (Dasburg)
(b. 1882 NYC – d. 1967)

Jones, Wendell
(b. 1899 Kansas – d. 1956) **WAC**

Karfiol, Bernard
(b. 1886 Hungary – d. 1952 NYS)

Kaz, Nathaniel
(b. 1917 NYC – d. 2010)

Kent, Rockwell
(b. 1882 NYS – d. 1971 NYS)

Killiam, Walter
(b. 1907 Rhode Island – d. 1979)

Klitgaard, Georgina
(b. 1893 NYC – d. 1976 Woodstock)

Koeniger, Walter
(b. 1881 Germany – d. 1993
Woodstock)

Komroff, Manuel
(b. 1890 NYC – 1974) **WAC**

Kroll, Leon
(b. 1884 NYC – d. 1974 NYC)

Kuniyoshi, Yasuo
(b. 1893 Japan – d. 1953 NYC) **WAC**

Lachaise, Gaston
(b. 1882 France – d. 1935 NYC)

Laufman, Sidney
(b. 1891 Ohio – d. 1985)

Lee, Doris
(b. 1905 Illinois – d. 1983
Woodstock) **WAC**

Lee, Russell
(b. 1903 Illinois – d. 1986)

Lever, Richard Hayley
(b. 1876 Australia – d. 1958 NYS)

Leith –Ross, Harry
(b. 1886 Mauritius – d. 1973)

Lindin, Carl Olaf Eric
(b. 1869 Sweden – d. 1942
Woodstock) **WAC**

London, Frank
(b. 1876 North Carolina – d. 1945
NYC)

Lowengrund, Margaret
(b. 1902 Pennsylvania – d. 1957
NYC)

Ludins, Eugene
(b. 1904 Russia – d. 1996
Woodstock) **WAC**

Macrum, George
(b. 1878 Pennsylvania – d. 1970
NYS)

Magafan, Ethel (Currie)
(b. 1916 Illinois – d. 1993
Woodstock) **WAC**

Magafan, Jenne (Chavez)
(b. 1916 Illinois – d. 1952 NYS) **WAC**

Mahler, Rebecca
(b. 1877 NYC – d. unknown)

Mandel, Howard
(b. 1917 NYC – d. 1999)

Maratta, Hardesty
(b. 1864 Illinois – d. 1924)

Marsh, Reginald
(b. 1898 France – d. 1954)

Martin, Fletcher
(b. 1904 Colorado – d. 1979 NYC)
WAC

Mason, Nan
(b. 1896 – d. 1982) **WAC**

Matteson, Bartow
(b. 1894 NYS – d. 1984 Woodstock)

Mattson, Henry
(b. 1887 Sweden – d. 1971
Woodstock) **WAC**

McClellan, John
(b. 1908 England – d. 1986
Woodstock) **WAC**

McFee, Henry Lee
(b. 1886 Missouri – d. 1953)

Mecklem, Austin
(b. 1894 Washington – d. 1951
Woodstock) **WAC**

Millman, Edward
(b. 1907 Illinois – d. 1964 Woodstock)
WAC

More, Hermon
(b. 1887 Massachusetts – d. 1968)

Mosca, August
(b. 1909 Italy – d. 2002 NYS)

Murphy, Hermann Dudley
(b. 1867 Massachusetts – d. 1945)

Noda, Hideo
(b. 1908 California – d. 1938)

Pachner, William
(b. 1915 Czechoslovakia – d. 2017
Woodstock) **WAC**

Pascin, Jules
(b. 1885 Bulgaria – d. 1930)

Pennell, Joseph
(b. 1857 Pennsylvania – d. 1926
NYC)

Perrine, Van Dearing
(b. 1868 Kansas – d. 1953)

Pike, John
(b. 1911 Massachusetts – d. 1979
Woodstock) **WAC**

Pittman, Hobson
(b. 1899 North Carolina – d. 1972)

Pollet, Joseph
(b. 1897 Germany – d. 1979 NYC)
WAC

Presser, Josef
(b. 1907 Poland – d. 1967) **WAC**

Refregier, Anton
(b. 1905 Russia – d. 1979) **WAC**

Reiss, Winold
(b. 1886 Germany – d. 1953)

Revzan, Daniel
(b. 1908 Illinois – d. 1996
Woodstock)

Rohland, Paul
(b. 1884 Virginia – d. 1953) **WAC**

Rosen, Charles
(b. 1878 Pennsylvania – d. 1950
Woodstock) **WAC**

Ruellan, Andrée (Taylor)
(b. 1905 NYC – d. 2006
Woodstock) **WAC**

Ryder, Chauncey Foster
(b. 1868 Connecticut – d. 1949)

Scarlett, Rolph
(b. 1889 Canada – d. 1984
Woodstock) **WAC**

Schmidt, Katherine (Kuniyoshi)
(b. 1889 Canada – d. 1984
Woodstock)

Schumacher, William Emile
(b. 1870 Belgium – d. 1931
Woodstock)

Serger, Frederick
(b. 1889 Czechoslovakia – d. 1965)

Shotwell, Helen Harvey
(b. 1908 NYC – d. 1989 NYC) **WAC**

Siegel, Adrian
(b. 1898 NYC – d. 1978)

Siporin, Mitchell
(b. 1910 NYC – d. 1976)

Sluizer, Kurt
(b. 1911 Holland – d. 1988
Woodstock)

Small, Hannah (Ludins)
(b. 1903 NYC – d. 1992 Woodstock)
WAC

Smith, David
(b. 1906 Indiana – d. 1965)

Smith, Judson
(b. 1880 Michigan – d. 1962
Woodstock) **WAC**

Sokole, Miron
(b. 1901 Russia – d. 1985 NYC) **WAC**

Spear, Caroline (Rohland)
(b. 1885 Massachusetts – d. 1965
NYC) **WAC**

Speicher, Eugene
(b. 1883 NYS – d. 1962 Woodstock)
WAC

Steele, Zulma
(b. 1881 Wisconsin – d. 1979 NYS)

Steffen, Bernard
(b. 1907 Kansas – d. 1980 NYC)
WAC

Sterner, Albert
(b. 1863 England – d. 1946 NYC)

Summers, Ivan
(b. 1889 Illinois – d. 1964
Woodstock) **WAC**

Tannin, Harriet
(b. 1928 NYC – d. 2011 Woodstock)
WAC

Taylor, John Williams
(b. 1897 Maryland – d. 1983
Woodstock) **WAC**

Tedlie, Harry
(b. 1898 Pennsylvania – d. 1983
Woodstock)

Thurber, Edna
(b. 1887 – d. 1981)

Tomlin, Bradley Walker
(b. 1899 NYS – d. 1953 NYC)

Towbin, Phoebe
(b. 1910 – d. 1995) **WAC**

Tschacbascov, Nahum
(b. 1899 Russia – d . 1984 NYC)

Turnbull, James
(b. 1909 Missouri – d. 1976)

Van de Bovenkamp, Hans
(b. 1938 Holland –

Varian, Dorothy
(b. 1895 NYC – d. 1985 NYC) **WAC**

Vukovic, Marko
(b. 1892 Yugoslavia – d. 1973) **WAC**

Walters, Carl
(b. 1883 Iowa – d. 1955 Woodstock)
WAC

Watson –Schutze, Eva
(b. 1867 New Jersey – d. 1935)
WAC

Wetterau, Margaret
(b. 1894 – d. 1989)

Wetterau, Rudolph
(b. 1890 Tennesee – d. 1953
Woodstock)

White, Hervey
(b. 1866 Iowa – d. 1944 Woodstock)

Whitehead, Ralph Radcliffe
(b. 1854 England – d. 1929
Woodstock) **WAC**

Whitney, Gertrude
(b. 1875 NYC – d. 1942 NYC)

Wilson, Reginald
(b. 1909 Ohio – d. 1993 Woodstock)

Wiltz, Arnold
(b. 1889 Germany – d. 1937
Woodstock) **WAC**

Winslow, Earl
(b. 1884 Michigan – d. 1969
Woodstock)

Winters, Denny
(b. 1907 Michigan – d. 1985)

Woiceske, Ronau
(b. 1887 Illinois – d. 1953
Woodstock)

Woodward, Dewing
(b. 1856 Pennsylvania – d. 1950)

Wuermer, Carl
(b. 1900 Germany – d. 1981)

Wylie, Samuel
(b. 1900 Indiana – d. 1957
Woodstock) **WAC**

INTRODUCTION

Norbert Heermann
(American, born Germany, 1891–1966)
Lady with Red Lips, c. 1940
Oil on canvas
24 x 20 in.

Rudolph Wetterau
(American, 1890–1953) and
Margaret Wetterau
(American, 1894–1989)
Map of Woodstock…Showing the location of some of the artists' homes, 1926
Ink on board
20 x 28.5 in.

BYRDCLIFFE

Bolton Brown
(American, 1864–1936)
Bowl, 1930
Polychrome glazed ceramic earthenware
3.5 x 5 in.

Bolton Brown
(American, 1864–1936)
Summer Shower, 1920
Lithograph on paper
10 x 14 in.

Bolton Brown
(American, 1864–1936)
Valley and Sky (Tonalist Mountains), 1904
Oil on canvas
22 x 23 in.

Birge Harrison
(American, 1854–1929)
St. Lawrence River Sunset, n.d.
Oil on canvas
25 x 39 in.

Hermann Dudley Murphy
(American, 1867–1945)
The Shower of Sunset (Woodstock), 1904
Oil on canvas
20 x 27 in.

William Schumacher
(Belgium, 1870–1930)
The Woodchopper, 1920
Oil on canvas
37.5 x 35.5 in.

Zulma Steele
(American, 1881–1979)
Zedware Bowl, c. 1935
Glazed ceramic
6.25 x 12.6 in.

Eva Watson-Schütze
(American, 1867–1935)
Yellow Callas, 1929
Oil on canvas
31 x 31 in.

MAVERICK ARTS COLONY

John Carroll
(American, 1892–1959)
Lydia, c. 1925
Oil on canvas
36 x 34 in.

Robert Winthrop Chanler
(American, 1872–1930)
Maverick Melodeon, n.d.
Hand-painted Mason & Hamlin melodeon organ
36 x 32 in.

Konrad Cramer
(American, born Germany, 1888–1963)
Hervey White, c. 1920
Photograph
10 x 8 in.

John Flannagan
(American, 1895–1942)
Maternal Bird, n.d.
Bronze
14.5 x 6 in.

Harry Gottlieb
(American, born Romania, 1895–1992)
Autumn in Woodstock, 1930
Oil on canvas
20.25 x 24 in.

Carl Walters
(American, 1883–1955)
Fan Dancer, 1923
Glazed terracotta
8 x 6 in.

Hervey White
(American, 1866–1944)
The First Maverick Festival, 1928
Manuscript, subsequently published in *The Saturday Morning,* Woodstock, New York, August 31, 1928.
12 x 9 in.

ART STUDENTS LEAGUE

George Ault
(American, 1891–1948)
Autumn Hillside, 1940
Gouache on paper
21 x 15.13 in.

Peggy Bacon
(American, 1895–1987)
Clams and Clodhoppers, 1933
Dry point on paper
8 x 10 in.

Peggy Bacon
(American, 1895–1987)
Lunch at the League, c. 1918
Etching on paper
4 x 5 in.

Otto Bierhals
(American, born Germany, 1879–1944)
Path in Woods, c. 1935
Hand-colored lithograph on paper
17.75 x 19.19 in.

Henry Billings
(American, 1901–1985)
Backyard Garden Path, n.d.
Oil on canvas
25.25 x 30.25 in.

Arnold Blanch
(American, 1896–1968)
Woodstock Farm, 1926
Watercolor on board
11 x 16 in.

Lucile Blanch
(American, 1895–1981)
Circus Acrobats, 1930
Watercolor on paper
5.75 x 3.25 in.

Alexander Brook
(American, 1898–1980)
Cottage on a Hillside, 1935
Oil on canvas
30 x 34 in.

Frank Swift Chase
(American, 1886–1958)
Catskills at Woodstock, 1927
Oil on canvas
22 x 28 in.

Cecil Chichester
(American, 1891–1963
*Willow Valley Near
Woodstock,* c. 1925
Oil on canvas
30 x 50 in.

Paul Fiene
(American, born Germany,
1899–1949)
*Portrait Bust of the Artist
(Paul Fiene),* 1932
Plaster
17.75 x 56 in.

Grace Mott Johnson
(American, 1882–1967)
*Young Greyhound
(Greyhound Pup),* 1911
Bronze
9 x 6 in.

Walter Koeniger
(American, born Germany,
1881–1943)
Catskill Winter Stream, c. 1925
Oil on canvas
28.25 x 36 in.

Paul Rohland
(American, 1884–1953)
Woodstock Autumn, 1923
Oil on canvas
26 x 30 in.

Judson Smith
(American, 1880–1962)
Two Sisters, 1923
Oil on canvas
58 x 52 in.

Eugene Speicher
(American, 1883–1962)
Last of the Sun, 1913
Oil on board
19.8 x 23.8 in.

Bradley Walker Tomlin
(American, 1899–1953)
*House with Dormer
and Cat,* 1926
Watercolor and pen and
ink on paper
16.25 x 14.75 in.

Gertrude Vanderbilt Whitney
(American, 1875–1942)
Young Girl, or Wallflower, 1913
Plaster with patina finish
4.96 x 4.96 in.

Dewing Woodward
(American, 1856–1950)
Woodland Nude, c. 1915
Oil on canvas
20.25 x 16.25 in.

GEORGE BELLOWS AND HIS CIRCLE

George Bellows
(American, 1882–1925)
Charles Rosen, c. 1922
Conte crayon on paper
11.5 x 10.25 in.

George Bellows
(American, 1882–1925)
Elsie, Emma, and Marjorie, 1921
Lithograph on paper
11.25 x 13.75 in.

George Bellows
(American, 1882–1925)
*Eugene Speicher Drawing
on a Stone,* 1921
Lithograph on paper
11.5 x 8.5 in

George Bellows
(American, 1882–1925)
Four Friends, 1921
Lithograph on paper
10.25 x 8 in.

George Bellows
(American, 1882–1925)
Hungry Dogs, 1916
Lithograph on paper
13.25 x 10 in.

George Bellows
(American, 1882–1925)
Portrait of John Carroll, c. 1922
Conte crayon on paper
11 x 8.5 in.

George Bellows
(American, 1882–1925)
Portrait of John Carroll, 1923
Lithograph on paper
12.5 x 9.75 in.

George Bellows
(American, 1882–1925)
Robert Henri, c. 1921
Graphite on paper
8 x 5 in.

George Bellows
(American, 1882–1925)
Self Portrait, c. 1921
Conte crayon on paper
9.5 x 6.75 in.

George Bellows
(American, 1882–1925)
Sniped (War Series), 1918
Lithograph on paper
9 x 11.25 in.

Robert Henri
(American, 1865–1929)
Three Studies, Madrid, 1906
Conte crayon on paper
19.5 x 9 in.

Leon Kroll
(American, 1884–1974)
Young Girl, c. 1930
Red chalk on paper
25 x 19 in.

Eugene Speicher
(American, 1883–1962)
Farmer in Overalls, c. 1925
Oil on canvas
29.5 x 23 in.

BOLTON BROWN AND LITHOGRAPHY

Grant Arnold
(American, 1904–1988)
Old Risely Barn, 1936
Lithograph on paper
9.25 x 14.5 in.

George Bellows
(American, 1882–1925)
Appeal to the People, 1923
Lithograph on paper
15 x 19 in.

Bolton Brown
(American, 1864–1936)
Choke Cherries, 1920
Lithograph on paper
9 x 12.75 in.

Bolton Brown,
(American, 1864–1936)
Little A, 1915
Lithograph in sanguine ink
on paper
12.5 x 12.75 in.

Bolton Brown
(American, 1864–1936)
Storm, 1923
Lithograph on paper
13 x 11 in.

Emil Ganso
(American, born Germany,
1895–1941)
Spring, n.d.
Color lithograph on paper
11.5 x 16 in.

Rosella Hartman
(American, 1895–1993)
Chickadees in the Snow, n.d.
Lithograph on paper
13.25 x 9.25 in.

Rockwell Kent
(American, 1882–1971)
Father and Son, 1920
Lithograph on paper
6.75 x 4.75 in.

Yasuo Kuniyoshi
(American, born Japan,
1889–1953)
Carnival, 1949
Lithograph on paper
9.5 x 14.5 in.

Pele de Lappe
(American, 1916–2007)
Picnic, 1932
Lithograph on paper
12.5 x 19 in.

John McClellan
(American, born England,
1908–1986)
Cat and Table, 1939
Lithograph on paper
9 x 6.25 in.

Albert Sterner
(American, born England,
1863–1946)
*African-American Couple
Playing Cards,* 1920
Lithograph on paper
13 x 17 in.

MODERNISM IN WOODSTOCK

Florence Ballin Cramer
(American, 1884–1962)
Cramer Homestead in Winter, 1926
Oil on board
20 x 24 in.

Konrad Cramer
(American, born Germany,
1888–1963)
Abstraction, c. 1945
Photograph
10 x 7.75 in.

Konrad Cramer
(American, born Germany,
1888–1963)
Still Life Abstraction #7, 1923
Lithograph on paper
9.5 x 12.5 in.

Andrew Dasburg
(American, born France, 1887–1979)
Cubist Landscape, c. 1920
Graphite on paper
10 x 12 in.

Ernest Fiene
(American, born Germany,
1894–1965)
Mountain Stream, 1938
Watercolor on paper
23 x 26 in.

Henry Lee McFee
(American, 1886–1953)
Portrait of Florence Ballin, c. 1916
Oil on panel
36 x 28 in.

Henry Lee McFee
(American, 1886–1953)
Still Life with Glass and Pipe, c. 1919
Graphite on paper
15 x 12 in.

Winold Reiss
(American, born Germany,
1886–1953)
*Woman in Black Hat
with Cigarette,* 1917
Pastel on paper
48 x 35 in.

Charles Rosen
(American, 1878–1950)
*River Boat No. 2,
Hudson River,* 1939
Oil on canvas
32 x 40 in.

1930S AND BEYOND

Arnold Blanch
(American, 1896–1968)
On the Hudson, c. 1930s
Tempera on panel
9 x 34.5 in.

Edward Chavez
(American, 1917–1995)
Abstraction, n.d.
Bronze
8 x 9 in.

Julio de Diego
(American, born Spain,
1900–1979)
Altitude 3000, 1946
Oil on board
24 x 30 in.

Julio de Diego
(American, born Spain,
1900–1979)
Nichos No. 2, 1947
Tempera on paper
17.75 x 24.5 in.

Julio de Diego
(American, born Spain,
1900–1979)
Woodstock Bugs, 1948
Watercolor on paper
10.63 x 13 in.

William Hunt Diederich
(American, born Hungary,
1884–1953)
Bullfight Silhouette, c. 1930s
Cut paper silhouette
14.6 x 16.625 in.

William Hunt Diederich
(American, born Hungary,
1884–1953)
Bullfight Silhouette, c. 1930s
Cut paper silhouette
14.6 x 16.625 in.

William Hunt Diederich
(American, born Hungary,
1884–1953)
Bullfight Silhouette, c. 1930s
Cut paper silhouette
14.6 x 16.625 in.

Alfeo Faggi
(American, born Italy, 1885–1966)
Greco Wrestlers, c. 1930
Terracotta
18 x 24 in.

Ernest Fiene
(American, born Germany,
1894–1965)
War bonds poster, c. 1942
Print on paper
15.5 x 11 in.

Karl Fortess
(American, born Belgium,
1907–1993)
Abstraction No. 5, c. 1950
Oil on canvas
40 x 24 in.

Mary Frank,
(American, born England, 1933)
Face and Hands, n.d.
Ceramic
11.5 x 8 in.

Mary Frank
(American, born England, 1933)
Figure with Deer, 1962
Ink on paper
10 x 7.75 in.

Marion Greenwood
(American, 1909–1970)
Study for Tennessee Mural, 1940s
Graphite on paper
12.5 x 9.75 in.

Al Held
(American, 1928–2005)
Stone Ridge #6, 1984
Colored etching on paper
26.50 x 39 in.

Doris Lee
(American, 1905–1983)
Still Life with Fruit, c. 1945
Lithograph on paper
9.5 x 14 in.

Margaret Lowengrund
(American, 1902–1957)
Coal Pickers, 1936
Lithograph on paper
10 x 13.75 in.

Jenne Magafan
(American, 1916–1952)
Autumn Wind (Cornstalks), 1942
Oil and tempera on board
24.5 x 18.25 in.

Jenne Magafan
(American, 1916–1952)
Cornstalks, 1942
Lithograph on paper
11 x 8.75 in.

Fletcher Martin
(American, 1904–1979)
Far Off City, 1946
Oil on canvas
27 x 44 in.

Josef Presser
(American, born Poland, 1909–1967)
*String Bass Player
(Abstraction),* c. 1945
Oil on canvas
50 x 39 in.

Anton Refregier
(American, born Russia, 1905–1979)
*Mural Study for 1939
World's Fair,* 1939
Gouache on paper
8 x 2.5 in.

Charles Rosen
(American, 1878–1950)
*WPA Mural Study
for the Poughkeepsie
Post Office,* c. 1939
Gouache on paper
8.46 x 34.02 in.

Rolph Scarlett
(American, born Canada,
1889–1984)
Abstract Composition, c. 1940
Gouache on paper
3.5 x 3 in.

David Smith
(American, 1906–1965)
*Horses and Figure
(Don Quixote),* 1954
Ink on paper
9 x 11.5 in.

Arnold Wiltz
(American, born Germany,
1889–1937)
Quarry Pool, 1936
Wood engraving
5.5 x 7.5 in

ESSAY CHECKLIST

COX ESSAY

Margaret Chapline Wetterau
(American, 20th century)
Woodstock Gallery Opening, c. 1950
Ink on paper
8 x 13.75 in.
James Cox Gallery

Key to Margaret Chapline Wetterau,
Woodstock Gallery Opening
James Cox Gallery

KEARNEY ESSAY

George Bellows
(American, 1882–1925)
Elsie & Gene Speicher, n.d.
Conte crayon on paper
Framed: 15.5 x 16.75 x 1.125 in
The Historic Woodstock Art Colony:
The Arthur A. Anderson Collection

George Bellows
(American, 1882–1925)
*Portrait of Eugene Speicher –
Profile,* 1921
Conte crayon on paper
7.5 x 4.5 in.
The Historic Woodstock Art Colony:
The Arthur A. Anderson Collection

George Bellows
(American, 1882–1925)
*Sketch of Bellows and Speicher
in a Car* (sketch in a letter to
Robert Henri, November 5, 1920)
Pen & ink on paper
5.5 x 10.5 in.
Robert Henri Papers. Yale Collection
of American Literature, Beinecke Rare
Book and Manuscript Library

George Bellows
(American, 1882–1925)
The Reader, 1920 or 1921
Conte crayon on paper
7.75 x 8.50 in.
The Historic Woodstock Art Colony:
The Arthur A. Anderson Collection

Budd Studios, New York, NY
*Eugene Speicher in his
Studio,* ca. 1957
Silver gelatin print
8 x 10 in.
Private Collection

Konrad Cramer
(American, born Germany,
1888–1963)
*Untitled, Gene Speicher and Anne
Bellows Kearney, Woodstock,* 1937
Silver gelatin print
8 x 10 in.
Private Collection

Eugene Speicher
(American, 1883–1962)
Kitchen Garden, n.d.
Oil on canvas
19 x 22 in.
The Historic Woodstock Art Colony:
The Arthur A. Anderson Collection

Eugene Speicher
(American, 1883–1962)
*Portrait of a Young Girl
(Jean Bellows),* ca. 1926 or 1927
Oil on canvas
20 x 16 in.
The Historic Woodstock Art Colony:
The Arthur A. Anderson Collection

LEVAL ESSAY

Julio de Diego
(American, born Spain, 1900–1979)
Love Chair, n.d.
Painted wood
32.5 x 22.5 x 20.5 in
The Historic Woodstock Art Colony:
The Arthur A. Anderson Collection

Julio de Diego
(American, born Spain, 1900–1979)
Self Portrait, 1955
Oil on board
18 x 12 in.
The Historic Woodstock Art Colony:
The Arthur A. Anderson Collection

Julio de Diego
(American, born Spain, 1900–1979)
Serraglio, 1948
Oil on canvas
22 x 28 in.
The Historic Woodstock Art Colony:
The Arthur A. Anderson Collection

Julio de Diego
(American, born Spain, 1900–1979)
Spring Fantasia from
Surrealisme en 1947, 1947
Lithograph on paper
9.5625 x 8.3125 x .375 in.
The Historic Woodstock Art Colony:
The Arthur A. Anderson Collection

ESSAY CHECKLIST (CONTINUED)

Julio de Diego
(American, born Spain, 1900–1979)
Two Nudes with Hand, 1950
Oil on canvas
32 x 48 in.
The Historic Woodstock Art Colony:
The Arthur A. Anderson Collection

Julio de Diego
(American, born Spain, 1900–1979)
*The Last Advance Officially
Reported,* 1942
Oil on board
47.5 x 29.5 in.
The Historic Woodstock Art Colony:
The Arthur A. Anderson Collection

MURPHY ESSAY

Arnold Wiltz
(German, 1889–1937)
American Landscape, 1936
Oil on canvas
25.25 x 35 in.
Gift of G. Evelyn Hutchinson, M.A.H. 1944
1991.88.1, Yale University Art Gallery

Arnold Wiltz
(German, 1889–1937)
The Causeway, 1932
Wood engraving
8 x 10 in.
Samuel Dorsky Museum of Art
Edward Coykendall Collection
1957.001.156

Arnold Wiltz
(German, 1889–1937)
Spillway, 1936
Woodblock print on paper
6 x 4.45 in.
The Historic Woodstock Art Colony:
The Arthur A. Anderson Collection

Arnold Wiltz
(German, 1889–1937)
Wood Chopper, 1936
Woodblock print on paper
5.25 x 7.2 in.
The Historic Woodstock Art Colony:
The Arthur A. Anderson Collection

QUINN ESSAY

Peggy Bacon
(American, 1895–1987)
Art Gallery #2, 1931
Conte crayon on paper
9.5 x 6.75 in.
The Historic Woodstock Art Colony:
The Arthur A. Anderson Collection

Peggy Bacon
(American, 1895–1987)
Black Eye "John Carroll", n.d.
Dry point on paper
5 x 4 in.
The Historic Woodstock Art Colony:
The Arthur A. Anderson Collection

Peggy Bacon
(American, 1895–1987)
Come Play With Me, n.d.
Lithograph on paper
6.75 x 5.25 in.
The Historic Woodstock Art Colony:
The Arthur A. Anderson Collection

Peggy Bacon
(American, 1895–1987)
Guy Pene du Bois, 1935
Conte crayon on paper
16.75 x 13.75 in
The Historic Woodstock Art Colony:
The Arthur A. Anderson Collection

Peggy Bacon
(American, 1895–1987)
Off With Their Heads, New York,
Robert M. McBride & Company,
1934, n.p.
12.5 x 9.5 in.
Private Collection

Peggy Bacon
(American, 1895–1987)
Portrait of Eugene Speicher, n.d.
Conte crayon on paper
7 x 6 in.
The Historic Woodstock Art Colony:
The Arthur A. Anderson Collection

Peggy Bacon
(American, 1895–1987)
Two Cats, n.d.
Pastel on paper
17.75 x 18 in.
The Historic Woodstock Art Colony:
The Arthur A. Anderson Collection

WEBER ESSAY

Peggy Bacon
(American, 1895–1987)
Lady Artist, 1925
Etching on paper
6 x 4 in.
The Historic Woodstock Art Colony:
The Arthur A. Anderson Collection

John F. Carlson
(American, born Sweden, 1875–1947)
Grey Mills, ca. 1920
Watercolor on paper
17.5 x 23.5 in.
The Historic Woodstock Art Colony:
The Arthur A. Anderson Collection

Allen Cochran
(American, 1888– 1971)
Winter Stream, n.d
Oil on canvas
25 x 30 in.
The Historic Woodstock Art Colony:
The Arthur A. Anderson Collection

Florence Ballin Cramer
(American, 1884–1962)
Hudson River at Rondout, ca. 1938
Oil on canvas
20 x 30 in.
The Historic Woodstock Art Colony:
The Arthur A. Anderson Collection

Birge Harrison
(American, 1854–1929)
*Woodstock Meadows
in Winter,* 1909
Oil on canvas
46 x 40.25 in.
Toledo Museum of Art (Toledo, Ohio),
Gift of Cora Baird Lacey, in memory
of Mary A. Dustin, 1912.1266

Alfred Hutty
(American, 1877–1954)
Summer Landscape, 1925
Oil on board
8 x 10 in.
The Historic Woodstock Art Colony:
The Arthur A. Anderson Collection

WOLF ESSAY

Abastenia St. Leger Eberle
(American, 1878–1942)
Mermaid, n.d.
Bronze
5 x 5.25 x 1.25 in.
The Historic Woodstock Art Colony:
The Arthur A. Anderson Collection

Alfred Hutty
(American, 1877–1954)
Nude Study, 1930
Graphite on paper
18 x 14 in.
The Historic Woodstock Art Colony:
The Arthur A. Anderson Collection

Zulma Steele
(American, 1881–1979)
Mountain Landscape, n.d.
Oil on canvas
27 x 36 in.
The Historic Woodstock Art Colony:
The Arthur A. Anderson Collection

Eva Watson-Schütze
(American, 1867–1935)
Martin Schütze at a Quarry, 1902
Photograph
6.5 x 4.5 in
Courtesy Samuel Dorsky Museum of Art
State University of New York – New Paltz
Gift of Howard Greenberg

Eva Watson-Schütze
(American, 1867–1935)
*Portrait of Two Children
by Waterfall,* 1902
Photograph
6.25 x 8.25 in
Courtesy Samuel Dorsky Museum of Art
State University of New York – New Paltz
Gift of Howard Greenberg

Dewing Woodward
(American, 1856–1950)
Paper Dolls, 1913
Oil on canvas
18 x 24 in
Woodstock Artists Association & Museum
Gift of Helen Sawyer, 2007-26-01

Being a part of Arthur's fascinating story and seeing his ongoing promotion of the cultural role of Woodstock has been, and will continue to be, an honor for me.

– James Cox, Director, James Cox Gallery at Woodstock